Decarbonizing transport is a critical challenge for the 2030 Agenda. It touches at the heart of several objectives, including not only reducing CO_2 emissions but also improving air quality and hence health and quality of life in cities.

The upheavals in France in 2019 followed the government's increases in petrol and diesel prices. The increases ostensibly were part of the government's climate action plan. The public's reactions, often violent, were driven by concerns about making ends meet and an absence of alternatives that are reliable, safe, clean, and affordable and that take one to destination at the desired time. The upheavals point to the need to engage the public in the policy conversation and to meet quality of life aspirations while addressing the climate challenge.

Electric vehicles are emerging as a policy tool of choices for a growing number of countries and cities, but they bring with them a number of non-negligible but imperative infrastructure shifts. This report, prepared by Boston University's Institute for Sustainable Energy, is a timely contribution exploring the opportunities and constraints for electric vehicles.

— Scott Foster, Director, Sustainable Energy Division,
United Nations Economic Commission of Europe

"The journey of a thousand miles begins with a single step."
— *Lao Tzu*

MELTING THE ICE

Lessons from China and the West in the Transition from
the Internal Combustion Engine to Electric Vehicles

The Critical Role of Public Charging Infrastructure

Editors
Peter Fox-Penner, PhD, Z. Justin Ren, PhD, and David O. Jermain

TABLE OF CONTENTS

ACKNOWLEDGEMENTS

Boston University and the Institute for Sustainability thank Bloomberg Philanthropies for a generous grant and support, which made this research and analysis possible.

We thank David B. Sandalow (Inaugural Fellow, Columbia University Center on Global Energy Policy), Yue (Sally) Qiu, and Anders Hove (Center on Global Energy Policy), our colleagues Han Huang, Fang Yang, Yang Zhao, and Shinning Zhang of Global Energy Infrastructure Development Cooperative Organization (GEIDCO) in Beijing and Mengrong (Shirley) Cheng, Feng Zhou, Qjankun Wang, and Yuan (Ryan) Ren of GEIDCO New York, Henry Kelly (ISE Advisory Board member), Katharine Lusk (Executive Director, Initiative on Cities at Boston University), Karen Wayland (kW Energy, and former Deputy Director, EPSA of the US Department of Energy), Gary Gero (LA County Chief Sustainability Officer), and Michelle Kinman (Director of Transportation, LACI), Katie Sloan (Director of Transportation Electrification), and Simon Horton of Southern California Edison, Todd Kirrane (Transportation Administrator), Maria Morelli (Senior Planner – Climate Action /Land Use, Department of Planning and Community Development), and Linda Pehike, (Brookline Selectmen Climate Action Committee Chair of the Township of Brookline, Massachusetts), and Peishan Wang (Research Scientist, Institute for Sustainable Energy) for providing very helpful comments and feedback on an early draft of this book. We are very grateful to all of the individuals who generously gave time for interviews and advice in support of the editors and authors of this work.

Dr. Pereira acknowledges the Portuguese National Foundation for Science and Technology (FCT) for supporting this work through the Doctoral Grant PD/BD/105841/2014, awarded under the framework of the MIT Portu-gal Program funded through the POPH/FSE. Additionally, this work has been partially supported by FCT project grant: UID/MULTI/00308/2019, SAICTPAC/0004/2015-POCI-01-0145-FEDER-016434, and by the Euro-pean Regional Development Fund through the COMPETE 2020 Program and FCT project T4ENERTEC POCI-01-0145-FEDER-029820, as well as by the Energy for Sustainability Initiative of the University of Coimbra.

Conflict of Interest Notification:

Dr. Fox-Penner holds equity in Energy Impact Partners, a utility-backed energy investment and innovation firm, and consults for Energy Impact Partners and the Brattle Group on energy technologies. Dr. Fox-Penner also conducts research in areas of interest similar to the business interests of Energy Impact Partners and the Brattle Group. The terms of this arrangement have been reviewed by Boston University in accordance with its financial conflicts of interest in research policies.

PREFACE

Peter Fox-Penner and David B. Sandalow

Electric vehicles reduce local air pollution, improve energy security and play an important role in decarbonizing the transport sector. They are fun to drive, winning rave reviews from many drivers.

The climate change benefits of electric vehicles are especially critical. Concentrations of heat-trapping gases are now higher than at any time since humans started walking the Earth—and climbing. We are already seeing the impacts, including more severe and frequent storms, floods, droughts and heat waves. More than 180 nations have now ratified the Paris Agreement, agreeing to work together to address this challenge and achieve net-zero emission globally by the second half of this century. That will require significant transformation in the transport sector with low carbon technologies such as electric drive trains.

Electric vehicles are a small part of the global vehicle fleet but growing rapidly. Growth is especially strong in China, where drivers bought more electric vehicles last year than in the rest of the world combined. Growth is also significant in the United States, Japan and much of western Europe. In 2018 more than half of new cars sold in Norway had electric drive trains.

These countries have many differences. Can they learn from each other with respect to electric vehicle deployment?

We believe the answer is yes. This volume focuses in particular on urban policies. The authors find that, despite differences in size, political organization and other factors, the five cities in three countries studied face similar challenges with respect to deployment of electric vehicle infrastructure. Each city faces land use and financing constraints. Each must contend with rapidly growing EV charging demand. Each city finds that technology changes in one part of the world rapidly have impacts everywhere.

Around the world, stakeholders working on the transition to electric vehicles have a great deal to learn from each other. We hope the information and experiences in this book and a recent companion paper from our joint project[1] can help speed this transition.

---

1   Hove, A. and Sandalow, D., *Electric Vehicle Charging in China and the United States*, Feb. 2019, Columbia Center on Global Energy Policy, Available at: https://energypolicy.columbia.edu/sites/default/files/file-uploads/EV_ChargingChina-CGEP_Report_Final.pdf.

PART I

MAPPING THE
INFRASTRUCTURE CHALLENGE

CHAPTER 1

Introduction

Z. Justin Ren, PhD

In the opening of his recent book, *Climate of Hope*, Michael Bloomberg wrote that "Cities are actually the key to saving the planet."[2] When it comes to replacing internal combustion engine (ICE) vehicles with electric ones (hence the title of this work *Melting the ICE*), the same applies: cities are the key to electrifying transportation. This work focuses on why and how cities around the world are driving the change toward faster and wider electric vehicle (EV) adoption.

Transportation is one of the leading sectors in the emission of greenhouse gases, which in turn is the leading cause of global warming. To reduce greenhouse gas emissions and reverse the warming trend, nations must decarbonize their transportation sector (as well as other sectors, such as electricity production, agriculture, and industrial activity). Electrification of transportation, i.e., replacing ICE vehicles with EVs, is on the critical path toward deep decarbonization.

Every EV needs charging. This work is about the need for public infrastructure EV charging, current impediments to its widespread deployment, and practical solutions to accelerating EV adoption by enhancing infrastructure deployment. It is organized into three sections. The first section offers a high-level summary (Chapter 1) and discusses several trends that are important to EV adoption and public charging infrastructure (Chapter 2). The middle section (Chapters 3–6) presents case studies of Los Angeles, Shanghai and Beijing, Oslo, and Brookline, Massachusetts (a small township in the heart of the Boston metropolitan area). The last section (Chapters 7–9) offers perspective and tools for EV infrastructure planning, based on case studies. Chapter 7 presents an analytical tool kit that city planners can use to refine planning for, and allocating resources in support of, public EV infrastructure charging investments. Chapter 8 applies a systems approach to EVSE infrastructure. Chapter 9 concludes with key points to guide city executives, planners, and academic researchers.

---

2   Bloomberg, M. and Pope, C., *Climate of Hope: How Cities, Businesses, and Citizens Can Save the Planet*, April 2017, New York: St. Martin's Press, Chapter 2: PLANYC.

1.1   Electrification of Mobility Must Be Accelerated

Recent research from the Intergovernmental Panel on Climate Change (IPCC) of the United Nations issued a dire warning to the world in October 2018.[3] Time is running out for reversing the trend of global warming. Carbon emissions must be severely reduced beginning immediately to prevent worst-case climate impact scenarios. Specifically, scientists warn that there are about 12 years remaining if global warming is to be kept to a maximum of 1.5°C, beyond which even a half-degree increase will result in much higher risks of severe consequences from extreme weather events. Figure 1.1 provides a summary of the IPCC report's emission impact scenarios.

FIGURE 1.1 Emission Impact Scenarios[4]

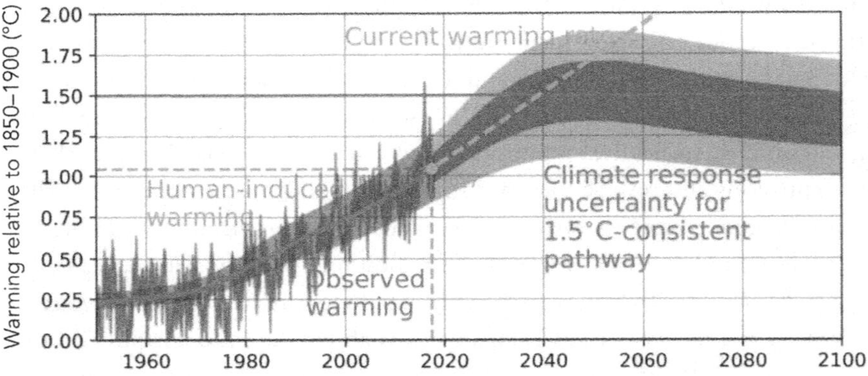

Note: The yellow solid line is the averaged actual warming trend up to 2018. The dashed yellow line is the projected warming trend based on status quo. The green and gray band after 2018 reflect the uncertainty around the 1.5° pathway scenario (i.e., with successful intervention). In this scenario, the global warming trend would reverse after 2040.

Transportation using internal combustion engine (ICE) vehicles is one of the leading contributors to atmospheric carbon buildup. Every day, transportation contributes significant carbon to the atmosphere. Most of the world's transportation systems are fossil fueled, using the ICE platform. In the United States alone, on-road transportation is the largest source of greenhouse gas contributing 1,556 Tg CO_2 Equivalent in 2016, almost 30% of US

---

3   IPCC, *Summary for Policymakers of IPCC special report on Global Warning of 1.5° approved by Governments*, Oct. 8, 2018, Available at: https://www.ipcc.ch/2018/10/08/summary-for-policymakers-of-ipcc-special-report-on-global-warming-of-1-5c-approved-by-governments/
4   Ibid., IPCC

carbon emissions.[5] Such percentage figures vary by state but can be as high as 41% in California.[6] See Figure 1.2.

FIGURE 1.2 Greenhouse Gas Emissions by Economic Sector: United States and the State of California[7]

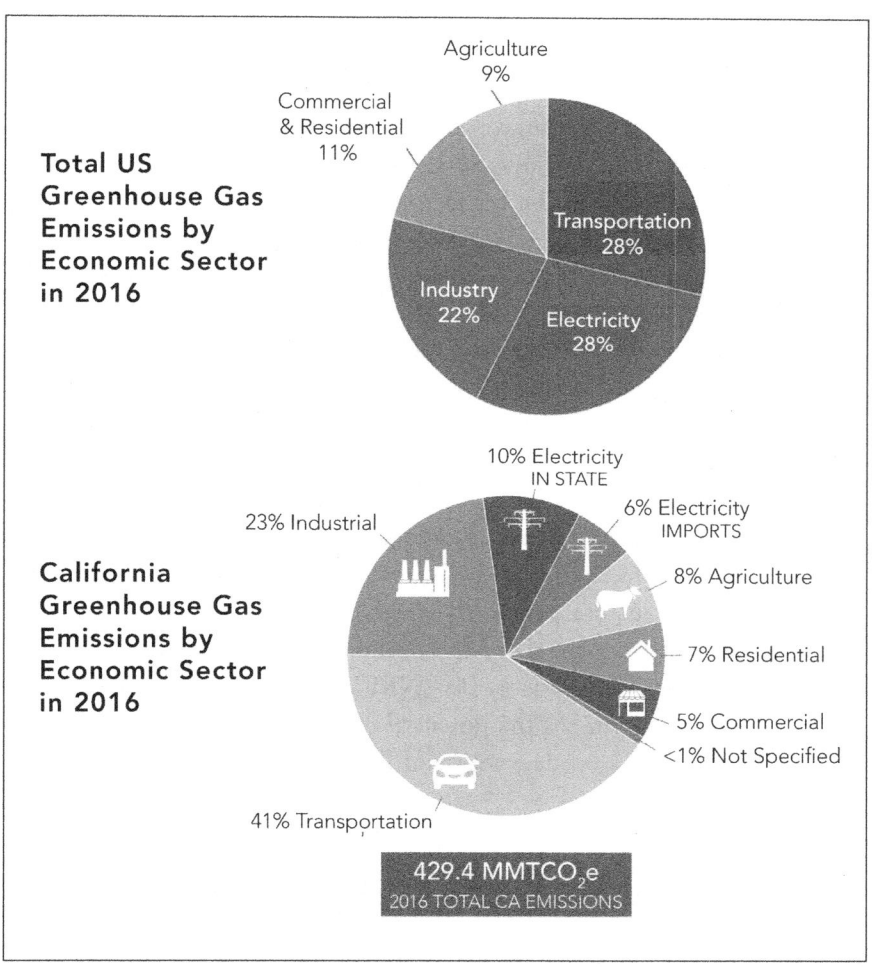

5   Tg CO2 Equivalent is Teragrams of CO2., Available at: http://www.odlt.org/dcd/
ballast/tg_co2_eq.html. EPA, *U.S. Transportation Sector Greenhouse Gas Emissions 1990-2016*,
July 2018, Available at: https://nepis.epa.gov/Exe/ZyPDF.cgi?Dockey=P100USI5.pdf
6   Ibid., EPA
7   Top figure: US Environmental Protection Agency, Available at: https://www.epa.gov/
sites/production/files/styles/large/public/2018-04/total_by_sector_2016.png; Bottom
figure: California Air Resources Board, *California Greenhouse Gas Emission Inventory—2018
Edition*, July 11, 2018, Available at: https://www.arb.ca.gov/cc/inventory/data/data.htm.

In European countries, the share of carbon contribution from transportation is similar to the United States.[8] In China, transportation contributes less to overall national carbon emissions compared to other sectors, in particular energy production.[9] However, as this 14 trillion-dollar economy (as of October 2018)[10] continues to grow, transport's share is expected to increase accordingly. China already has over 30 million more motor vehicles on the road than the United States, and Chinese vehicles are known to produce more CO_2 on a per-vehicle basis.[11]

Because of the predominant role of transportation in greenhouse gas emissions, almost all decarbonization pathway studies have identified electrification of transportation as one of the key factors in achieving decarbonization. For example, the US Middle-Century Strategy for Deep Carbonization (MCS) report released by the US White House in 2016 has the following statement in its executive summary:

> Shifting to clean electricity and low-carbon fuels in transportation, buildings, and industry: The vast majority of energy for transportation is currently provided by petroleum, while the industry and buildings sectors are powered by a mix of fuels including natural gas, coal, petroleum, and electricity. With a clean electricity system comes opportunities to reduce fossil fuel usage in these sectors: for example, electric vehicles displace petroleum use and electric heat pumps avoid the use of natural gas and oil for space and water heating in buildings.[12]

A recent electrification and decarbonization report authored by researchers at the National Renewable Energy Lab (NREL), stated:

> Electrification has the potential to address the direct combustion emissions associated with end use services in the transportation,

8   European Environment Agency, Nov. 22 2018, Available at: https://www.eea.europa.eu/data-and-maps/indicators/transport-emissions-of-greenhouse-gases/transport-emissions-of-greenhouse-gases-11.

9   Shan, Y., Guan, D., Zheng, H., Ou, J., Li, Y., Meng, J., Mi, Z., Liu, Z. and Zhang, Q., *China CO 2 emission accounts 1997–2015*. 2018, Scientific Data 5, 170201, Available at: https:// www.nature.com/articles/sdata2017201.

10   International Monetary Fund, n.d., Available at: https://www.imf.org/external/datamapper/NGDPD@WEO/OEMDC/ADVEC/WEOWORLD/C.

11   Center for Strategic and International Studies, *China Power Project, How is China Managing its Greenhouse Gas Emissions?*, n.d., Available at: https://chinapower.csis.org/china-greenhouse-gas-emissions/#top-emitters-of-carbon-dioxide.

12   The White House, *US Middle-Century Strategy for Deep Carbonization (MCS) Report*, Nov. 2016, Washington, DC: US Government, page 8, Available at: https://www.ipcc.ch/2018/10/08/summary-for-policymakers-of-ipcc-special-report-on-global-warming-of-1-5c-approved-by-governments/.

industrial, and buildings sectors, which accounted for 3,158 Mt CO_2-e emissions, or 46% of total US GHG emissions in 2014 (EPA 2016a). The transportation sector made up the largest share of direct combustion emissions (1,754 Mt CO_2-e) and, as a result, has a large potential for direct emissions reductions (EPA 2016a). Furthermore, Figure...demonstrates that emissions in the transportation sector are almost entirely due to direct fossil fuel combustion. Thus, given sufficient feasibility to substitute electric vehicles (EVs) for conventional vehicles and lowering carbon intensity of the grid, electrification in the transportation sector could represent a large potential for GHG reductions.[13]

It is worth noting that in the short- and medium-terms, greenhouse gas emissions could be reduced effectively by imposing more efficient fuel standards as well as incremental improvements in ICE technologies. However, it is evident from the aforementioned studies that deep decarbonization can be achieved only by displacing ICE vehicles with electrified, zero-emission vehicles (i.e., battery powered EVs, or via other carbon-free fuels such as fuel-cell vehicles operating on carbon-free hydrogen).

Electrification of transportation brings other important benefits beyond climate mitigation, such as energy security. This is especially important for countries that are concerned with their nonrenewable energy sources.[14] Another benefit is a cleaner environment. Certainly, EV supply chains are not necessarily clean, because EV manufacturing processes and their components, especially batteries, may not be environmentally friendly. But most scientific studies conclude that overall an EV-based transportation system is cleaner than an ICE-based system, especially so if battery manufacturing technologies and other critical components continue to improve in cleanliness.[15]

Electrification of transportation alone will not achieve desired deep decarbonization outcomes. In fact, electrification of transportation is necessary but not sufficient. The most recent report from the Deep Decarbonization

13 Steinberg, D., Bielen, D., Eichman, J., Eurek, K., Logan, J., Mai, T., McMillan, C., Parker, A., Vimmerstedt, L. and Wilson, E., *Electrification & Decarbonization: Exploring U.S. Energy Use and Greenhouse Gas Emissions in Scenarios with Widespread Electrification and Power Sector Decarbonization*, July 2017, Golden, CO: National Renewable Energy Laboratory, page 3, Available at: https://www.nrel.gov/docs/fy17osti/68214.pdf.
14 See, for example, a review of the security aspect of renewable energy sources by Johansson, B., *Security aspects of future renewable energy systems—A short overview, Energy*, Nov. 2013, vol. 61, 1, pages 598-605, Available at: https://www.sciencedirect.com/science/article/pii/S0360544213007743.
15 The Union of Concerned Scientists. *Cleaner Cars from Cradle to Grave*, 2015, Available at: https://www.ucsusa.org/clean-vehicles/electric-vehicles/life-cycle-ev-emissions.

Pathway Project (DDPP), a global consortium of decarbonization research teams, states:

> All deep decarbonization pathways incorporate "three pillars" of energy system transformation: energy efficiency and conservation, decarbonizing electricity and fuels, and switching end uses to low-carbon supplies. These measures were all implemented using technologies that are commercially available or expected to be in the time frame of the analysis. The DDPs show multiple ways of implementing the three pillars, with country-specific strategies, technology mixes, and sequences of action. However, because of the interactive effects between them—for example, using low-carbon electricity in combination with the electrification of vehicles—deep decarbonization cannot be achieved if any of the pillars is absent or implemented at insufficient scale.[16]

In addition, expanding and modernizing public transit at the city level remains an effective strategy for many cities combating congestion, which contributes to reducing carbon footprints. Deep decarbonization plans for cities, such as *Carbon Free Boston*,[17] contain analyses of the full range of transport strategies, their dollar costs, and their CO_2 savings potential. These and other deep decarbonization studies spotlight interconnected factors as well as the uniqueness of each locality, which requires solutions fitted to specific local needs. Deep decarbonization plans demonstrate the value of a "multivariate framework" that maps major factors related to EV infrastructure deployment for cities (see Chapter 7), and a "systems approach" that focuses on these factors (see Chapter 8).

This work primarily emphasizes the electrification of passenger vehicles. Attention to EV buses, trucks or other commercial vehicles is not emphasized because the majority (about 60–70%) of transport CO_2 emissions are from passenger vehicles.[18] However, much of the Electric Vehicle Supply Equipment (EVSE) created by cities will also serve freight vehicles, and electrification of fleet-based EVs. Attention to autonomous vehicles will be noted where relevant as will decarbonization of freight transport.

---

16 Sustainable Development Solutions Network, *Deep Decarbonization Pathway Project (DDPP) report*, Sept. 2015, page 6. Available at: http://deepdecarbonization.org/wp-content/uploads/2015/12/DDPP_EXESUM-1.pdf.

17 Cleveland, C., et al. *Carbon Free Boston Stakeholder Report*, March 2019, Available at: https://www.bu.edu/ise/research/cfb/.

18 OECD, *Reducing Transport Greenhouse Gas Emissions: Trends and Data, 2010*, Available at: https://www.nature.com/articles/sdata2017201; See also Tran, M., Banister, D., Bishop, D.K. J. and McCulloch, D. M., *Nature Climate Change*, 2012, vol. 2, pages 328–333, Available at: https://www.nature.com/articles/nclimate1429#ref6.

1.2 Cities Play a Pivotal Role in Electrifying Transportation

A fundamental trend happening worldwide is population migration from rural to urban areas. According to United Nations estimates, the percentage of people living in urban areas will increase to 86.6% by 2050 for more developed countries, and 65.6% for less developed countries, as depicted in Figure 1.3.

FIGURE 1.3 Percentage of Population at Mid-Year in Urban Areas, 1950–2050[19]

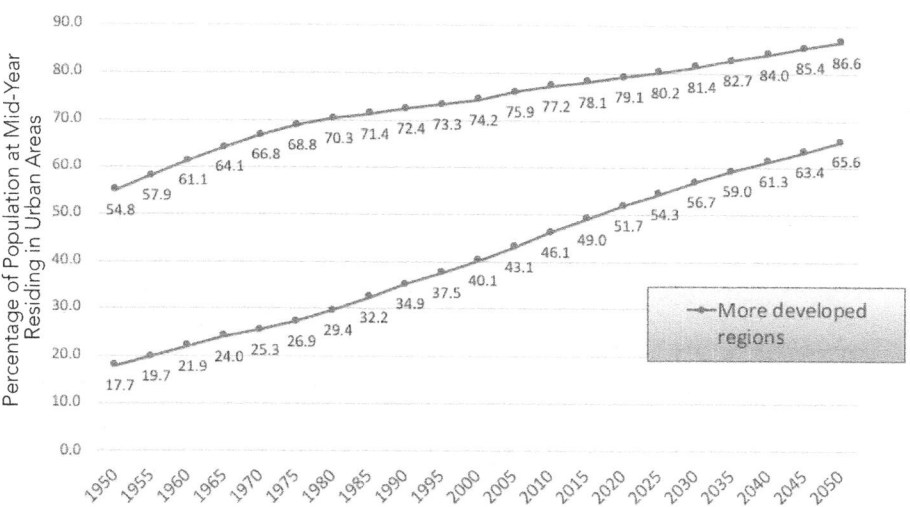

With more population living in urban areas, there will be more private and public transportation vehicles on roads, and increased vehicle miles traveled. Moreover, research shows that when the rubber meets the road, cities are the main actors and influencers in decarbonizing and electrifying mobility.[20]

Figure 1.4 maps the variation of EV adoption in the United States. The map shows that there is a steep hill to climb for most cities, if cities are to be leaders in decarbonizing and electrifying mobility.

---

19   UN Department of Economic and Social Affairs, *Worlds Urbanization Prospects 2018*, 2018, Available at: https://population.un.org/wup/Download/. Figure compiled by author.

20   Phocas, R., Prochazka, B. and Ritchotte, J., *Fulfilling America's Pledge—Climate Mayors, Leading Cities, and New Partnerships Lead America's Electric Transportation Future*, Dec. 20, 2018, Bloomberg Philanthropies Blog, Available at: https://www.bloomberg.org/blog/fulfilling-americas-pledge-climate-mayors-20-leading-cities-new-partnerships-lead-americas-electric-transportation-future.

FIGURE 1.4 Variation of EV Adoption in the United States[21]

Electric vehicle share of new 2017 vehicle registrations by metropolitan area.

☐ 0%–0.5%   0.5%–1%   ▦ 1%–1.5%   ▦ 1.5%–2%   ▦ 2%–3%   ▦ 3%–4%   ■ 4%–5%

State-level policies that provide incentives for EV adoption are clearly visible in the Figure 1.4 above. For example, many cities in California have higher adoption rates than cities in other states. California has comparatively stronger policies to support greater EV adoption than other states in the United States (ZE, the "Zero-Emission Vehicle" mandate, which requires that a minimum percentage of a vehicle manufacturer's statewide sales must be of vehicles that produce no tailpipe emissions).[22]

However, the large variances in EV adoption across cities cannot be explained by national- or state-level policies or incentives alone. For example, EV market shares in various California cities are quite different, even though, as a whole, the state comprises the largest portion of EV sales in the United States. This illustrates that cities across the United States can be very different in their effectiveness electrifying transportation. On the other hand, looking at cities as a whole, they are leading the charge in EV adoption. Worldwide, about 25

---

21 Slowik, P. and Lutsey, N., *The Continued Transition to Electric Vehicles in U.S. Cities*, 2018, ICCT, Available at: https://www.theicct.org/publications/continued-EV-transition-us-cities-2018. New vehicle registration data from IHS Automotive.
22 California Air Resources Board, *The Zero Emission Vehicle (ZEV) Regulation*, Oct. 24, 2018, Available at: https://www.arb.ca.gov/msprog/zevprog/factsheets/zev_regulation_factsheet_082418.pdf.

cities account for nearly half of the total EVs in use. Los Angeles, Beijing, and Shanghai each host about 5% of the total EVs in the world, while Shenzhen and Oslo each contain 3%. See more details in Figure 1.5.

FIGURE 1.5 EV Market Shares in Select Cities Worldwide[23]

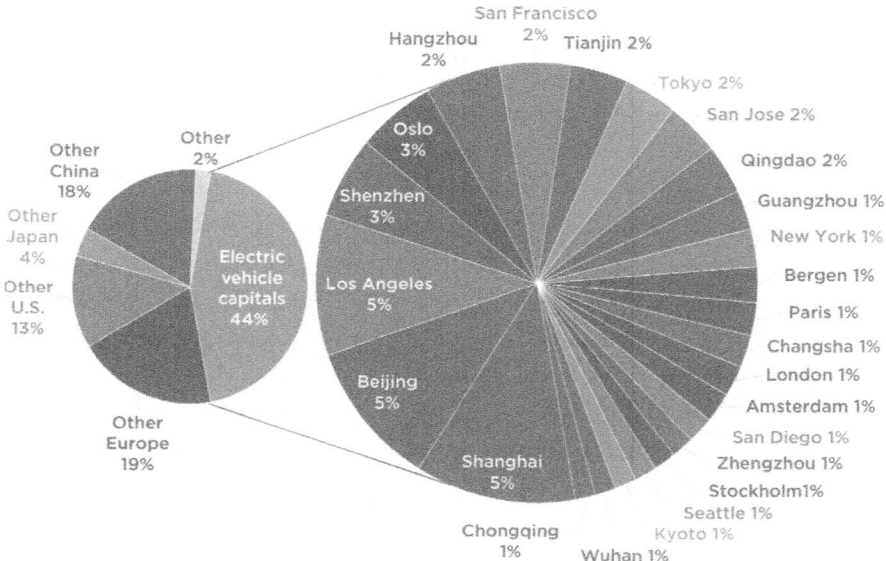

Such high concentrations of EVs in metropolitan areas highlight the importance of cities in accelerating EV growth. The research herein sheds light on why cities are the driving force in electrifying mobility. It starts by recognizing that EV adoption depends on current infrastructure. It features detailed case studies of four of the five previously mentioned cities (Los Angeles, Beijing, Shanghai, Oslo) and examines why, how, and what each of the case study cities are doing in electrifying transportation and building up needed EV infrastructure.

23   Hall, D., Cui, H. and Lutsey, N., *Electric Vehicle Capitals: Accelerating the Global Transition to Electric Drive, The International Council on Clean Transportation*, Oct. 30, 2018, Available at: https://www.theicct.org/publications/ev-capitals-of-the-world-2018.

1.3 Electrifying Mobility Depends on Various Stakeholders, Multiple Infrastructures, and Local Characteristics

Electric vehicles depend on local electricity grids and other city infrastructure, including but not limited to roads, traffic signals, the underlying communications backbones of cities, and safety and security systems. Infrastructure interdependency is a main reason why cities must approach electrifying mobility systematically, particularly with respect to EVs. Moreover, electrifying mobility is not just about installing more chargers. It is also about mayors, city executives, planners, and administrators adopting a holistic systems approach to propelling accelerated EV use. (This is discussed in depth Chapter 8.)

Consider the example of fueling systems. The ICE fueling system, composed of gas stations for cars, trucks, and fleets, may be renovated, in part, to accommodate EV charging; something a number of petroleum companies are doing. That is, service stations may be repurposed to integrate EVSEs while continuing to serve ICE vehicle fueling requirements.

The shift from ICE to EV will involve a multitude of stakeholders. These include EV customers, automakers, auto distributors and service providers, EVSEs, oil and gas, electric and gas utilities, wireless communications platforms, real estate owners and developers, retailers, and federal, state, and municipal governments. A systems approach (see Chapter 8) can help guide infrastructure design, development, deployment, and policies, which support continuing, and possibly accelerating, EV adoption.

The roles of various stakeholders are likely to evolve as EV adoption increases.[24] Take for example the role of utilities. With increased EV adoption, utilities may adopt new technologies, such as battery storage and smart grid solutions in order to better manage load impacts from growing EV market share. In the United States, some utilities may be allowed to build more EV chargers themselves, while others may enter into some form of partnership in building out EV charging infrastructure. In China, a similar pattern appears to be emerging, where the State Grid is deploying charging infrastructure while private enterprises are doing so as well. Also, some utilities in the United States and elsewhere may move into providing transportation services. For all of these possibilities, utilities need to work with multiple branches of local governments as well with their own customers.

---

24 Smith, S., Sanborn, S. and Slaughter, A., *Powering the future of mobility: How the electric power sector can prepare for its critical role in the new transportation ecosystem*, Oct. 16, 2017, Deloitte Insights, Available at: https://www2.deloitte.com/insights/us/en/focus/future-of-mobility/power-utilities-future-of-electric-vehicles.html.

One of the most important lessons learned from researching each city's EV transition trajectory is that each successful city is successful in its own way, while unsuccessful cities tend to be alike. A visual representation is presented as Figure 1.6 (more details are found in Chapter 7).

FIGURE 1.6 Each Successful City Is Successful in Its Own Way[25]

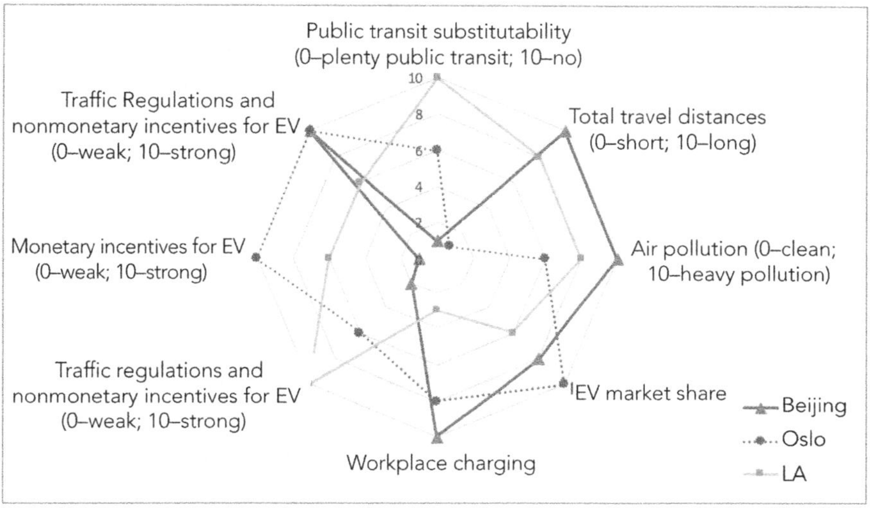

Note: Each polygon represents a city. Each vertex represents a score on a factor (there are a total of 8 factors).

In the above figure, major factors that are related to EV infrastructure deployment for three cities are plotted: Beijing, Oslo, and Los Angeles. All three cities are considered to be successful in EV adoption and supporting it with charging infrastructure. The major factors considered include:

- Monetary incentives
- Traffic regulations and other nonmonetary incentives
- Home charging availability
- Workplace charging availability
- EV market share
- Local air pollution
- Total travel distance
- Public transit

All the above factors are related to EV adoption and EV infrastructure deployment. Figure 1.6 shows that the three cities are quite different in the key

25 Source: By author

dimensions mapped in Figure 1.6, and yet each city has developed its own effective policies, which encourage city residents to switch from ICE vehicles to EVs.

For example, Oslo built up its high EV rolling stock mainly by using Norway's significant financial incentives to drive EV adoption. In contrast, Beijing managed to drive large-scale EV adoption by installing strong nonfinancial disincentives to own ICE vehicles (e.g., it uses a lottery system with an extremely low chance of being awarded ICE license plates). The disincentive is also an incentive to adopt EVs because EV license plates are available without a lottery. Los Angeles gives EV drivers the right to use HOV lanes, which become a major incentive for owning an EV in the face of heavy congestion on its freeways. These distinctive approaches strongly suggest that each locality needs to design its own basket of incentives that are based on unique local circumstances to successfully advance EV adoption.

1.4 The Future of EV Infrastructure Will Be "Smart": Digital, Interconnected, and Innovation-Driven

Just as next-generation power supplies will be "smart power"[26] and next-generation EVs will be "smart vehicles," next-generation EV infrastructure will be smart.

While not all EV chargers will be smart chargers, it is generally expected that most of the EV charging infrastructure will have the capability for real-time Internet communication and various cloud-based services for downloading and uploading relevant information and executing transactions. EV charging networks are expected to be integrated with smart grids to contribute to managing grid system reliability and supporting resilience requirements through Vehicle-to-Grid (V2G) or Vehicle-to-Home (V2H) technologies.

Another emerging trend is the integration of autonomous vehicles (AV) with EVs. There are many reasons why AVs most likely will be electric: (a) EVs require less maintenance and therefore can be in continuous operations longer; (b) EV charging can be fully autonomous while ICE refueling requires human intervention; (c) EVs are cheaper in the long run; and (d) they are cleaner.[27] For this emerging trend to continue, adoption of electric AVs will require better,

---

26 Fox-Penner, P., *Smart Power: Climate Change, the Smart Grid, and the Future of Electric Utilities*, 2010, Island Press.
27 For a deeper discussion, see Hatch, J. and Helveston, J., *Will Autonomous Vehicles be Electric?*, 2018, Boston University Institute of Sustainable Energy, Available at: https:// www.bu.edu/ise/2018/08/27/will-autonomous-vehicles-be-electric/.

smarter charging infrastructure. Over time, smart EV infrastructure is expected to work seamlessly with AVs, which together may have the potential to revamp cities' mobility infrastructure and fundamentally change cities themselves.

1.5 Home/Residential Charging Is Essential, but Not Sufficient

A fundamental difference between EVs and ICE vehicles is that EV charging occurs mostly at residential locations, which means a new "fueling" platform is emerging with electric utilities and third-party chargers as service providers.

A recent survey of 3,247 individuals, conducted by Plug Insights, shows that 81% of EV charging occurs at home. Seven percent occurs at workplaces and 10% at public charging stations.[28] These numbers are consistent with other studies (such studies will be noted later in this Chapter and in Chapter 8) as well as with the practical experience of city officials from cases studied. Consequently, city planners and specialized transportation planners may conclude that a lower level of public charge point assets will be sufficient for serving the needs of EV users.

The National Renewable Energy Laboratory (NREL), a Department of Energy research center, recently published a scenario-driven study focused on EV infrastructure requirements in the United States.[29] The research was model based, with scenarios analyzed for EV charging requirements in urban and rural communities, and along interstate highways. Research addressed not only the scale of public EV charging infrastructure needed but also how its deployment might be phased, based on EV adoption rates and patterns.

The high points of the study are as follows:

- An EV location with 15 million EVs on the road is estimated to require from 100,000 to 1.2 million charge points (with Level 2 dominating the mix of levels—see Figure 1.7).
- Fewer charging stations will be required to support long-distance highway trips.

---

28   Inside EVs, *81% of Electric Vehicle Charging is Done at Home*, 2018, Available at: https://insideevs.com/most-electric-vehicle-owners-charge-at-home-in-other-news-the-sky-is-blue/.

29   Presentation by Wood, E., Rames, C., Muratori, M., Raghavan, S. and Melaina, M., *National Plug-In Electric Vehicle Infrastructure Analysis,* Jan. 8, 2018, National Renewable Energy Laboratory (NREL), Available at: https://www.nrel.gov/docs/fy18osti/70779. pdf; For the full report, see: https://www.nrel.gov/docs/fy17osti/69031.pdf.

As its EV rolling stock has grown rapidly, Oslo, and some areas of Los Angeles, have learned that public charging infrastructure can be stressed by higher volumes of EVs needing to use available charging assets. This happens even where the number of EVs on the road rises by only a small percentage. Norway, and Oslo in particular, recognize that home charging by far is preferred, so the city is emphasizing it as EV adoption increases. For Oslo, it means finding ways to enable more home charging in multifamily dwellings and apartment buildings. Oslo's experience with the challenges stemming from accelerated EV adoption should be studied by other cities when their own EV adoption rates grow. See Chapter 5 for additional discussion.

Still, home charging must be complemented by public charging infrastructure. Recent research demonstrates how important ready access to public charging is in mitigating the anxiety related to range and charging wait times.[30]

New charging infrastructure is evolving while it overlaps with existing fueling methods for ICE vehicles. Charging services can be added to gas stations, as noted. These locations eventually may be fully repurposed as EV charging service centers or plazas, which may also integrate a broader menu of retail options compared to present-day convenience-vending services, or the age of the fueling station may be coming to an end.[31]

---

30   For an in-depth report on EV charging infrastructure in China and the United States, see Ibid., Hove, A. and Sandalow, D.

31   CarPay Diem, *Future of Fuel Stations: None, shopping malls or else?*, Available at: https://www.carpay-diem.com/2018/05/11/future-of-fuel-stations-none-shopping-malls-or-else/. Also, Mounce, R. and Nelson, J. D., *On the potential for one-way electric vehicle car-sharing in future mobility systems, Transportation Research Policy: Part A: Policy and Practice*, Feb. 2019, vol. 120, pages 17–30; Mounce, et al., examine the integration of one-way EV use with other transportation systems pointing to a future where conventional fueling stations are much less relevant. A view to the end of gasoline stations is articulated by Buhr, M., Gas stations will disappear sooner than you think, Oct. 1, 2017, The Hill, Available at: https://thehill.com/opinion/technology/352884-gas-stations-will-disappear-sooner-than-you-think.

FIGURE 1.7 Profile of Charging Levels[32]

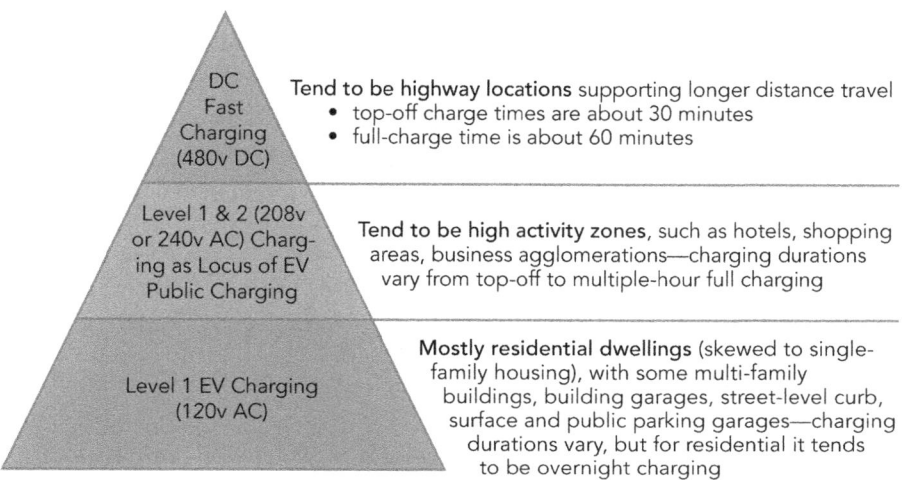

DC Fast Charging (480v DC)
Tend to be highway locations supporting longer distance travel
- top-off charge times are about 30 minutes
- full-charge time is about 60 minutes

Level 1 & 2 (208v or 240v AC) Charging as Locus of EV Public Charging
Tend to be high activity zones, such as hotels, shopping areas, business agglomerations—charging durations vary from top-off to multiple-hour full charging

Level 1 EV Charging (120v AC)
Mostly residential dwellings (skewed to single-family housing), with some multi-family buildings, building garages, street-level curb, surface and public parking garages—charging durations vary, but for residential it tends to be overnight charging

Another difference between the infrastructure of ICE fueling and that of EV public charging is that the latter must be widely available. This is true for many reasons, from dispelling range anxiety to enabling EV users to top-off their battery charge levels to continually maximize available vehicle trip range. Also, this approach helps to minimize negative effects on core power plant battery integrity by limiting the frequency of long-duration deep recharging.

The definition of EV public charging infrastructure used in this work includes some forms of charging at residential locations (the line between public and private charging infrastructure can be blurred when private charging stations start to be shared, which is seen already in some localities around the world). Home charging is typically considered with regard to single-family dwellings, but most urban areas contain many types of multifamily residential structures, from duplexes to large apartment buildings. In most cities, maintaining home charging that optimizes public infrastructure access (as EV adoption grows) requires significant effort to include "multifamily dwelling home charging" solutions as part of the overall "home charging category."

As EV adoption increases, cities may find it necessary to require owners of apartment buildings to install EV chargers in their buildings or in adjacent buildings or nearby surface parking lots. Owners should be rewarded for doing so and for ensuring that tenants have access to efficient charge points. Likewise, incentives for condominiums and other owner-occupied multifamily dwellings

---

32 Source: The pyramid diagram is presented in many ways across multiple publications in research journals and research institutes and centers. This depiction is the author's adaptation based on several similar EV charging graphics using a pyramid.

should be provided to spur and ease the adoption of Level 1 and Level 2 home charging infrastructure.

Unlike a public charging location, EV charging for a multifamily dwelling must be viewed as one readily available, easily accessible charger for each EV. Since home charging for multifamily dwellings has been under-emphasized until recently, the policies, guidelines, building codes, parking codes, and zoning requirements to support this type of EV charging have remained only partially designed and deployed in most cities.

1.6   Success Recipes for Accelerating City-Level EV Deployment

To summarize, here are several ways to spur accelerated EV infrastructure deployment so that it coevolves with accelerating EV adoption:

1. **Keep the big picture in mind, identify key influencing factors.** Mobility is at the heart of the intersection of smart grids and smart cities, so cities need to take an approach that integrates overall city plans and vision. For example, in 2015 Eric Garcetti, the Major of Los Angeles, unveiled LA's first-ever comprehensive Sustainable City plan,[33] which targets 14 categories to improve the city's environment, economy, and equity. The City of Boston, in its Carbon-Free Boston plan, has set its goal to be carbon-neutral by 2050.[34] Norway has longstanding policies requiring all new cars to be zero-emission by 2030.[35] As noted above, Chapter 7 contains a framework with eight categories of factors (monetary incentives, traffic regulations and other nonmonetary incentives, home charging availability, workplace charging availability, EV market share, local air pollution, total travel distance, and public transit) that city planners can use to identify which among them are most relevant to each locality.

---

33   The pLAn. Available at: http://plan.lamayor.org/.

34   Ibid., Cleveland, C., et al.

35   Voelcker, J., *Norway's Goal: All New Cars Will Be Emission-Free By 2025 To Cut Carbon*, Aug. 4, 2015, Green Car Reports, Available at: https://www.greencarreports.com/news/1099324_norways-goal-all-new-cars-will-be-electric-by-2025-to-cut-carbon; Elvestuen, O., Minister of Climate and Environment, Norway's Low Emissions Policy, July 11, 2018, Statement at The EU's Vision for a Modern, Clean, and Competitive Economy, stakeholder consultation high-level public event, Brussels, Available at: https://www.regjeringen.no/en/aktuelt/norways-low-emissions-strategy/id2607245/.

2. **Establish a clear goal, a measurement system and a process.** Each city should have a clear goal with a definitive deadline. For example, the City of Los Angeles's sustainability plan established a clear goal for EV adoption: increase the percentage of electric and zero emission vehicles in the city to 10% by 2025 and 25% by 2035. Once there is a clear goal, the next step is to build a process to craft an execution plan and to measure its progress. This is where each city needs to come up with its own creative solution. Figure 1.8 is a sample process flow chart.

FIGURE 1.8 A Sample Process Flow Toward Accelerated City-Level EV Infrastructure Deployment[36]

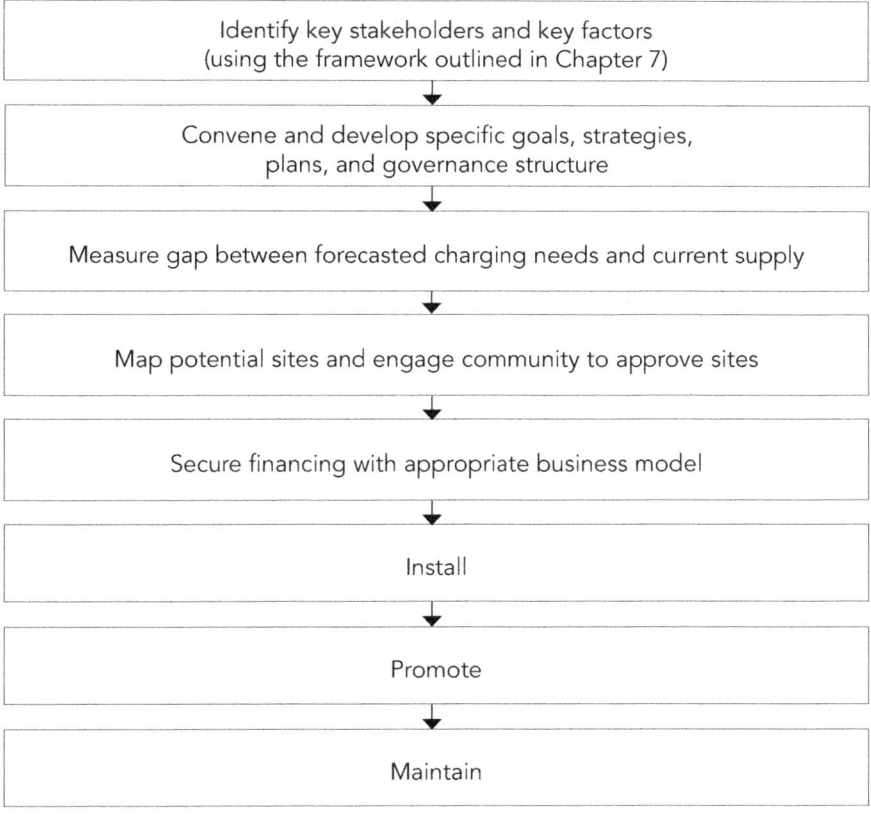

36 Source: By author. Katharine Lusk, Executive Director, Initiative on Cities at Boston University, suggested an early version of the above process flow.

3. **Tailor incentives.** Set up EV incentives (or disincentives) tailored to the specific needs of each locality. One of the main findings of this work is that there is no "silver bullet" that will solve every city's EV adoption challenges. Each city's situation is distinct, so its solutions also must be distinct. Still, most solutions will include financial or nonfinancial incentives, public charging infrastructure access, home charging, and workplace charging. Included in this work is a framework for holistically evaluating each city's EV infrastructure (Chapter 7). The lessons outlined in each case study (Chapter 3–6) serve as guidelines for city leaders as they craft distinctive solutions and plans that fit their specific cities.

4. **Develop and improve EV-related policies, standards, and practices**, and let a regional EV infrastructure organization, third party, or public-private partnership do the heavy lifting of infrastructure deployment (e.g., adjusting city zoning rules, building codes, and traffic management requirements) to facilitate EV adoption and charging access.

5. **Leverage existing infrastructure.** Home charging may be a priority, but private businesses, utilities, and other stakeholders must be involved in mapping the scale and scope of public charging infrastructure as EV adoption rates increase. This means leveraging existing infrastructure as much as possible to broaden the geographic accessibility of pubic charging, keep costs low, and maximize structural flexibility. Continuously evaluating the multiple dimensions of existing infrastructure such as public transportation and the availability of home charging and workplace charging is important as well. Chapter 7 presents an index tool to help city planners visualize their EV-related infrastructure.

6. **Set EV charging costs wisely to help achieve a city's specific goals.** Providers might consider offering electricity charging at no cost in the early phases of EV adoption, which is a compelling incentive. However, as market penetration grows and stresses on public charging infrastructure increase, pricing of electricity (or integrating it into the cost of parking) might be an effective way to optimize charge point use.

7. **Plan for and implement EV deployment at a scale that simplifies financing and allows cities and jurisdictions in a metropolitan area to work together more efficiently.** For example, place EV supply equipment (EVSE) responsibility within an existing transit district or agency, or create a specific regional EV organization to speed adoption and keep pace with the charging infrastructure requirements as EV adoption continues.

8. Create and support dynamic cross-learning and experience-sharing opportunities, which help city operations managers and staff stay up to date on state-of-the-art operational challenges and solutions. This work strives to serve this need.

Cities are on the frontlines in the EV transition, and leaders and community stakeholders must urge higher-level government entities to increase their funding in a timely manner and at the scale needed.

Cities are vastly complex information systems, especially with regard to transportation. Detailed information can be leveraged to locate EV charging infrastructure that aligns with existing utility infrastructure. Such information can also support utility funding requests for system upgrades necessary for EV deployments to utility regulators or municipal utility boards. These system upgrades can be funded through conventional rate-making processes or other financial mechanisms. These issues are discussed in Chapter 8.

To illustrate possibilities arising from aligning city and utility infrastructure, consider metropolitan Los Angeles and its expanding light rail system. Utility infrastructure changes must occur along rail lines to power electrified rail cars as well as provide power for nodal development at station stops. This is an ideal moment to plan for and prepare to integrate charge points with new and existing light rail infrastructure. In many light rail systems in the United States, small steps in this direction are occurring. The point is that the value of leveraging existing infrastructure may warrant greater attention by city leaders and planners, if it is not already under consideration.

A hypothetical example: If charge points were easily portable, moving them around a city to help deal with queuing and charging congestion issues could be a low-cost solution when EV agglomerations affect accessibility to local charging infrastructure. Mobile charging services might be deployed to ease wait times and assuage wait anxiety while granting time to plan and deploy more permanent EV public charging infrastructure.

Portable or easily accessible relocation charge points are established technologies. Using existing infrastructure is also on city planners' radar, but aggressively leveraging multiple infrastructures to enhance EV charging access is less common. For example, Royal Dutch Shell (Shell) and BP are redesigning their retail fueling stations to accommodate EV fueling, whether for electrons poured into BEVs or hydrogen poured into fuel-cell-powered vehicles. Also, BP is investing in portable EV charging solutions. This is discussed more the next chapter.

Another leverageable infrastructure, where electricity service is easily accessed, involves street lighting systems. Some street lighting platforms have enough power to enable parasitic charge point deployment to support accelerated buildout of needed EV charging infrastructure. In other cases, the electricity in low-power street lighting systems must be upgraded in order to provide EV charging services while continuing to illuminate streets. Using existing street lighting for EV charging may be less expensive than creating wholly new charging systems, even if electricity service must be upgraded on some street lighting systems.[37]

One interviewee for a city case study characterized cities' importance and power this way: "We own the roads." In other words, cities are responsible for how traffic flows on roads as well for the physical roadway itself. Cities have the administrative power to deploy EV infrastructure aggressively, but that administrative power depends first and foremost on adopting the leadership necessary to manage existing interdependent infrastructures and shape new infrastructure.

The next chapter (Chapter 2) discusses several trends that are important to EV adoption and public charging infrastructure.[38]

---

[37] Street lighting examples were gleaned by the authors from interviews with utility executives in Southern California for the Los Angeles case study in Chapter 3, and from discussion with city officials of Brookline, MA.

[38] A brief aside may be a useful way to illustrate the extraordinary power that a committed mayor and influential stakeholders can have when it comes to driving transportation and urban structural changes. Consider what transformed Portland, Oregon, from being an economically depressed city to one the *Wall Street Journal* has called an "urban mecca" for city planners. In the 1970s, a highway called Harbor Drive largely prevented the public from accessing the Willamette River, which flows through the city. The mayor decided to literally tear up Harbor Drive from one end of the city to the other and replace it with a vast public space composed of a continuous park with amenities and events that attracted people to the city. This extraordinary action was the first of many that led to Portland's renaissance. Others included building a light rail system and creating a downtown residential district (the Pearl). The critical success factor in this story? Personal leadership and determination along with the shared political will of stakeholders and influential entities, including the local electric utilities. The same opportunity is there for the taking by every city mayor. http://www.preservenet.com/freeways/FreewaysHarbor.html.

CHAPTER 2

Major Trends in Electrifying Mobility

Z. Justin Ren, PhD and David O. Jermain

2.1. EV Adoption and EV Infrastructure Deployment Is Accelerating

A report published by the Office of Economic Cooperation and Development (OECD) and the International Energy Agency (IEA) in 2018 documented global EV adoption from 2005 to 2017. Its calculations show global adoption at just over three million vehicles,[39] illustrated in Figure 2.1.

The figure shows that China and the United States are leading the charge in EV adoption. In a recent study by Columbia University on EV infrastructure in China and the United States, it is reported that in 2018 alone 1.25 million EVs were sold in China and 0.36 million in the United States. As of January 2019, there were about 2.6 million EVs in China and 1.1 million in the United States.[40]

Furthermore, for almost all countries, the rate of EV adoption is also accelerating (albeit at a slower rate). In Norway, EVs have outsold ICE counterparts—58.4% of all new cars sold in March 2019 were Battery EVs (BEV).[41] This is being viewed as a tipping point as EVs are outselling ICE vehicles in the country.[42]

---

39 OECD/IEA, *Global EV Outlook 2018: Toward Cross-Modal Electrification*, n.d., page 107. Available at: http://www.oecd.org/about/publishing/Corrigendum_GEVO2018.pdf.
40 Ibid., Hove, A. and Sandalow, D., and Brown, P., *Norway sells more EVs than traditional cars for the first time*, April 2, 2019, Electronic 360, Available at: https://electronics360.globalspec.com/article/13612/norway-sells-more-evs-than-traditional-cars-for-the-first-time.
41 Ibid., Brown, P.
42 AP, *In Norway, electric cars outsell traditional ones for the first time*, Apr. 1, 2019, MarketWatch, Available at: https://www.marketwatch.com/story/in-norway-electric-cars-outsell-traditional-ones-for-the-first-time-2019-04-01.

FIGURE 2.1 Electric Vehicle Car Stock (Bev and Phev) by Country, 2005–2017 (thousands)[43]

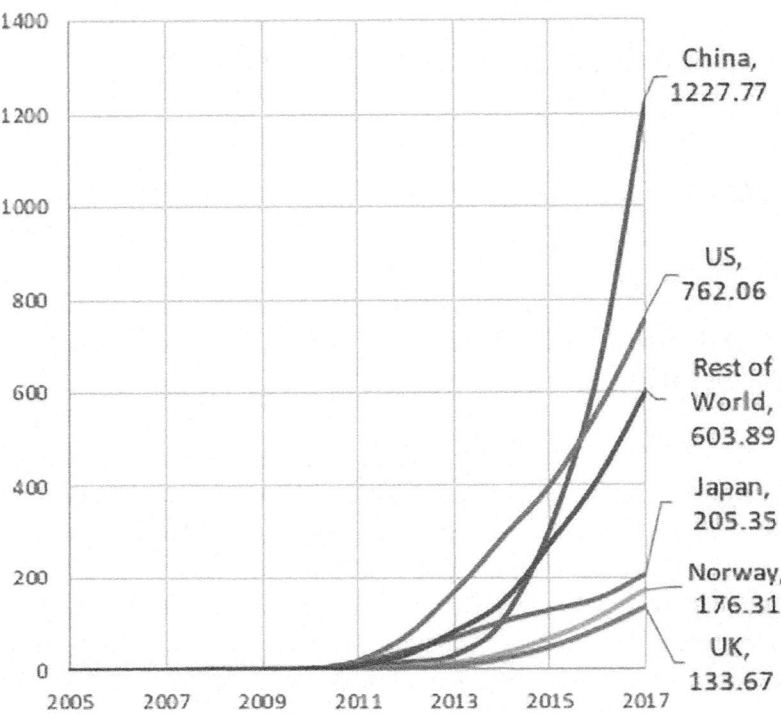

The latest figures from the aforementioned Columbia University report show that as of January 2019 there were roughly 330,000 public chargers in China, and about 67,000 "non-residential chargers" in the United States.

Comparing Figures 2.1 and 2.2 shows EV adoption aligns closely with the growth of charging infrastructure.[44] The OECD/IEA report describes the linkage as follows:

43 *Global EV Outlook 2018: Toward Cross-Modal Electrification*, n.d., Available at: http://www.oecd.org/about/publishing/Corrigendum_GEVO2018.pdf.

44 "Close alignment" is a general term. EV literature is rich with varying calculations and conclusions about the optimal ratio of public to private charging infrastructure. This topic will be covered throughout this work. See, for example, the following authors: Wolbertus, R., Kroesen, M., Hoed, R. van den, and Chorus, C., *Fully charged: An empirical study into the factors that influence connection times at EV-charging stations*, 2018, Energy Policy, 123, pages 1–7, Available at: https://doi.org/10.106/j.enpol.2018.08.030; Helmus, J.R., Spoelstra, J.C., Refa, N., Lees, M. and Hoed, R., *Assessment of public charging infrastructure push and pull rollout strategies: The case of the Netherlands*, 2018, Energy Policy, 121, pages 33–47, Available at: https://doi.org/10.1016/j.enpol.2018.06.011; Hall, D., and Lutsey, N., *Emerging Best Practices for Electric Vehicle Charging Infrastructure*, 2017, The International Council on Clean Transportation.

FIGURE 2.2 Publicly Accessible Chargers (slow and fast) by Country, 2005–2017[45]

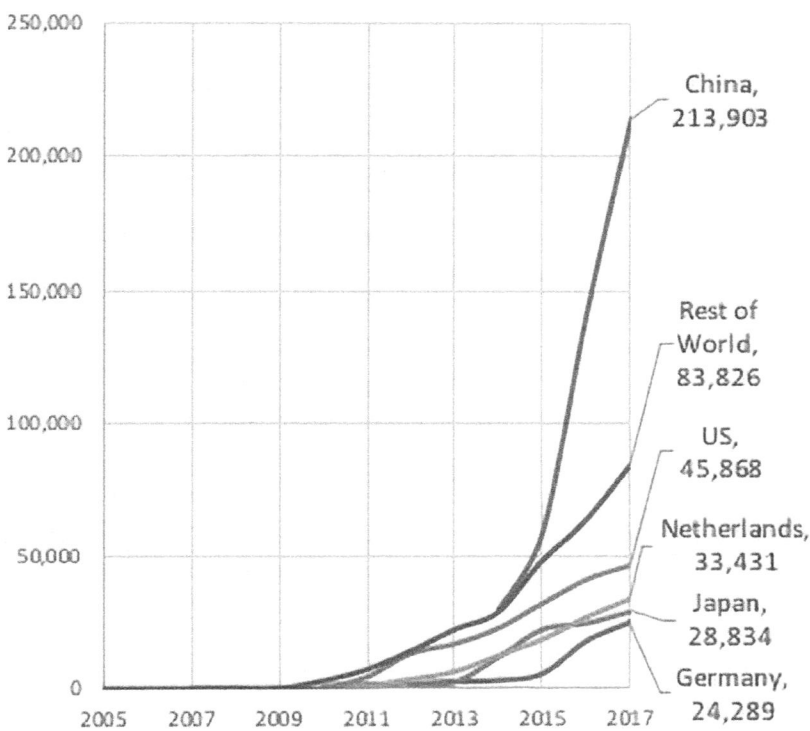

In 2017, private chargers at residences and workplaces, estimated to number almost 3 million worldwide, were the most widely used charging installations for electric cars owned by households and fleets. Charging outlets on private property for fleets (primarily buses) number some 366,000 units, almost all in China.[46]

The OECD/IEA report, as well as a recent report by ICCT,[47] emphasized that *publicly accessible* EV chargers are an important element in the EVSE system. Most public charging infrastructure provides service at Level 1 and Level 2. Fast chargers (Level 3) may play a more significant role in urban areas as EV adoption continues. One key variable that is likely to influence deployment of

45   *Global EV Outlook 2018: Toward Cross-Modal Electrification*, n.d., page 112, Available at: http://www.oecd.org/about/publishing/Corrigendum_GEVO2018.pdf.
46   Ibid., OECD/IEA, page 10.
47   Ibid., Hall, D., and Lutsey, N.

fast chargers is the displacement of "range anxiety" by anxiety over wait times to recharge and how cities assuage such worries.[48]

2.2 EV Adoption Drives the Need for Infrastructure, and Vice Versa

2.2.1 Public Infrastructure Charging

EV adoption generally correlates with accessible public charging infrastructure. Many studies suggest that different ratios of EVs to public charge point availability are optimal.[49] Figure 2.3 shows a modeled estimate of the gap between adoption and public charge point accessibility over the last few years.

If present trends continue, considerably more public charging infrastructure will be needed (absent an unexpected revolution in battery technology, or another mode of electrification). Public charging infrastructure can be costly and take time to deploy. As with other industries, overbuilding EV infrastructure can result in underutilized charging assets; but underbuilding can expose city leaders, executives, and managers to dissatisfaction from EV users and other EV stakeholders.

---

[48] Patel, V.J., *Forget About Range Anxiety, EV Owners Now Face 'Charging Time Trauma'*, Oct. 12, 2017, FutureCar, Available at: https://www.futurecar.com/1527/Forget-About-Range-Anxiety-EV-Owners-now-Face-Charging-Time-Trauma.

[49] Ratios of EVs to EV charge points are plentiful in literature, illustrating the complexity of planning for EV infrastructure deployment. An EV–to–EV-charge-point ratio may vary by location and density of EVs in a specific location. The layout of a city's traffic network, and the convenience of EVs' drivers can influence local grid power losses and a degradation in voltage profiles at some nodes. In such circumstances, the location-specific ratio may differ from a nonpower-supply-affected distribution-system node. Here are useful papers illustrating the complexity of something that seems to be a simple and useful metric. Liu, Z., Wen, F., Ledwich, G., *Optimal Planning of Electric-Vehicle Charging Stations in Distribution Systems*, Nov. 27, 2012, IEEEDigital Library, Available at: https://ieeexplore.ieee.org/abstract/document/6362255. Mozafara, R. M., Moradib, H. M., Aminicd, H. M., *A simultaneous approach for optimal allocation of renewable energy sources and electric vehicle charging stations in smart grids based on improved GA-PSO algorithm*, July 2017, Sustainable Cities and Society, Vol. 32, pages 627-637. Yassir A. Alhazmiab, Y.A., Mostafaa Magdy, H.A. and Salamaa, M.A., *Optimal allocation for electric vehicle charging stations using Trip Success Ratio*, Oct. 2017, International Journal of Electrical Power and Energy Systems, vol. 91, pages 101-116; Wei, Z., Li, G. and Wang, L., *Locating Charging Stations for Electric Vehicles*, Aug. 2018, Transportation Policy. Ibid., Hall and Lutsy. Note that this paper includes multiple references to the specific question of charge point to EV ratios.

FIGURE 2.3 Growth of Electric Vehicles and Public Charge Points in the United States, 2011–2017[50]

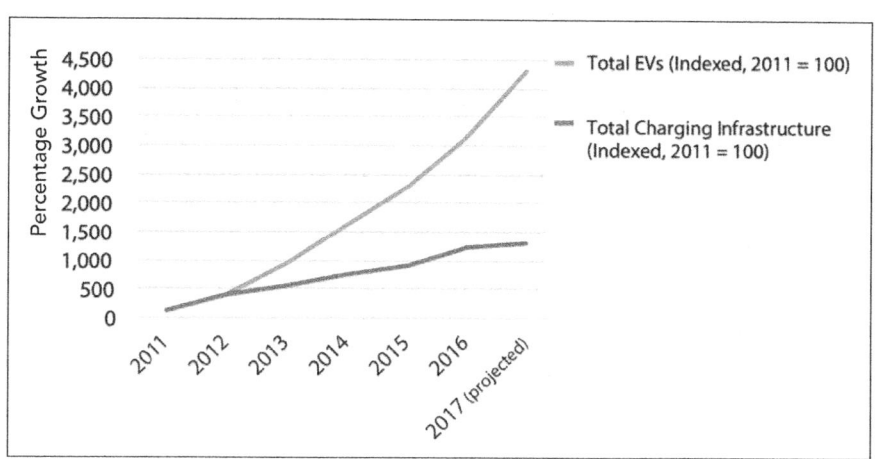

Further, misaligned pricing can lead to either over- or under-utilization. Consequently, as EV adoption and use patterns evolve, so too must city infrastructure deployment plans and actions evolve, including coordination with utilities and third-party vendors.

For instance, diverse infrastructure modalities (e.g., on-street and off-street public charge point locations, prescheduled or reserved charge point use, number of vehicles simultaneously charging at a specific charge point or station, in-street or in-parking stall induction charging) should be fitted to local community and neighborhood circumstances. Areas where single-family dwellings dominate may need fewer public charging options, since most EV charging occurs at home.[51] But locations with high concentrations of multifamily dwellings will require a mix of in-building, on-street, and nearby surface parking facilities with a mix of Level 1, 2, and 3 chargers.[52] As autonomous vehicles become widely adopted, localized EV charging plazas—possibly integrated with bus malls or multimodal transportation complexes—may be cost effective

50   Miller, A., Morris, T. and Masur, D., *Plugging In: Readying America's Cities for the Arrival of Electric Vehicles*, Winter 2018. PennEnvironment. Available at: https://pennenvironment. org/sites/environment/files/reports/PA%20Plugging%20In%20Feb18.pdf.
51   Office of Energy Efficiency & Renewable Energy, *Charging at Home*, n.d., US DOE, Available at: https://www.energy.gov/eere/electricvehicles/charging-home.
52   Lopez-Behar, D., Tran, M., Froese, T., Mayaud, R. J., Herrera, E. O. and Merida, W., *Charging infrastructure for electric vehicles in Multi-Unit Residential Buildings: Mapping feedbacks and policy recommendations*, March 2019, Energy Policy, 126, pages 444–451.

as a service model, reducing today's concerns over how ubiquitously available public EV charging must be to meet EV user needs.[53]

Figure 1.7 in Chapter 1 depicted the present array of charging level options city planners and transportation engineers have at their disposal for tailoring infrastructure to fit specific locations within a city. However, even faster charging technology already is coming to markets. ABB has released a charger capable of adding 120 miles of driving range to BEVs in about eight minutes, and VW has installed and is operating its first DC fast-charger system in the United States.[54] Shell has begun to introduce super-chargers in the United States,[55] and Tesla in 2019 is rolling out its ultra-fast Supercharger v3 stations that feature charging rates at 250 kW.[56] Also, the city of Oslo is reportedly installing wireless charging infrastructure for its taxi fleets that can charge at a rate of 75 kW.[57] One key implication is that city planners may find themselves striving to optimize public charging with more than three levels of charging (that is, with even faster charge rates on the horizon, if charger technology innovations continue as expected[58]).

Until the "ratio standard" of EVs to EV charging infrastructure is more rigorous than that evident in current research, cities planning future public EV infrastructure must navigate a challenging mix of interdependencies, which influence priorities for and timing of deployment. An illustration of such interdependencies of key elements regarding EV infrastructure deployment is offered in Figure 2.4.

A key takeaway from Figure 2.4 is the importance of looking at EV deployment from a portfolio perspective. Making incremental decisions to allocate

---

53 These observations are authors' interpretations, stemming from interviews for city case studies, which follow in Chapters 3–6.

54 Blain, L., *World's fastest EV charger gives drivers 120 miles in 8 minutes*, April 26, 2018, New Atlas, Available at: https://newatlas.com/abb-350kw-fast-charger/54377/and https://electrek.co/2018/12/06/electrify-america-first-350kw-charger-california.

55 Vaughn, A., *Shell starts rollout of ultrafast electric car chargers in Europe: First in network of chargers three times faster than current models installed near Paris*, Oct. 25, 2018, The Guardian, Available at: https://www.theguardian.com/environment/2018/oct/25/shell-starts-rollout-of-ultrafast-electric-car-chargers-in-europe.

56 *The Tesla Team, Introducing V3 Supercharging*, March 6, 2019, Available at: https://www.tesla.com/blog/introducing-v3-supercharging.

57 Nick Statt, *Norway will install the world's first wireless electric car charging stations for Oslo taxis*, Mar 21, 2019, The Verge, Available at: https://www.theverge.com/2019/3/21/18276541/norway-oslo-wireless-charging-electric-taxis-car-zero-emissions-induction.

58 Shareef, H., Islamb, M. and Mohamed, A., *A review of the stage-of-the-art charging technologies, placement methodologies, and impacts of electric vehicles*, Oct. 2016, Renewable and Sustainable Energy Reviews, vol. 64, pages 403-420.

EV infrastructure (whether single or multiple charge points) to one location at a time, or on a first-come, first-served basis may yield suboptimal EV deployments. Considering EV deployment plans based on location, facilities, EVSE configuration, operation-related and management-related costs, deployment timing, and overall safety makes effective deployment success more likely.

FIGURE 2.4 Interdependencies Influencing Decisions Regarding EV Infrastructure Deployment in Cities[59]

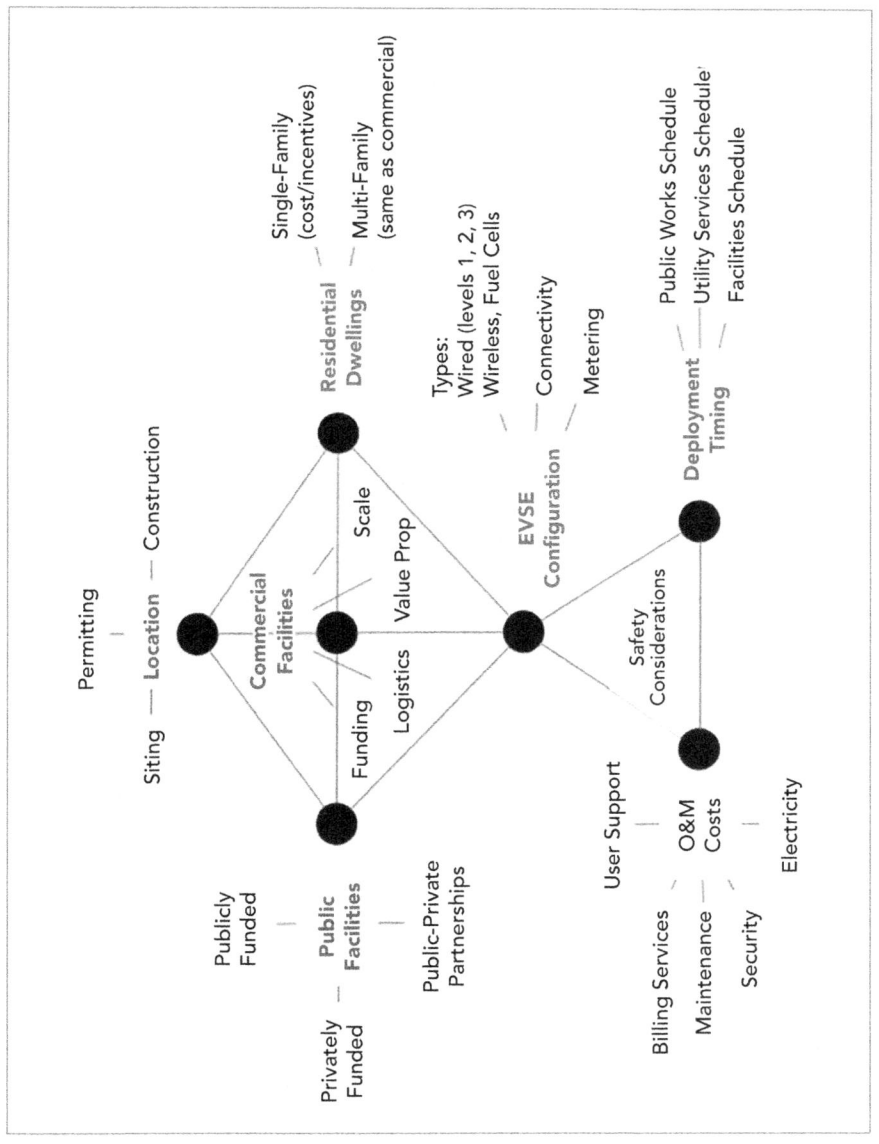

59 Figure 2.4 by authors.

2.2.2 Capacity Utilization and Public Charging Infrastructure

In EV charging systems, capacity utilization is challenging. Most EV public charging infrastructure shows capacity use of 50% or less.[60] In large cities in China, utilization rate for pubic chargers is especially low, in the low single digits (largely due to higher prices, but there are other factors as well; see more discussion in Chapter 4). However, for private charging services (regardless of city), enterprise capacity utilization per charger is critical to revenue growth and earnings performance.

For city and traffic planners specifically, there is more to consider than per-charger utilization rates when it comes to planning for both scale and location allocation in EV charging infrastructure deployment. Effects of charger placement on traffic congestion, pedestrian safety, road maintenance, and many other factors come into play.[61] For instance, placing a charge point on a street with head-in parking spaces and narrow lanes for traffic can lead to EV congestion as drivers wait for access while other users charge up. If the street is heavily traversed, especially by numerous delivery trucks, the flow of traffic can be, from time to time, very slow or stopped. The situation can be further complicated if EVs try to turn around to exit the congestion.[62] Thus, traffic flow can affect charging access and vice versa.

City planners and traffic managers must distinctively define "congestion" and "capacity utilization" for EV charging infrastructure, because they may differ from ICE patterns, if best-fit EV charge point placement and network design is to be realized. For example, the following questions are likely to yield different answers for EV congestion management than conventional, well-established ICE vehicle/traffic management.

City planners and traffic managers must distinctively define "congestion" and "capacity utilization" for EV charging infrastructure, because they may differ from ICE patterns, if best-fit EV charge point placement and network design are to be realized. For example, the following questions are likely to yield different answers for EV congestion management than conventional, well-established ICE vehicle/traffic management.

---

60 Wolbertus, R., Hoed, R. van den, Maase, S. Benchmarking Charging Infrastructure Utilization, June 19-22, 2016, EVS29 Symposium. Montreal, Québec, Canada. A Dutch measure of utilization identified a 15% increase year over year but did not indicate the actual average per charger utilization rates. *Public Charging Benchmark: Accelerating progress to a mature market 2018*, Jan. 2019 Available at: https://www.nklnederland.com/news/public-charging-benchmark-2018/.

61 Ibid., Shareef, H., Islamb, M. and Mohamed, A., pages 403–420.

62 This specific event was witnessed by the authors in Oslo in September 2018.

- Is charge point capacity utilization limited only to use of a specific charge point, or should it include effects on surrounding traffic flows? For instance, should there be calculation of a wait time congestion factor in a Key Performance Indicator (KPI) for individual active charge points?
- Is capacity utilization as a value metric for an entire network a more meaningful KPI than per unit utilization rates?
- Is there a meaningful social value metric[63] to be developed to aid city planners?

A parallel challenge in specific locations may involve impacts on local utility electricity delivery. For instance, if multiple Level 2 chargers are located in the same place and all are charging simultaneously, what are the risks, if any, to local electricity system reliability?[64] Should cities insist upon an onsite electricity source, such as solar plus battery assets, for all or part of electricity service delivered to charge points?[65]

---

63   The term "social value metric" means in this context locationally specific impacts related to EV infrastructure deployment, which can be aggregated into a citywide set of KPIs. For instance, do EV charge points enhance local businesses or increase utilization of public facilities, such as libraries and parks? Alternatively, are they focal points for theft of EV equipment, leaving the area appearance suboptimal? Are EV charge point deployments energy and environmentally just? Each city's social value metrics should be designed to fit the characteristics of its urban environment.

64   This topic is widely analyzed and modeled in published literature. Here is a sampling of the diverse perspectives addressing this question. An example of a technical analysis is Gholami, S., Wadood, A. F., Khurshaid, T., Chang-Hwan, K., and Sang-Bong, R., *Minimizing static VAR compensator capacitor size by using SMC and ASRFC controllers in smart grid with connected EV charger*, May 2019, International Journal of Electrical Power and Energy Systems, vol. 107, pages 656–667, Available at: https://doi.org/10.1016/j.ijepes.2018.12.029; For a load impact perspective see Fischera, D., Harbrechtab, A., Surmanna, A. and McKennab, R., *Electric vehicles' impacts on residential electric local profiles—A stochastic modelling approach considering socio-economic, behavioral and spatial factors*, Jan. 1, 2019, Applied Energy, vol. 233–234, pages 644–658. For a grid impact perspective see M. Taljegard, L. Göransson, M. Odenberger and F. Johnsson, *Impacts of electric vehicles on the electricity generation portfolio—A Scandinavian-German case study*, Feb. 1, 2019, Applied Energy, vol. 235, pages 1637–1650.

65   For example, Hilton, G., Kiaee, M., Bryden, T., Cruden, A. and Mortimer, A., *The case for energy storage installations at high rate EV chargers to enable solar energy integration in the UK—An optimised approach*, The Journal of Energy Storage, Feb. 2019, vol. 21, pages 435–444. See the following: McKinsey & Company, *Travel and logistics: data drives the race for customers*, May 2018. Sumalee, A. and Ho, H.W., *Smarter and more connected: Future intelligent transportation system*, 2018, IATSS Research, 42, pages 67–71. Atzori, L., Floris, A., Girau, R., Nitti, M. and Pau, G., *Toward the implementation of the Social Internet of Vehicles, n.d., Computer Networks*, 2018, 147, pages 132–145.

2.3 The Transportation Ecosystem Is Becoming More Complex

The authors view the ecology of today's vehicle transportation system as composed of multiple interdependent factors:

- There is the core manufacturing supply chain, which applies to all vehicle manufacturers in some form.
- There are operational and transition-enabling platforms that continually support, evolve, manage, and finance the transportation sector.
- Today's vehicle transportation system is increasingly connected to a sociocultural, public policy, and capital investment shift, prompting continual improvement on matters related to environmental sustainability principles and practices.
- Physical and cyber safety and security matters influence execution within the other three factors. This leads to vehicle operations that depend on the highest levels of security available, due to the rapid digitalization of the transportation sector.[66]
- Autonomous vehicles (AVs) will be more than experimental or pilot projects in select cities.[67] AVs are likely to reshape mobility within and between cities. Because AVs are closely tied with EV transition and shared mobility, AVs offer exciting possibilities of reducing total car volume, vehicle emissions as well as traffic congestion. Starting in 2016, Bloomberg Philanthropies announced a new initiative to help cities transition to AVs. There are still a lot of uncertainties and challenges to moving toward a driverless future.[68] But city and transportation planners designing EV infrastructure, absent recognition of the

---

66   See the following: McKinsey & Company, *Travel and logistics: data drives the race for customers*, May 2018. Ibid., Agachai Sumalee and Hug Wai, pages 6771. Ibid., Atzori, L., Floris, A., Girau, R., Nitti, M. and Pau, G., pages 132–145.

67   Chase, N., *Autonomous Vehicles: Uncertainties and Energy Implications*, June 5, 2018, 2018 EIA Energy Conference, Washington, DC. Webb, J., Wilson, C. and Kulartne, T., *Will people accept shared autonomous electric vehicles? A survey before and after receipt of the costs and benefits*, Feb. 2019, Economic Analysis and Policy, article in press. Walker, J., *The Self-Driving Car Timeline—Predictions from the Top 11 Global Automakers*, Jan. 30, 2019, Emerj; Lavasani, M., Jin, X. and Du, Y., *Market Penetration Model for Autonomous Vehicles on the Basis of Earlier Technology Adoption Experience*, 2016, Journal of the Transportation Research Board, vol. 259.

68   Bloomberg Philanthropies, *Bloomberg Philanthropies Launches First-Ever Autonomous Vehicles Map, A Living Inventory of Cities Planning for a Driverless Future*, Oct. 23, 2017, Available at: https://www.bloomberg.org/press/releases/bloomberg-philanthropies-launches-first-ever-autonomous-vehicles-map-living-inventory-cities-planning-driverless-future/.

impending impacts of AVs entering the marketplace, risk misallocating resources toward possibly structural underutilization of EVSE assets.

Figures 2.5 depicts, in a much-simplified fashion, the ecology of today's transportation system.

The visualization illustrates the following.

- The underlying digital integration of the ecosystem enables very fast information flows, alerts, and notifications, which can influence traffic flows, congestion, and overall vehicle efficiency for both ICE and EV platforms.
- Culture, through social networking and internet service platforms (e.g., shared mobility pioneered by ride-hailing services, such as Uber and Lyft) is reshaping how people move around, within, and between cities.
- All vehicles are likely, ultimately, to become smart, interconnected, and generally governed by the same communications platforms used across industries, including (but not limited to) wireless mobile and wi-fi, microwave, and Bluetooth.

FIGURE 2.5 Electrified Mobility Is an Automotive-Communications-Infrastructure-People-Flow Ecosystem on a Continually Improving Technology Platform[69]

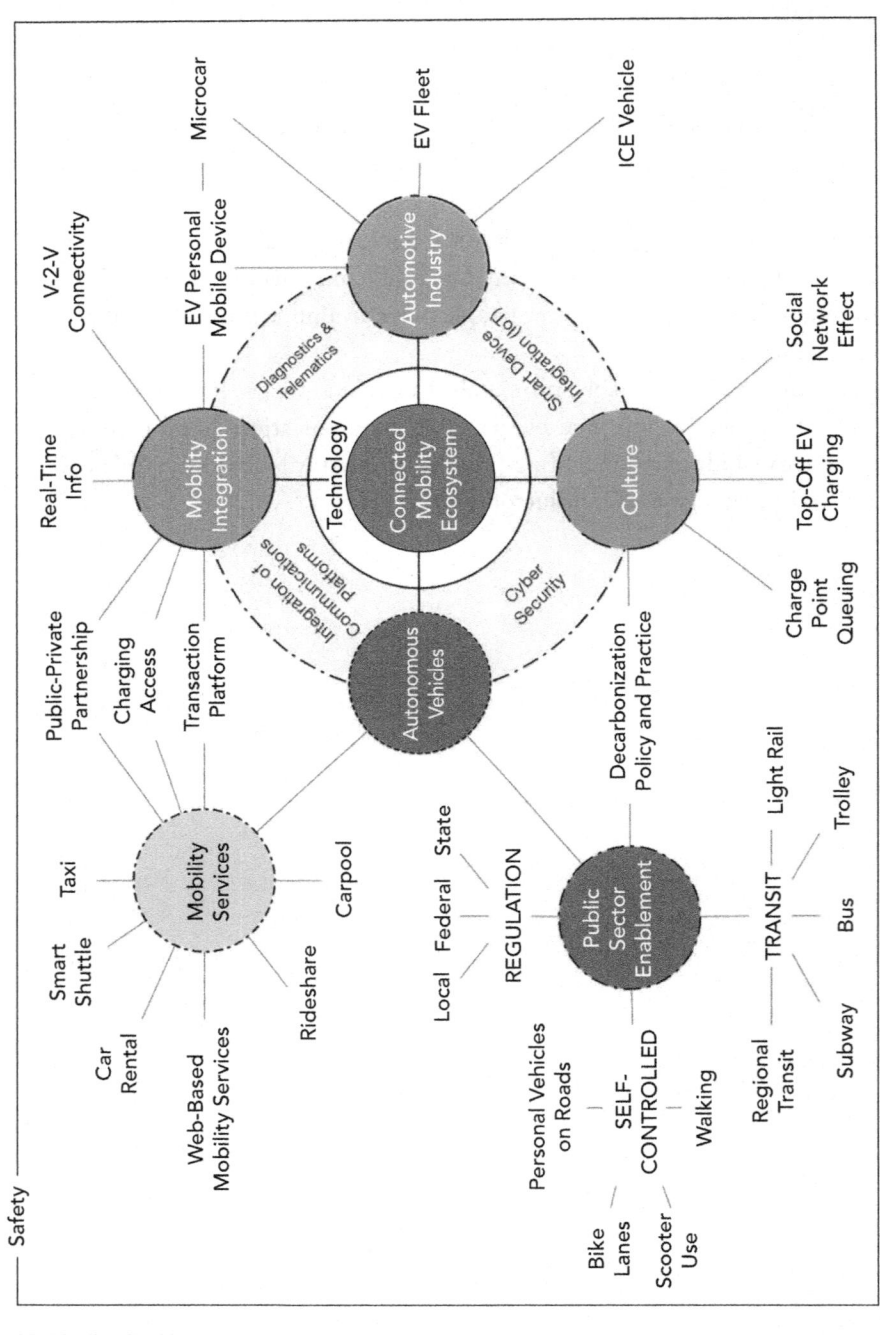

All these changes are significant to city planners. As EV deployment continues and ICE vehicles recede in significance, city planners will be particularly challenged to look at transportation transitions from an ecological perspective. This may include:

- A greater focus on energy flows as key to infrastructure design, which includes emphasizing the importance of anticipating EV charging and utility service infrastructure changes that may be required in urban locations where there is growing EV adoption.
- Inclusion of energy storage facilities (in particular battery storage) in infrastructure design as (a) backup power for individual or constellations of charge points, (b) two-way flows of power between grid needs and aggregations of EVs across one or more charging networks (sometimes referred to as V-2-G), and (c) the role of EVs as energy storage for homes or at workplaces.
- Specification of incremental energy-efficiency requirements for EV public infrastructure charging networks year-on-year; a modality that is consistent with ecosystems, which optimize energy consumption against energy storage, because energy storage can facilitate a more stable transportation ecosystem.[70]

2.4 Stakeholder Engagement Is Becoming More Important

Public institutions engage stakeholders in decision-making processes, regardless of government type. In China, national policy is executed at the local level, but local stakeholders can influence how national policy is implemented.

In the United States, stakeholder engagement is paramount in most cities, even though each city has its own approach. In Brookline, Massachusetts, for instance, an active community committee supported by Brookline township staff has been involved in longer-term EV planning. In Los Angeles, cities, counties, and a regional transportation agency, along with representatives of various departments of state government, engage with stakeholders from local neighborhoods, national special interest groups, academic institutions, and businesses.

Regardless of how stakeholders engage, when charge points are to be deployed, the first steps for installation and operation are navigating permits, meeting safety compliance measures, engaging with local electric utilities, and

---

70 Authors' extrapolation based on the work of Howard T. Odum and B. Odum, *Concepts and methods of ecological engineering*, 2003, Ecological Engineering, 20, pages 339–361.

scheduling construction around city road management schedules (and sometimes utility field operations work schedules as well). In some cases, police have to regulate traffic flow during installation.

The processes for engaging utilities and cities regarding charge point deployment generally fall within established city processes and regulated utility requirements for responding to requests. As an example, if an array of charge points stress utility electricity transformers nearby, transformers may require an upgrade. At minimum, that will add to deployment time, and it might create the need for spending approvals from utility regulators or municipal utility oversight boards.[71] This example illustrates that EV infrastructure deployment includes many moving parts, each of which takes time to complete. In cities that still have a slow adoption rate, the challenge of keeping EV volumes aligned with charging infrastructure may be standard operating procedure. However, adjustments to city standard operating procedures may be needed as EV adoption accelerates. Along with procedural adjustments, contingency planning for different scenarios may become more important.

2.5 Some ICE-Based Incumbents Are Trying to Adapt, but It Is Still Too Early to Tell

Global oil and gas companies have a significant stake in the melting of the ICE platform. Some are taking steps to remain relevant and competitive as the electrification of transportation progresses. For example, BP's *Energy Outlook 2018* forecasts that more than 300 million electric cars on the road by 2040, and that 15% of worldwide vehicle rolling stock in 2040 will be EVs.[72]

Royal Dutch Shell's (Shell's) scenario planning analysis points to a more aggressive shift to EVs. Shell forecasts that oil consumption will peak globally in the early 2030s; if high usage of clean biofuels is added to the mix, peak demand

---

71   These characteristics are noted based on the authors' professional experience with electric utilities and actual experience managing EV operational activities for a US electric utility.

72   BP, *Electric Vehicles*, Available at: https://www.bp.com/en/global/corporate/sustainability/climate-change/a-low-carbon-future/electric-vehicles.html.

for oil could occur in the late 2020s.[73] Shell scenarios forecast 100% penetration of EVs in Europe in the same time frame (late 2020s to early 2030s). Still, Shell notes that planes, ships, and heavy trucks are likely to remain predominantly ICE powered at least through mid-century.[74] Evidence of Shell's recognition of where its future resides came at a recent conference where it announced that it seeks to be the world's largest electricity company by 2030.[75]

Whether the ICE is fully melted by mid-century or earlier, the two afore-mentioned companies are trying to adapt to the pace of EV adoption. For example, BP has invested in FreeWire Technologies—which produces an electric charging station on wheels—with near-term plans to roll them out at some of its retail gas stations in Europe.[76] Shell's immediate moves toward realizing its global electricity enterprise future can be seen in its investments in EVSE activities, including starting its rollout of super-fast EV charging stations in Europe so as to be one of the leaders in EV infrastructure deployment.[77] Further, Shell is heavily invested in all other parts of the clean energy supply chain. For instance, the company is investing $1.0 billion per year in renewable biofuels and hydrogen (as well as teaming with Total on hydrogen product development). In 2017, it acquired New Motion, a company that manages 30,000 residential

73   Bousso, R. and Schaps, K., *Shell sees oil demand peaking by late 2020s as electric car sales grow*, July 27, 2017, Reuters, Available at: https://www.reuters.com/article/us-oil-demand-shell/shell-sees-oil-demand-peaking-by-late-2020s-as-electric-car-sales-grow-idUSKBN1AC1MG. This article focuses on Shell's acquisition of New Motion: Casey, T., *It's Over: Oil Giant Shell Doubles Down On EV Charging Stations*, Oct. 16, 2017, Clean Technica, Available at: https://cleantechnica.com/2017/10/16/oil-giant-shell-doubles-ev-charging-stations/. Shell's US-based EV service offering can be found on its website: *Shell Recharge Plus: Managed Smart Charging for Electric Vehicles*, n.d., Available at: https://www.shell.us/business-customers/shellrechargeplus.html; Vaughn, A. *Shell starts rollout of ultrafast electric car chargers in Europe: First in network of chargers three times faster than current models installed near Paris*, Oct. 25, 2018, The Guardian, Available at: https://www.theguardian.com/environment/2018/oct/25/shell-starts-rollout-of-ultrafast-electric-car-chargers-in-europe.
74   Ron Bousso and Karolin Schaps, *Shell sees oil demand peaking by late 2020s as electric car sales grow*, July 27, 2017, Reuters, Available at: https://www.reuters.com/article/us-oil-demand-shell/shell-sees-oil-demand-peaking-by-late-2020s-as-electric-car-sales-grow-idUSKBN1AC1MG.
75   Crooks, E. and Raval, A., *Shell aims to become world's largest electricity company: Oil major prepares for fundamental shift towards lower-carbon energy sources*, March 13, 2019, Financial Times.
76   Business Wire, *FreeWire Technologies Raises $15 Million Series A Financing*, Dec. 4, 2018, Available at: https://www.businesswire.com/news/home/20181204005329/en/FreeWire-Technologies-Raises-15-Million-Series-Financing.
77   Lambert, F., *Oil giant Shell accelerates electric vehicle effort with acquisition of network with over 30,000 chargers*, Oct. 13, 2017, Electrek, Available at: https://electrek.co/2017/10/13/oil-giant-shell-electric-vehicle-chargers/.

FIGURE 2.6 Multiple EV Infrastructure Pathways Developing Through at Least Mid-Century

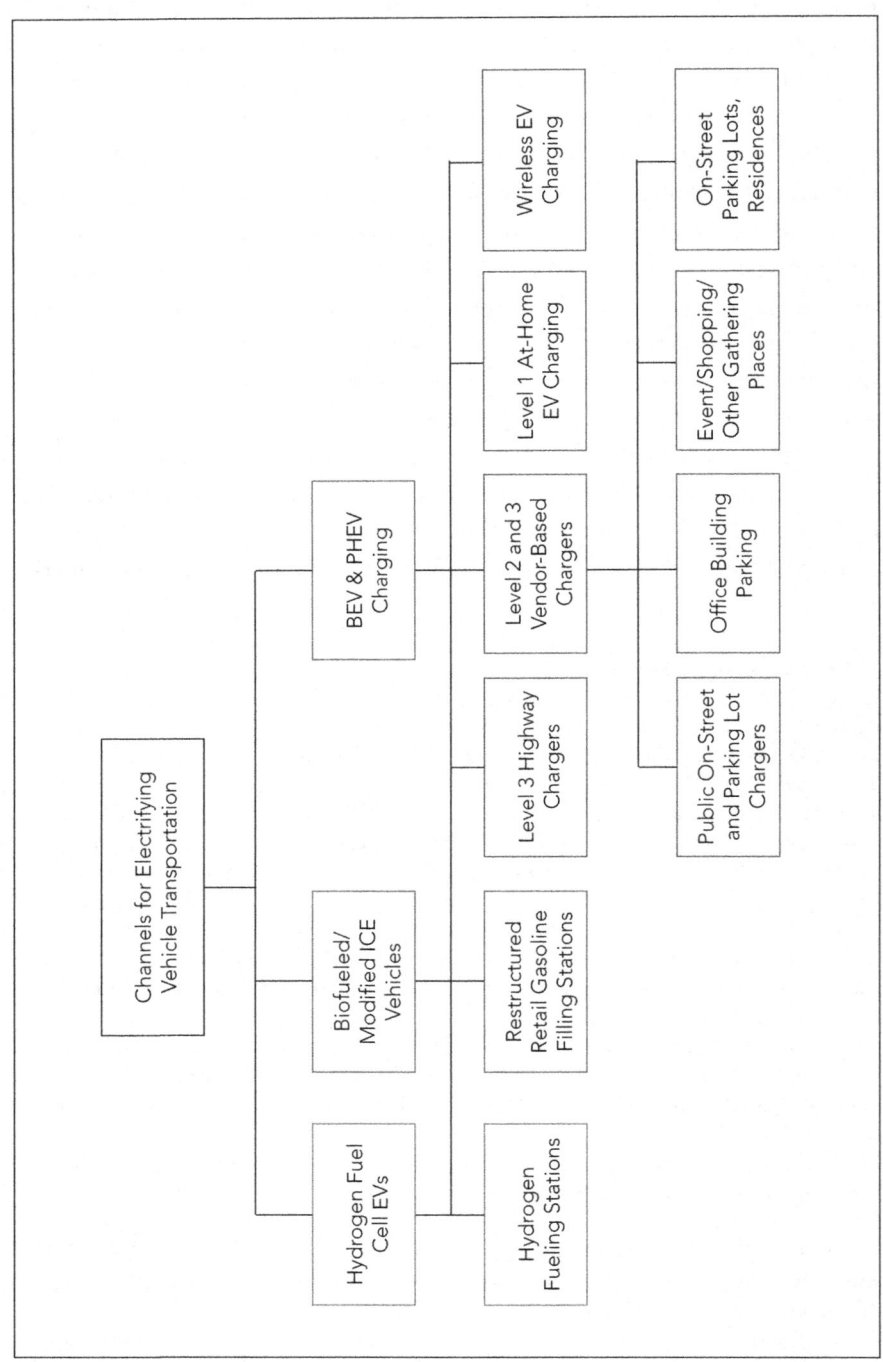

and business charging stations and offers access to 50,000 more. Shell sees both of its initiatives as a natural progression and a big step from oil and gas into electricity as the transportation "fuel" of the future.[78]

It is too early to tell if and how the entire oil industry will adapt to the transport electrification movement, as Shell and BP collectively represent a minor slice of the entire industry (less than 10% of world market[79]). As EV adoption continues, it remains to be seen to what extent existing retail fuel distribution platforms (local gasoline stations, highway fueling plazas, and large commercial vehicle fueling infrastructure) can evolve into part of EV public charging infrastructure.

With multiple fuel sources coexisting, Figure 2.7 visually depicts the somewhat contingent nature of EV infrastructure deployment, which city leaders and planners are likely to confront as adoption continues, if not accelerates.

While Figure 2.7 presents only one mix of pathways leading to an electrified transportation future, it is a reminder that cities' planning, investment priorities, and deployment efforts should remain flexible. Technological changes and vehicle market share competition could produce a surprising mix of solutions, which might require infrastructure adapting to support "surprising outcomes." Finally, as technology advances and new disruptions emerge, Figure 2.7 merits continual updating to keep policymakers, planners, and operations people aware of "what this way comes." Policy direction and market development coevolve as both complementary and oppositional forces. For instance, shifts in mobility patterns and user behaviors influence city planning for road improvements, road and pedestrian changes, and additions to roads, which can lead to changes

---

78   Foehringer, E., *Shell Buys Slice of the Electric vehicle market with purchase of NewMotion*, Oct. 13, 2017, Available at: https://www.greentechmedia.com/articles/read/shell-buys-charging-company-newmotion-electric-vehicle-market#gs.CSkreQ4. Note that Shell has teamed with Total to invest nearly $11 billion in the next five years on hydrogen product development.
79   List of largest oil and gas companies by revenue, Available at: https://en.wikipedia.org/wiki/List_of_largest_oil_and_gas_companies_by_revenue

in traffic patterns, as well.[80] Also, parking design and management, and demonstrable environmental improvements through decarbonization and improved air quality, yield visible changes to urban environmental quality and overall quality of urban life.[81]

2.6 The Role of Utilities Is Increasing (and shifting as well)

With increased EV adoption, the roles of utilities become even more important. Consider such roles according to two of the most common EV charging challenges: home charging, and public charging.

For home charging, EVs bring multiple challenges. The first consideration has to do with load changes – the extent that load growth actually happens and if so, how fast it occurs. Currently an average American household consumes about 28.5 kWh per day.[82] Such consumption is at the low end of a BEV's charging requirements. As an example, the Tesla Model 3, the most popular BEV on the market in 2019, has a battery capacity of 75 kWh on its production model with a range of 310 miles. This means that the electricity load of a typical EV charging session is equivalent to that of 2 or 3 households. Many utility street-

---

80   Literature on this subject is longstanding. The articles herein cited spotlight new tools intended to help city planners improve road management activities: Liu, K., Gao, S. and Lu, F., *Identifying spatial interaction patterns of vehicle movements on urban road networks by topic modelling*, 2019, Computers, Environment and Urban Systems, 74, pages 50–61. Another relevant article profiles constellations of research and analysis related to improving city planning using big data for more granular understanding of traffic patterns and road-related impacts: Chen, S., Wei, X., Xia, N., Yan, Z., Yuan, Y., Zhang, H., Li, M. and Cheng, L., *Understanding road performance using online traffic condition data*, Journal of Transport Geography, 2019, 74, pages 382–394. The following article is representative of new analytical tools that help city road and traffic planners better prioritize and focus their management efforts: Goto, A. and Nkamura, H., *Functional Hierarchical Road Classification Considering the Area Characteristics for the Performance-oriented Road Planning*, n.d., Transportation Research Procedia, vol. 15, 2016, pages 732–748. City road planning and traffic management principles and processes are evolving as sustainable mobility principles are increasingly adopted. This article is an example: Hickman, R., Hall, P. and Banister, D., *Planning more for sustainable mobility*, 2013, Journal of Transport Geography, 33, pages 210–219.
81   Emodi, N. V., Chaiechi, T. and Beg, A.B.M. R. A., *A techno-economic and environmental assessment of long-term energy policies and climate variability impact on the energy system, 2019*, Energy Policy, 128, pages 329–346. Bonges, H.A. III and Lusk, A.C., *Addressing electric vehicle (EV) sales and range anxiety through parking layout, policy and regulation*, 2016, Transportation Research Part A, 83, pages 63–73. Silvester, S., Beella, S.K., Timmeren, A., Bauer, P., Quist, J. and Dijk, S., *Exploring design scenarios for large-scale implementation of electric vehicles; the Amsterdam Airport Schiphol case*, 2013, Journal of Cleaner Production, 48, pages 211–219.
82   EIA, Available at: https://www.eia.gov/tools/faqs/faq.php?id=97&t=3.

level residential transformers will not be able to handle increased power supply requirements from EV adoption. Larger transformer failures can affect the stability of much larger grid networks, as well.

One occasionally underappreciated impact of overnight EV charging has to do with transformer life cycles. For locations with higher concentrations of EVs charging overnight on a single transformer, the design for the nighttime cooling process of the transformer is either abbreviated or eliminated, in turn reducing the life of the unit. This can lead to utilities needing to change out transformers more frequently and/or increasing the capacity of a transformer, in both cases increasing utility operating costs.[83]

Certainly, there are complexities in how EV and grid interactions occur. For example, transformer stresses vary as a function of the number of EVs drawing power from a single transformer and as a function of when this is occurring. Power draws overnight differ in impact from high EV charging activities occurring during a period where, for instance, high air conditioning demand is in-flight. Also, residences with rooftop solar (some with battery storage as well) enable EV charging essentially off-grid, in turn reducing the stresses on individual transformers.

A second consideration is born of research showing that, even at low EV adoption levels, uncoordinated residential EV charging could significantly change the shape of the local aggregate electricity demand curve.[84] Possibly, wider local network effects could occur as well. This could lead utilities to invest in distribution infrastructure upgrades, as noted above. Such upgrades might include smart grid solutions (e.g., grid-side battery storage for better monitoring and load management, as well as improved load-shifting and load-shaping processes that involve two-way flows of power between utilities and their customers—where planning for V-2-G engagement already is extensively underway in many utilities).[85]

---

83   These insights come from the experience of the authors at a large US utility managing internal EV deployment operations related processes.

84   Muratori, M., *Impact of uncoordinated plug-in electric vehicle charging on residential power demand*, Jan. 2018, Nature Energy, Available at: https://www.nature.com/articles/s41560-017-0074-z.

85   Three examples of a large and growing literature include: Triviño-Cabrera, A., Aguado, J. A. and Torre, S., *Joint routing and scheduling for electric vehicles in smart grids with V2G*, May 15, 2019, Energy, vol. 175, pages 113–122. Zecchino, A., Prostejovsky, A., Ziras, C. and Marinelli, M., *Large-scale provision of frequency control via V2G: The Bornholm power system case*, May 2019, Electric Power Systems Research, vol. 170, Pages 25-34. Kestera, J., Noel, L., Lin, X., Rubens, G.Z., and Sovacoola, B.K., *The coproduction of electric mobility: Selectivity, conformity and fragmentation in the sociotechnical acceptance of vehicle-to-grid (V2G) standards*, Jan. 10, 2019, Journal of Clean Energy Production, volume 207, pages 400–410.

Utilities are exploring their future roles with respect to EV charging infrastructure.[86] In some jurisdictions (in the United States and certain European countries) utilities have options with respect to how they can support the evolution of EV infrastructure deployment, driven in part by regulatory directions and by enterprise investment and operational interests.[87] Utility-private enterprise partnerships regarding EVSE deployment are one of the options being piloted and deployed, as well.[88]

EV charging systems will require improved integration into current grid system operations to ensure efficient capacity utilization both for utilities and for EV owners.[89] Managing peak EV demand on chargers also shall merit more attention as adoption increases.[90] Sprawling urban spaces such as Los Angeles, Phoenix, or Houston mean that EV trip radii can be elongated compared to that of more compact large-scale cities, such as those on the East Coast of the United States. More public charging infrastructure may be re-

---

86 Jones, B.M., *Electric Vehicles and the Roles of the Utility*, June 14, 2017, Presentation to the LIPA Board Development & Education Workshop, MJB&A, Available at: https://www.lipower.org/wp-content/uploads/2017/03/EV20Infrastructure20Presentation1.pdf. A similar presentation was put before the Rhode Island PUC, May 31, 2017; Available at: http://www.ripuc.org/utilityinfo/electric/PST_BE_5_31_P_MJBA.pdf. The authors have direct experience with California's investor-owned utilities with respect to their efforts to shape an appropriate role for utilities, as well.

87 Hall, D., and Lutsey, N., *Literature Review on Power Utility Best Practices Regarding Electric Vehicles*, 2017, ICCT, see whole report, and summaries of relevant regulatory matters on pages 10-13, Available at: https://www.theicct.org/sites/default/files/publications/Power-utility-best-practices-EVs_white-paper_14022017_vF.pdf. See also, MJB&A, *Accelerating the Electric Vehicle Market*, March 2017, pages 13 - 15, Available at: https://www.mjbradley.com/sites/default/files/MJB&A_Accelerating_the_Electric_Vehicle_Market_FINAL.pdf.

88 Allen, P., Horn, G., Goetz, M., Bradley, J. and Zyla, K., *Utility Investment in Electric Vehicle Charging Infrastructure: Key Regulatory Considerations*, Nov. 2017, MJB&A and Georgetown Climate Center, Available at: https://www.georgetownclimate.org/files/report/GCC-MJBA_Utility-Investment-in-EV-Charging-Infrastructure.pdf. Deign, J., *Oil owns gas stations. Who will own EV charging stations?*, Aug. 14, 2018, Green Tech Media, Available at: https://www.greentechmedia.com/articles/read/oil-owns-gas-stations-who-will-own-ev-charging-stations#gs.7z5ge8.

89 Here are representative examples of a rich literature on EV recharging behavior. Robinson, A.P., Byth, P.T., Bell, M.C., Hubner, Y., and Hill, G.A., *Analysis of Electric Vehicle Driver Recharging Demand Profiles and Subsequent Impacts on the Carbon Content of Electric Vehicle Trips*, Oct. 2013, Energy Policy, vol. 61, pages 337–348. Schauble, J., Kaschub, T., Ennslen, A., Jochem, P. and Fichtner, W., *Generating electric vehicle load profiles from empirical data of three EV fleets in Southwest Germany*, 2017, Journal of Cleaner Production, 150, pages 253–266. Brady, J. and O'Mahony, M., *Modeling Charging Profiles of Electric Vehicles Based on Real World Electric Vehicle Charging Data*, 2016, Sustainable Cities and Society, 26, pages 203–216.

90 This article begins to get to the point being made concerning capacity utilization of charge points and charging systems. Ibid., Wolbertus, R., Hoed, R. van den and Maase, S.

quired when cross-city trips and longer commutes are common features of an urban landscape.[91]

Large metropolitan areas that are composed of many small cities create another complication. Streets and roads may fall into the legal boundaries of more than one city. That is, the legal boundaries of each city may overlay the same streets or highways. In some cases, road maintenance and appearance differ according to which city is responsible for a particular segment of a road. The LA metropolitan area exhibits such patterns, as do many US cities.

For intra-city deployment, EV charging infrastructure location allocation may vary if adjoining cities and towns have public charging infrastructure on one of the city's borders. Such is the case with Brookline, Massachusetts, discussed in Chapter 6. If one city advances EV charging before or more densely than surrounding cities, the latter might eventually lean on the investments of the former. "Leaning" in this case means residents of one city might use EV charging in another city near residential or workplace locations. The "leaning city" may avoid increased operating costs of securing and maintaining chargers as well as costs related to enabling charge point deployment, changes in road and pedestrian configurations, and policing against damaging and/or theft of EVSE assets.

The possibility of leaning and the cost-carry of underused charging infrastructure suggest that metropolitan-wide design would best ensure that EV user needs are met at the lowest cost and with the best fit. Many metropolitan areas have used multi-jurisdictional entities (e.g., transit districts) to deal with similar challenges concerning various forms of mass transit, such as mitigating commuting congestion through investment in mass light rail systems.[92] These established entities may be worthy candidates for enabling a metropolitan-wide funding and governance of EV infrastructure buildout (where public, public-private, and private investment pathways can function efficiently without having to sort infrastructure for individual cities and towns within a large metropolitan area). For instance, such a metro-level scaling approach is being used in Los Angeles (see Chapter 3).

91 Wolbertus, R., Kroesev, M., Hoed, R. van den and Chorus, C., *Fully charged: an empirical study into the factors that influence connection time at EV-charging stations*, Dec. 2018, Energy Policy, 123, pages 1–7.

92 For a quick survey of the main regional transit authorities, see: *List of United States rapid transit systems by ridership*, Available at: https://en.wikipedia.org/wiki/List_of_United_States_rapid_transit_systems_by_ridership. For a more thorough look, see: American Public Transportation Association, *2017 Transportation Fact Book*, March 2018. https://www.apta.com/resources/statistics/Documents/FactBook/2017-APTA-Fact-Book.pdf.

2.7 Governments Both at the National and Local Levels Are Playing an Increasingly Active Role

The global deployment of EVs tends to be government-policy directed. In Europe, several countries have passed laws prohibiting the sale of ICE vehicles after a specified year. The no-ICE rule occurs in 2025, 2030, and other out-years, depending on country.[93] Table 2.1, on the next page, inventories national "de-ICEing" initiatives underway, worldwide.

While prohibiting ICE vehicles is a definitive *stick* to drive EV adoption, incentive *carrots* have been instrumental in driving early EV market development.

- In China, for instance, obtaining registration for an ICE vehicle can take years, but for EVs the registration process is fast.[94]
- In European countries, varying bundles of incentives are driving EV adoption, including tax benefits, parking privileges, free EV charging, access to special highway lanes, and more.[95]
- In the United States, EV adoption has been prompted primarily through a combination of state and federal incentives; at the federal level, the emphasis is principally upon tax credits.[96]

---

93 Oslo, 2019; Madrid, 2020; Chengdu, China, 2020; Copenhagen, 2025; Britain-wide, 2040, see the article by Leanna Garfield, *13 cities that are starting to ban cars*, Jun. 1, 2018, Business Insider, Available at:. https://www.businessinsider.com/cities-going-car-free-ban-2017-8#new-york-city-is-decreasing-car-traffic-in-small-doses-13 France will ban ICE vehicles after 2040: available at: https://qz.com/1341155/nine-countries-say-they-will-ban-internal-combustion-engines-none-have-a-law-to-do-so/.

94 Information obtained from Chinese staff at the Institute for Sustainable Energy, and from discussions between authors and colleagues at Global Energy Infrastructure Development Cooperation Organization (GEIDCO). Also, see Bloomberg, *China Pushes Drivers Toward Electric Vehicles out of Necessity*, May 23, 2018, Available at: https://skift.com/2018/05/23/china-pushes-drivers-toward-electric-vehicles-out-of-necessity/.

95 For an inventory of country-specific incentives, see European Automobile Manufacturers Association, *Overview on tax incentives for electric vehicles in the EU*, Available at: https://www.acea.be/uploads/publications/EV_incentives_overview_2018.pdf.

96 Office of Energy Efficiency & Renewable Energy, *Electric vehicles: tax credits and other incentives*, n.d., Available at: https://www.energy.gov/eere/electricvehicles/electric-vehicles-tax-credits-and-other-incentives. Plug-In America, Inventory of State-level and Federal subsidies, n.d., Available at: https://pluginamerica.org/why-go-plug-in/state-federal-incentives/?location=ks.

TABLE 2.1   Country-Specific "De-ICEing" Actions[97]

Country	Status of ICE Vehicle (ICEV) Phase Out	Action Date
Austria	Official target: no new ICEVs sold after 2020	4/2016
Britain	Official target: no new ICEVs sold after 2040 (does not include hybrids)	7/2017
China	Official target: end production and sales of ICEVs by 2020	9/2017
Costa Rica	Initiate complete phase-out of ICEVs by 2021	4/2018
Denmark	Official target: 5,000 EVs on the road by 2019, tax incentive in place	2008
France	Official target: no new ICEVs sold after 2040	7/2017
Germany	No registration of ICEVs by 2030 (passed legislation); cities can ban diesel cars, federal ruling supports law	10/2016
India	Official target: no new ICEVs sold after 2030 (will likely hit 30% by 2030)	4/2017
Ireland	Official target: no new ICEVs sold after 2030, incentive program in place for EV sales	7/2017
Israel	Official target: no new ICEV imports after 2030	2/2018
Japan	Incentive program in place for EV sales	1996
Netherlands	Official target: no new ICEVs sold after 2030, phase-out begins 2025	10/2017
Norway	Incentive program in place for EV sales; official target—only sell EVs by 2025	1990
Portugal	Official target and incentive program in place for EV sales	2010
Scotland	Official target: no new ICEVs sold after 2032	9/2017
South Korea	Official target: EVs account of 30% of auto sales by 2020	6/2016
Spain	Government program: Movea 2017 Plan, an incentive package to promote sale of alternative energy vehicles	6/2017
Taiwan	Official target: phase out fossil-fuel motorcycles by 2035 and fossil-fuel vehicles by 2040. Replace all government vehicles and public buses with EVs by 2030.	12/2017

97 The table is replicated from: Burk, I., and Gilchrist, J., *Survey of Global Activity to Phase Out Internal Combustion Engine Vehicles*, revised Sept. 2018, Center for Climate Protection, Available at: https://climateprotection.org/wp-content/uploads/2018/10/Survey-on-Global-Activities-to-Phase-Out-ICE-Vehicles-FINAL-Oct-3-2018.pdf.

Incentive providers in the United States are mainly governments (city, state, and federal); but in some areas of the country, public utility commissions have either approved or ordered utilities to provide special rates for EVs on the premise that EV charging costs meaningfully influence buying decisions.[98] US city and state incentives include free parking, High Occupancy Vehicle (HOV) lane access, and vehicle licensing cost reductions, depending on the city.[99]

Home charging is one area that warrants more incentive support. In general, home charging occurs at night. Growing numbers of Level 2 chargers are in the public domain, especially at workplaces. For EV owners unable to charge at home—still common at many multifamily dwellings (even with parking garages)—workplace charging can be important.

Integrating home charging may influence the scale, scope, and location of public charging infrastructure. Many multifamily dwellings have limited access to charging because buildings have insufficient parking and on-street parking can be limited.[100] Such limitations complicate structuring charging levels by location. For example, is it possible to use low-cost Level 1 on-street charging in areas with high concentrations of multifamily dwellings? Perhaps the question is best answered by asking a different question: How much flexibility is needed to deploy public charging infrastructure?[101]

Charging requirements (for concentration of chargers, wait time for access, and cost of charging) are altered by potential changes in battery technology, autonomous vehicle deployment, and other innovations. These dynamics argue for city planning that maximizes charging infrastructure design and deployment flexibility.[102]

98   California Public Utility Commission, Order Instituting Rulemaking to Continue the Development of Rates and Infrastructure for Vehicle Electrification and Closing Rulemaking 13-11-007. Dec. 13, 2018.

99   Hartman, K. and Dowd, E., *State Efforts to Promote Hybrid and Electric Vehicles*, Sept. 26, 2017, National Conference of State Legislatures, Available at: http://www.ncsl. org/research/energy/state-electric-vehicle-incentives-state-chart.aspx.

100 Lopez-Behar, D., Tran, M., Froese, T., Mayaud, J.R., Herrera, O. E. and Merida, W., *Charging infrastructure for electric vehicles in Multi-Unit Residential Buildings: Mapping feedbacks and policy recommendations*, March 2019, Energy Policy, Volume 126, pages 444-451.

101 Amjada, M., Ahmad, A., Rehmani, M.H., and Umer, T., *A review of EVs charging: From the perspective of energy optimization, optimization approaches, and charging techniques*, July 2018, Transportation Research Part D: Transport and Environment, Volume 62, Pages 386–417.

102 Flexibility is defined by how easy and low cost it is to make changes in EVSE assets and processes as next-version technology comes to market.

Research indicates that public charging infrastructure is important in enabling EV adoption.[103] Still, policy makers and planners in cities must ask, and answer, certain questions on a city-by-city basis.

- Do institutional processes and procedures (e.g., government approval processes, government operations management) deter timely infrastructure expansion?
- How important is the deployment of Level 2 and Level 3-DC fast charging for stimulating EV adoption, compared to other factors such as incentive carrots and sticks for EV adoption?
- How tightly linked must growth in market share of EVs and growth in public charging infrastructure be to ensure sustained progress on the electrification of transportation?
- How slow can infrastructure buildout be without slowing down the pace of EV adoption? Conversely, how far ahead must public charging infrastructure deployment be to ensure sustained public support as adoption of EVs accelerates?
- Does the cause of infrastructure "deployment lag" make a difference to prospective EV buyers? For instance, if EV infrastructure is tied to new road construction or major road renovations, are prospective buyers inclined to make purchases because the infrastructure is essentially confirmed given the construction in progress (regardless of how long before access is available after road construction completion)?

Core elements of effective planning still need better "validating standards." For instance:

- Is the optimal charge-point-to-EV-volume ratio meaningful in itself, or does its importance depend on how location-specific it is?
- Is the relationship between EV market share and EV charging infrastructure consistent over time? At what point and under what circumstances do one-to-one, or more-chargers-to-one-EV become necessary, if at all?

103 Szczepanek, A., and Botsford, C., *Electric Vehicle Infrastructure Development: An Enabler for Electric Vehicle Adoption*, May 13–16, 2009, EVS24, Stavanger, Norway. Kestera, J., Noela, L., Rubensa, G.Z., and Sovacoolab, B.K., *Policy mechanisms to accelerate electric vehicle adoption: A qualitative review from the Nordic region*, Oct. 2018, Renewable and Sustainable Energy Reviews, vol. 94, pages 719–731; Levinson, R.S., and West, T.H., *Impact of Convenient Away-from-Home Charging Infrastructure*, Dec. 2018, Transportation Research Part D: Transport and Environment, vol. 65, pages 288–299; Levinson, R.S. and West, T.H., *Impact of public electric vehicle charging infrastructure, Transportation Research Part D: Transport and Environment*, Oct. 2018, Volume 64, pages 158–177.

The case studies that follow are meant to add insights from experienced field practitioners to assist city leaders and planners in preparing for EV public charging infrastructure deployment and management.

PART II

MILESTONES ON THE ROAD TO TRANSITION

CHAPTER 3

The Transition to Electric Vehicles in Los Angeles, California

Guillermo Ivan Pereira, PhD

3.1 Introduction

This chapter examines the City of Los Angeles and the greater LA metropolitan area. Los Angeles is the pinnacle of the ICE vehicle in the United States with a culture built around the car.[104] As such, its approach to the electrification of mobility offers worthwhile lessons for other US cities, as well as cities in China and Europe. There are lessons to learn on managing design, deploying infrastructure, organizing a metro-wide approach to deployment involving multiple cities and other public organizations, and integrating the complex array of stakeholders that both help and hinder city policymaking and operations.

The accelerating diffusion of electric vehicles (EV) in Europe, China, and the United States calls for reassessments of transportation support policies of cities and how these policies support or impede the deployment of electric vehicle charging infrastructure as well as whether new policies may be needed.

In this case study, the electric vehicle market for Los Angeles is analyzed, providing information about the EV markets, adoption rates and patterns, and governance of electric vehicle deployment in one of the world's most populated cities and one of the largest vehicle markets in the United States.

Los Angeles is California's largest city, with a population of 3.98 million and one of the highest per-capita car ownership rates in the United States, with 1.64 million vehicles on the city's roads (see Table 3.1).

----

104 In this chapter, "Los Angeles region," "LA," or "LA region" shall refer to the greater metropolitan area. Where the city proper is referenced, "City of Los Angeles" shall be used to distinguish it from greater LA. For other jurisdictions, such as the County of Los Angeles, the formal name of the jurisdiction shall be used.

TABLE 3.1 Population and Vehicle Market Indicators, 2018[105]

KEY INDICATORS			
City of LA population	**3,900,00**	**LA County population**	**10,170,000**
Cars per fuel type in the City of LA		**Cars per fuel type in LA County**	
Battery electric	9,948	Battery electric	41,936
Diesel	35,305	Diesel	35,305
Diesel hybrid	56	Diesel hybrid	238
Ethanol	84,067	Ethanol	368,436
Gasoline	1,426,959	Gasoline	6,561,503
Fuel cell	191	Fuel cell	1,139
Hybrid gas	70,369	Hybrid gas	284,304
Plug-in hybrid	8,841	Plug-in hybrid	46,871
Butane	2	Butane	7
Compressed natural gas	1,716	Compressed natural gas	2,402
Methanol	263	Methanol	1,012
Methane	39	Methane	46
Natural gas	3,584	Natural gas	10,450
Propane	664	Propane	1,358
Total	1,642,004	Total	7,519,469

Table 3.1 provides key indicators on population and vehicles for both the City of Los Angeles and LA County. The City of Los Angeles operates 18,789 registered EVs, representing 1.14% of its total vehicle fleet. LA County operates 88,807 registered EVs, representing 1.18% of its total vehicle fleet.

---

105 California Department of Motor Vehicles, 2018, Vehicles by fuel type by city as of Jan. 1, 2018, Available at: https://www.dmv.ca.gov/portal/wcm/connect/c24637c9-5faf-4fe2-9375-9b5221a2ef4a/motorvehiclefueltypes_city.pdf?MOD=AJPERES&CVID=; California Department of Motor Vehicles, 2018, Vehicles by fuel type by county as of Jan. 1, 2018, Available at: https://www.dmv.ca.gov/ portal/wcm/connect/2156a052-c137-4fad-9d4f-db658c11c5c9/MotorVehicleFuelTypes_County.pdf?MOD=AJPERES; US Census Bureau, 2018, Los Angeles, California, Quickfacts, Available at: https://www.census.gov/quickfacts/fact/table/losangelescountycalifornia,ca/PST045217.

The LA metropolitan area often has been considered a leader in charging infrastructure deployment.[106] The city's sustainability plan calls for 10% of the vehicles in the city to be electric by 2025, and for 35% by 2035.[107] Considering the 2018 vehicle data presented in Table 3.1, the number of EVs on the city's roads could be around 164,200 by 2025 and 410,501 by 2035.

As electrification of mobility gains momentum, it is important to understand how LA governments are managing the transition from Internal Combustion Engine (ICE) vehicles to EVs. Accordingly, existing policies, programs, and processes pertaining to EV adoption and infrastructure deployment are of particular interest.

The LA region has a history of supporting EV deployment, with government efforts dating back to 1997.[108] This early EV support was part of California's statewide efforts undertaken in the 1990s when the United States' first Zero Emission Vehicle (ZEV) mandate was implemented. It supported the rollout of the first Plug-in Electric Vehicles (PEV), such as the General Motors' EV-1, Toyota's RAV4-EV, and Honda's EV-Plus.[109]

An analysis of recent EV sales for the City of Los Angeles and for LA County provides additional information necessary to understand the evolution of the current region-wide EV rolling stock and possible future trends.[110] Figure 3.1 depicts the boundaries of the City of Los Angeles and LA County.

106 Farrell, J., and Weinmann, K., *Choosing the Electric Avenue: Unlocking Savings, Emissions Reductions, and Community Benefits of Electric Vehicles*, 2017, Minneapolis, Minnesota, Available at: https://ilsr.org/wp-content/uploads/2017/06/Electric-Vehicles-Report-Final.pdf.

107 City of Los Angeles, *Los Angeles Sustainable City Plan*, 2015, Los Angeles, Available at: http://plan.lamayor.org/wp-content/uploads/2017/03/the-plan.pdf. Miller, A., and Morris, T., *Plugging In: Speeding the Adoption of Electric Vehicles in California with Smart Local Policies*, 2018, Available at: https://environmentcalifornia.org/reports/cae/plugging-speeding-adoption-electric-vehicles-california-smart-local-policies.

108 City of Los Angeles, *Citywide plan for electric vehicle charging infrastructure*, 2017, Los Angeles, Available at: http://clkrep.lacity.org/onlinedocs/2014/14-0079-s2_rpt_GSD_03-10-2017.pdf ; International Energy Agency, *EV city casebook: A look at the global electric vehicle movement*, 2012, Paris, Available at: https://www.iea.org/publications/freepublications/publication/EVCityCasebook.pdf.

109 US Department of Energy, *Los Angeles Sets the Stage for Plug-In Electric Vehicles*, 2014, Available at: http://www .afdc.energy .gov/case/1002.

110 Given the scale of Los Angeles County, as depicted in Figure 3.1, its data is used as indicative of region-wide patterns when region-wide data was not available.

FIGURE 3.1 City of Los Angeles and LA County

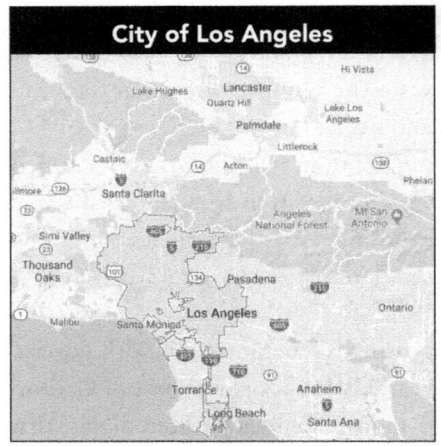

In 2017, EV sales in the LA region accounted for 5% of the light-duty vehicles market, compared to 1% for the national market.[111] Overall, between 2010 and 2017, LA metropolitan area sales totaled 143,000. For the same period, the City of San Francisco registered 71,000 in sales, while San Jose accounted for 54,000 EVs.

Figure 3.2 displays the top 30 cities in California by EV sales in 2017, and growth percentages from 2016. It gives sales figures for the City of Los Angeles, which was the leading city, with approximately 12,000 new vehicles purchased, representing a 17% increase over 2016 registered sales. As EV penetration in the city increases, the need to deploy charging infrastructure becomes a priority. In addition to the importance of charging infrastructure availability, accessibility is key to supporting growing shares of EVs within city areas.

The increasing availability of EV charging infrastructure in the City of Los Angeles indicates a consistent drive to support market uptake. In 2015, 740 public charging stations were available for use;[112] in 2017, that number rose to 1,456.[113] The latest data, from 2018, indicates that 1,591 charging stations (76.1%) are available to the public in the City of Los Angeles.[114]

---

111 Lutsey, N., *California's continued electric vehicle market development*, 2018, Available at: https://www.theicct.org/sites/default/files/publications/CA-cityEV-Briefing-20180507.pdf.

112 Ibid, Lutsey, N. NOTE: this graphic was replicated by authors to decrease the blur in the copy of the original. Any variances from the original are unintended.

113 Farrell, J. and Weinmann, K., *Choosing the Electric Avenue: Unlocking Savings, Emissions Reductions, and Community Benefits of Electric Vehicles*, 2017, Minneapolis, Minnesota, Available at: https://ilsr.org/wp-content/uploads/2017/06/Electric-Vehicles-Report-Final.pdf.

114 Ibid., Miller, A. and Morris, T.

FIGURE 3.2 Top 30 Cities in California with the Most EV Sales in 2017 and Percent Growth from 2017[115]

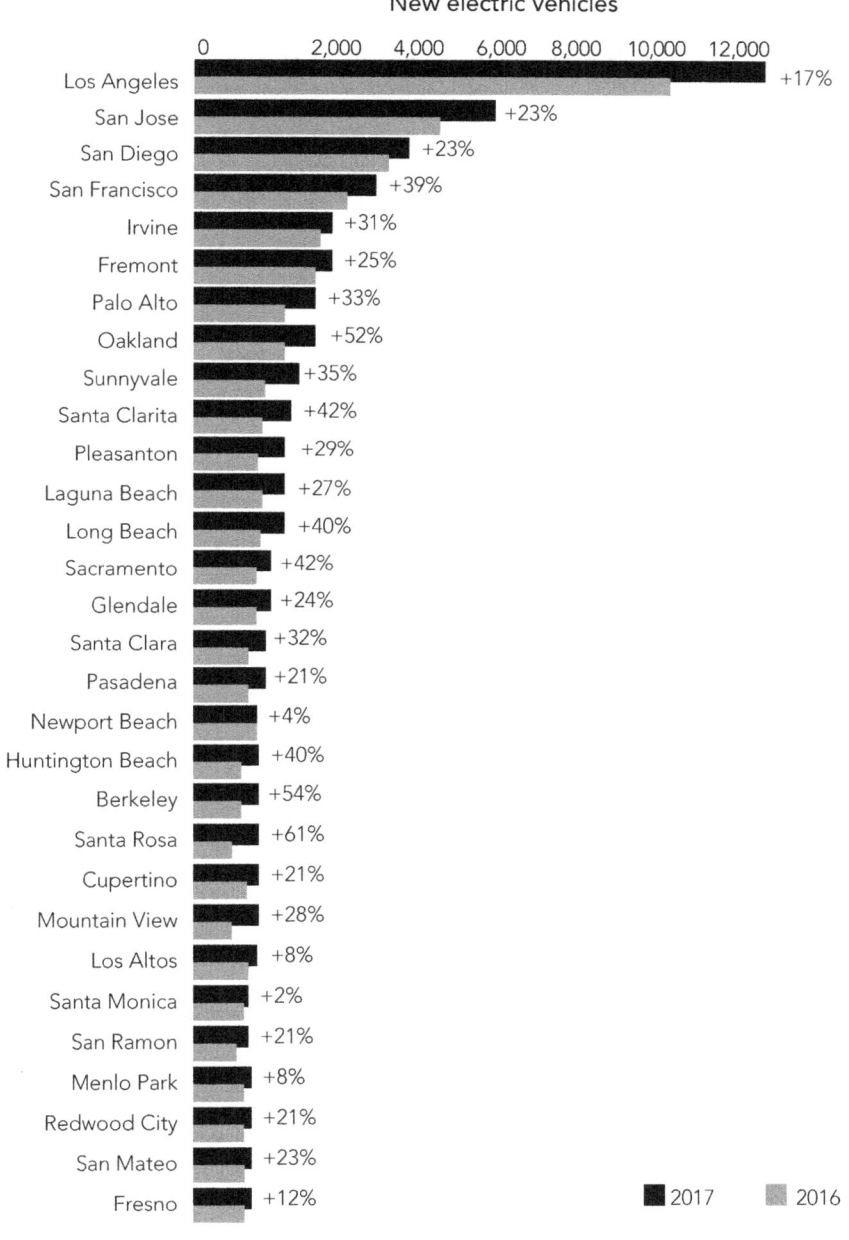

115 Lutsey, N, *California's continued electric vehicle market development*, 2018, Available at: https://www.theicct.org/sites/default/files/publications/CA-cityEV -Briefing-20180507. pdf NOTE: this graphic was replicated by authors to decrease the blur in the copy of the original. Any variances from the original are unintended.

Table 3.2 breaks down charging station availability in 2018 according to charger levels and accessibility.

TABLE 3.2 Summary of Public Charging Infrastructure Available in the City of Los Angeles, 2018[116,117]

	Charger Type			
	Level 1	Level 2	DCFC	Total
Public Charger Accessibility	11	1,539	41	1,594 (76.1%)
Private Charger Accessibility	46	448	5	499 (23.9%)
Total	57 (2.7%)	1,987 (95.1%)	46 (2.2%)	2,090

While about 95% of the mix of chargers are Level 2 technology, it is worth noting that within the Level 2 category, 448 chargers—or about 30% of the supply—are privately owned.[118] Also noteworthy is how California defines accessibility with respect to EVs. Generally, accessibility means being able to safely access charging equipment, move around vehicle and equipment while charging, and traverse areas between chargers and surrounding facilities. Also, it means adhering to relevant state and federal laws intended to ensure that special cases, such as people with disabilities, can fully access charging facilities.[119]

116 Ibid., US Department of Energy.
117 California defines public accessibility and private accessibility thusly: "private accessibility" means Electric Vehicle Charging Stations (EVCS) not available to the general public (example: EVCS that charge public and private fleet vehicles) and intended for use by a designated vehicle or driver (example: EVCS assigned to an employee) or EVCS intended for use by an EV owner or operator at their residence. "Public accessibility" means that an EV space shall be located adjacent to an accessible parking space with shared access aisle, or EV space shall be accessible according to the specified requirements in CALGreen and located on an accessible route to the building. Further, in multifamily public housing facilities, EV spaces provided in a visitor or unassigned parking area shall be accessible according to California Building Code (CBC) Chapter 11B scoping and technical requirements. More details can be found at: https://www. green-technology.org/gcsummit18/images/Accessibility-Regs-EVCS.pdf.
118 Ibid., CDOT. More details can be found at: https://www.green-technology.org/ gcsummit18/images/Accessibility-Regs-EVCS.pdf .
119 Details on accessibility can be found here: DSA, *Electric Vehicle Charging Stations, Accessibility, FAQs*, Available at: https://www.documents.dgs.ca.gov/dsa/access/EVCS_ FAQ_09-20-17.pdf , however a comprehensive documentation of all aspects of accessibility requires a review of relevant laws that are both directly related to EVs and indirectly related through requirements to accommodate special cases, such as people with disabilities.

While federal and state jurisdictions in the United States may dictate terms, as illustrated above, cities can take a leading role in supporting the deployment of EV charging infrastructure, as well. For instance, they can drive adoption through procurement (to be discussed later in the chapter) by shifting to an EV fleet for city government use. Cities can implement greenhouse gas emission reduction targets that include EVs as part of the transition to a low carbon economy, as well.

3.2 Cross-Cutting EV Deployment Initiatives

3.2.1 EV Task Force—City of Los Angeles

The City of Los Angeles implemented an EV task force to help develop recommendations on the acquisition of EVs and implement charging infrastructure. The task force continues its work and is responsible for organizing how the city approaches electric vehicles. Its activities include designing and implementing the processes necessary for city EV procurements; supporting departments considering buying EVs by providing clarification and additional information; and identifying funding sources to support the city's transition to EVs.

The City of Los Angeles's EV task force is coordinated by the Mayor's Office and includes the following city departments: Department of General Services (GSD); Bureau of Street Lighting (BSL); Department of Water and Power (LADWP); Department of Transportation (LADOT); Fire Department (LAFD); Police Department (LAPD); World Airports (LAWA); Port of Los Angeles (POLA); Recreation and Parks (RAP); Office of the Chief Legislative Analyst (CLA); City Administrative Officer (CAO); additional departments may be called when specific needs arise. The task force is supported through departmental collaboration, which allows organizations in the city to share knowledge gained from completed projects. See Figure 3.3.[120]

---

120 Ibid., City of Los Angeles.

FIGURE 3.3 Organization of the City of Los Angeles and EV Task Force Participating Departments[121]

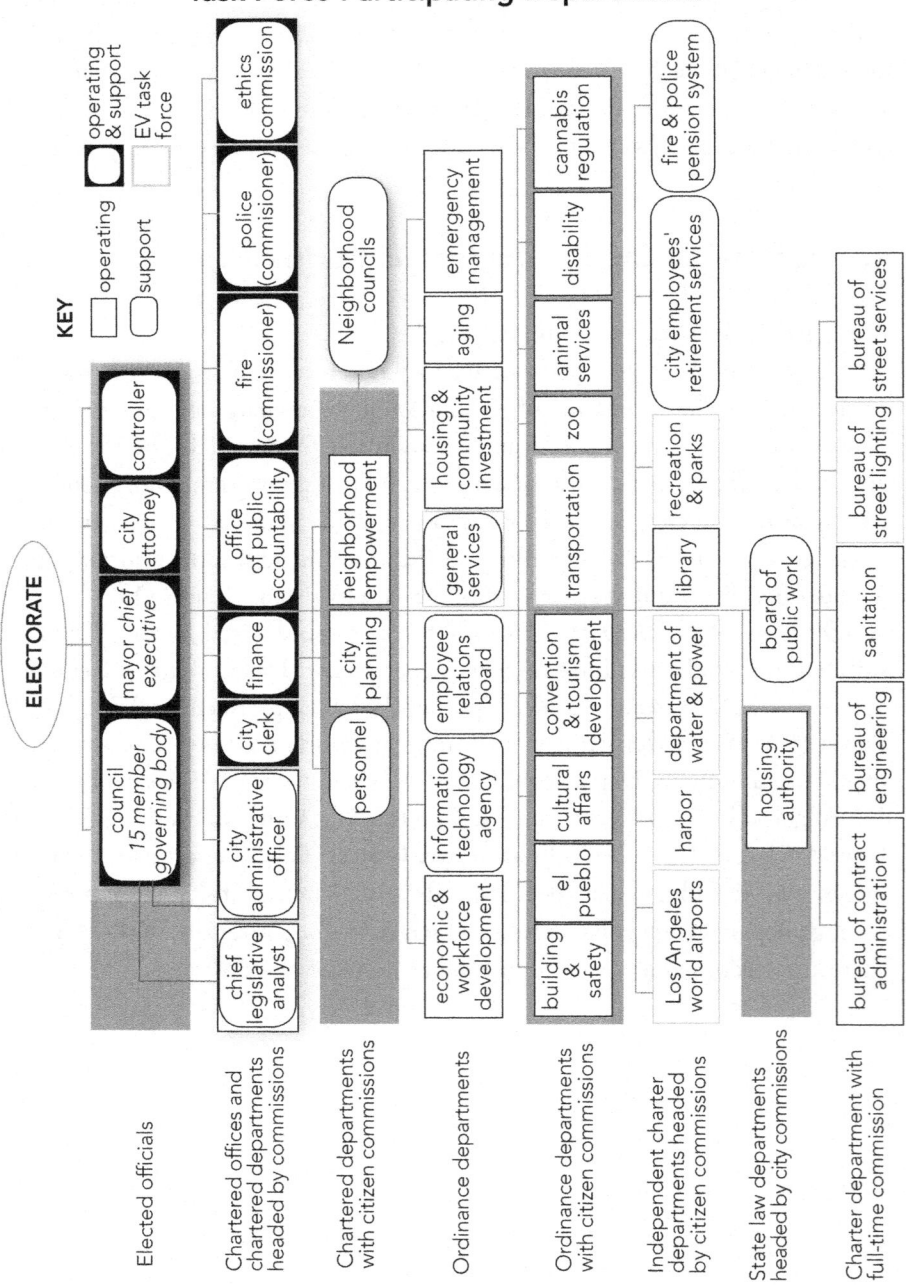

121 City of Los Angeles, *Organization of the City of Los Angeles*, 2018e, City of Los Angeles, Available at: http://cao.lacity.org/misc/LAorgchart.pdf. Graphic is editor's replication of a published organization chart for purposes of increasing visual clarity. No content changes were made in the graphic from its original.

The task force breaks down into working groups to tackle specific challenges. Once a working group completes the work at hand, its members report back to the Mayor with insights and policy proposals. The ongoing work by the EV task force focuses on the following issues:

- **Networked vs. Nonnetworked EV charging infrastructure.** This working group is focused on identifying the added value of installing networked chargers. Networked chargers make remote control and monitoring of usage possible, communicate the amount of electricity consumed, and can provide information when a charger is faulty. Because the costs of networked vs. nonnetworked chargers and the associated infrastructure for deployment differ, this task force aims to map the locations where networked and nonnetworked chargers should be deployed.
- **Fee for charging.** Given that no uniform policy on fees for EV charging has been implemented, this working group aims to analyze current practices, policies, and fee structures and to provide guidance on possible approaches to implement fees for charging services.
- **Parking policy.** The deployment of EV charging infrastructure as well as dedicated parking spaces created a need to reevaluate the city's parking policy. This working group focuses on understanding how parking policies should evolve. For instance, it will be important to evaluate how long EV owners can park in EV-dedicated spaces. Traffic regulations were recently adjusted to prevent ICE vehicles from inappropriately using EV-charging-dedicated spaces.
- **Joint EV procurement.** The purchase of EVs through a centralized process can contribute to unlocking economies of scale at the city level. This working group is streamlining a collaborative process for city departments and LA County. The goal is to have these entities develop EV specifications together. Ongoing work is targeting the procurement of long-range EV sedans.

An example of the added value and relevance of joint EV procurement programs is the procurement process established by the Climate Mayors collaborative, of which the City of Los Angeles Mayor Garcetti participates in partnership with other city Mayors. In this case, joint procurement is enabled through an online portal which aims to lower the cost of acquiring EVs by enabling cities to make joint bids in larger quantities. This also serves to demonstrate of how cities can work together to reduce existing barriers and accelerate EV adoption.[122]

122 Climate Mayors, *What is the collaborative?*, 2019, Available at:: https://driveevfleets. org/what-is-the-collaborative/; and Climate Mayors, *Procurement process*, 2019, Available at: https://driveevfleets.org/procurement-process/.

- **Pilot programs.** The EV market continues to evolve, with new models, technologies, and features released by different vendors. This task force focuses on designing pilot programs that expose the city to different vehicle types for different city-level needs. This is expected to enable experimentation and knowledge dissemination among departments that test different EVs and charging technologies. Ongoing work is focusing on developing pilot programs for EV vans and trash trucks.

3.2.2 EV Charge Plan—City of Los Angeles

The city's EV Charge Plan is a multiyear strategic initiative focusing on deploying charger infrastructure for the City of Los Angeles. Its scope and ambition further advance the work developed within the EV task force previously described. The EV Charge Plan is a cooperative development involving the Department of General Services (GSD), the Bureau of Engineering (BOE), and the Bureau of Street Lighting (BSL). Through this plan, the city aims to increase the charging network to benefit city residents, employees, and visitors. In terms of implementation, the EV Charge Plan was designed to be flexible and scalable, depending on the evolution of costs, available funding, and technology.

The goal of this plan is to contribute to cleaner air in the city, by supporting the transition to low- and zero- emission vehicles, where EVs are a key to success. By increasing the charger network, the city aims to provide the necessary infrastructure for public (i.e., city and county) departments to transition to EV fleets. Through this initiative, the city intends to complement private efforts dedicated to meet the growing need for charge points. The EV Charge Plan is responsible for selecting the deployment of public charging infrastructure projects. A set of criteria has been developed to provide guidance when the city is selecting charging station deployment projects. Through the established criteria, the EV Charge Plan can prioritize and identify the projects to be implemented. The criteria being considered include:

1. **Electrical capacity and building readiness.** The BOE will certify the facilities' ability to handle the load impacts caused by EV chargers.[123] This is important, because existing buildings may not have spare electrical capacity (i.e., increased electricity service infrastructure and/or capacity may be required). All municipal installations will require a demand study to ensure that the increase in load does not affect other buildings' systems.

---

123 "Load" is a term used by the electric power industry to reference how much demand from consumers is being placed on grid operations and system assets, such as transformers or substations. "Load impact" refers to specific effects of demand and demand patterns on grid operations.

2. **Public and city employee demand**. One of the factors to be considered when selecting projects is the demonstrated demand from city employees and the public for charging at a given location. An example of demonstrated demand occurred at City Hall East, where due to high demand and limited charging infrastructure availability, city employees had to organize in groups to facilitate sharing. The employees used a shared spreadsheet to keep track of the reserved spaces and waiting line.

3. **Size, location, and geographic distribution**. This criterion aims to ensure that deployed public charging infrastructure serves a significant portion of the population at the location of installation, reflected as the number of EV charge point parking spaces available compared to the total number of parking spaces. Geographic distribution will also be considered to ensure that infrastructure is available throughout the city to ease movement among facilities.

4. **Funding**. Availability of funding will be key in selecting the projects to be implemented. The EV Charge Plan aims to pursue the most cost-effective projects first.

Public charging projects are selected based on the previously described criteria. Their implementation follows a structured process. The process clarifies the stages of implementation, which may vary by how much time and effort each project requires, depending on the readiness of buildings targeted for charging infrastructure deployment. Some sites have electrical panels, and the appropriate capacity and proximity to install charging infrastructure, while others require additional transformers, panels, and electrical infrastructure to service the planned buildout of EV chargers. This difference in readiness among projects may result in two stages of deployment. In the first stage, buildings ready to receive charging infrastructure are prioritized. In a subsequent stage, reinforcement of buildings' electrical infrastructure occurs so that charging infrastructure can be deployed.

The implementation process includes the following steps:

1. **Facilities assessment—BOE and GSD**. The designated project designer collects a building's electrical plan, building plant, and historical utility data. The project designer can either be a city employee or an external contractor. BOE and GSD cooperate with the project designer to provide information needed and to conduct a site assessment. Different degrees of complexity may require additional data, depending on the available electrical capacity and number of chargers to be installed. Additional necessary information may relate to consumption patterns to provide a sufficiently detailed understanding of a building's load.

2. **Design and permitting—BOE and Department of Building and Safety (DBS).** The project's implementation design is prepared for permitting, using the data collected. BOE is involved throughout project implementation and design steps. The bureau might give approval or suggest that design elements be modified. The DBS is consulted for a pre-plan check in the later stages of project design implementation readiness.

3. **Construction—GSD and related departments.** Once design and permitting for the installation are complete, construction starts. During preconstruction, the relevant stakeholders meet to prepare a construction plan. In cases where the installation is small and not complex, construction may occur without interruptions. More complex installations may need to be built in sections, depending on location and facility characteristics. Construction includes the configuration and addition of electrical power sources for EV charging, the installation of the EV chargers, parking space striping that easily identifies a space as designated for EV charging, and associated signals that simplify identification.

4. **Commissioning—GSD and related departments.** Nonnetworked charger installation is completed and ready for use after the construction phase. After successfully completing construction, networked chargers are commissioned. This process includes data connection and setting up charger software. Software-enabled features include payment capabilities, station monitoring, and remote reporting.

3.2.3 Transportation Electrification Partnership—LA Region

The Transportation Electrification Partnership (TEP) started at the Los Angeles Cleantech Incubator in early 2018. The goal of the public-private partnership among local, regional and state stakeholders is to reduce greenhouse gas emissions and air pollution in the Greater Los Angeles region by accelerating transportation electrification in advance of the 2028 Olympic and Paralympic Games, which will be held in Los Angeles. The partnership is led by a group including the California Air Resources Board (CARB), City of Los Angeles Mayor Eric Garcetti, LA County, Los Angeles County Metropolitan Transportation Authority (LA Metro), Los Angeles Department of Water and Power (LADWP), Southern California Edison (SCE), and Los Angeles Cleantech Incubator (LACI).[124] In addition to the leading members, the partnership's work is supported through an advisory group including automakers, industry representa-

---

124 Los Angeles Cleantech Incubator, *Transportation Electrification Initiative Zero Emissions Roadmap 2028*, 2018, Los Angeles, Available at: http://roadmap.laci.org/.

tives, and also representatives from smaller cities in LA County and other public sector agencies (e.g., South Coast Air Quality Management District).

The work of the TEP is guided by a strategic action roadmap—the Zero Emissions 2028 Roadmap. The roadmap was developed through a collaborative, multi-stakeholder process identifying opportunities to enable a transition to a zero emissions movement of people and transportation of goods. The development of this roadmap was motivated by the effects of climate change in the LA region, namely, increased heat, droughts, and wildfires. The plan emphasizes the need for increased regional climate action as well as efforts to propel a shift to electrified mobility. The region is preparing for the 2028 Olympics, which will also help transform Los Angeles's transportation system.

The Zero Emissions 2028 Roadmap centers on four guiding principles: (1) when visitors and athletes arrive for the Olympics, people and goods will move emissions-free; (2) range anxiety will be eliminated thanks to adequate charging infrastructure availability; (3) equity will be enhanced by improving air quality and access to mobility options and good jobs; and (4) the Greater LA regional economy will grow via transportation electrification and development of an advanced transportation industry. These four guiding principles translate into three main sectors where project and programmatic actions drive implementation of the roadmap—movement of people, movement of goods, and the energy-transportation nexus.[125]

- **People movement.** Vehicles used to transport people are the largest emitters within the transportation sector. Electrifying this segment of the transportation sector can greatly improve air quality in Los Angeles. Through its actions in this sector, the TEP aims to ensure: (a) equal access to zero-emission transportation; (b) that the future of autonomous vehicles is electric and does not result in an increase in miles traveled; and (c) that first- and last-mile options complement the public transport services available. Figure 3.4 describes the targets for essentially decarbonizing people movement.

125 Ibid., Los Angeles Cleantech Incubator.

FIGURE 3.4 People Movement Targets[126]

Charging infrastructure	**Light-duty private vehicles**	**Shared cars**	**Local transit**
60,000 to 130,000 public chargers installed	20–45% of all light-duty private vehicles on the road are electric	50–100% of shared cars (e.g., taxis and TNCs) are electric	80–100% of Metro and LADOT buses on the road, and 100% of new buses being introduced are electric
Low: Based on current commitments of utilities in county	Low: SCE 2030 pathway scaled to 2028	Low: Estimated proportion of electric TNC rides based on Lyft's 1B AV EV goal by 2025	Low: Estimated progress to reach commitments by 2030
High: Based on projected needs to support a higher range of light-duty electric vehicles	High: Ambitious goal to achieve partnership pathway	High: Ambitious goal to achieve partnership pathway	High: Commitments of Metro & IAOOT to attempt to move up current 2030 100% commitments to 2028.

Commuter rail	**Light electric vehicles** (LEVs) active transit	**Aerial transit**
Begin planning for electrification of one or more commuter-rail lines with key partners	All disadvantaged communities with a walkscore of less than 65 have LEV hubs to reduce single-occupancy vehicle (SOV) trips	Ensure short-haul and VTOL transit is electric

---

126 Ibid, Los Angeles Cleantech Incubator .

- **Goods movement.** Vehicles used for goods movement are also large-volume carbon emitters in the LA region. Medium- and heavy-duty trucks represent the second-largest emitters in the transportation sector. Also, they are the largest source of local air pollution. Further, focusing on decarbonizing goods movement gains relevance considering that 40% of all the goods that enter the US travel through the ports of Los Angeles and Long Beach, thus reflecting the scale of goods movement in the region.

  To mitigate these emissions, the roadmap aims to plan for and invest in zero-emission freight corridors to support the transition to zero-emission goods transport and to help improve the competitiveness and economic development of the freight sector in Greater Los Angeles. Figure 3.5 describes the targets presented for this sector.

FIGURE 3.5 Goods Movement Targets[127]

Goods charging infrastructure	Heavy-duty drayage trucks	Heavy-duty long-haul trucks
10,000–100,000 zero emission chargers installed for goods movement	10-40% of drayage trucks on the road are zero emissions	5–25% of trucks on the road are zero-emission vehicles
Low: SCE target based on May 2018 CPUC decision	Low: SCE target for 2030 scaled to 2028	Low: SCE target for 2030 scaled to 2028
High: Based on number of heavy-duty and medium trucks	High: Aggressive target to support Paris and to meet Clean Air Action Plan to meet zero emissions by 2035	High: Aggressive target to support Paris

Medium-duty delivery trucks	Marine shipping & freight trains	Aerial
25–50% are electric	Begin electrification of shipping and freight rail in the region	Ensure local delivery drones are electric
Low: UPS target 25% by 2025		
High: 100% is based on discussions with GM on desire for delivery electrification		

---

127 Ibid., Los Angeles Cleantech Incubator .

- **Energy-transportation nexus.** The roadmap focuses on the relationship between the electrification of transportation and energy infrastructure, recognizing a future in which renewable energy and need for related capacity will increase due to the growing EV loads. This sector's goals include expanding grid infrastructure to promote large-scale EV adoption, ensuring that the additional electricity demand resulting from electrification of mobility is met with renewable energy, and ensuring a local grid that addresses the opportunities and needs for integrating EV-related technology. Figure 3.6 describes this sector's targets.

FIGURE 3.6 Energy Transportation Nexus Targets[128]

Grid capacity	**Grid intelligence and EV-grid interconnection**	**Digital tools and autonomy**
The electricity grid in the region—increasingly comprised of clean energy sources—has sufficient capacity to meet the rising needs from the electrification.	Smart grid and storage technologies are incorporated into the grid and utility interconnection, and permitting processes for electric charging infrastructure are streamlined to enable greater use of electric vehicles and efficient dispatch of energy as needed.	Current and emerging technological and digital innovations—such as autonomous vehicles, connectivity, data, IoT, and blockchain—integrate with and help advance transportation electrification and emissions reductions.

Having established these guiding principles, sectors, and sector-specific targets, the TEP's short-term goals for 2019 include:

- Conducting advanced greenhouse gas modeling to narrow the target ranges for the deployment of various vehicle classes and the needed charging infrastructure in alignment with the Leadership Group's commitment to reduce GHG emissions an additional 25 percent by 2028.

---

128 Ibid., Los Angeles Cleantech Incubator.

- Engaging stakeholders in working groups to identify solutions needed to reach the targets set forth in the movement of people, the transportation of goods, and the energy-transportation nexus.
- Identifying pilot projects to implement, which will help meet target ranges.
- Publishing a Zero Emissions 2028 Roadmap update in September 2019, including refined target ranges and information on policy, funding, infrastructure, technology and behavioral solutions identified by the working group to advance progress toward the targets.

3.2.4 E4 Mobility Alliance—LA County

The Los Angeles County Economic Development Corporation (LAEDC) created the E4 Mobility Alliance to position Southern California as a leader in advanced transportation solutions. The alliance's involvement includes research and development, commercialization of autonomous vehicles, increasing plug-in electric vehicles on the roads, and increasing natural gas and fuel-cell vehicle adoption. In addition, the alliance aims to motivate fleet conversion and ride sharing and to implement electric mobility solutions that contribute to a robust manufacturing cluster and infrastructure deployment. This is expected to result in job growth and to attract investment. This initiative provides a wider-ranging platform to enable regional economic development that benefits residents while supporting the transition to a low-carbon economy.[129]

The alliance's goals are to:
- Spread awareness of LA County as an Advanced Transportation Capital
- Leverage the region's intellectual property, research, and workforce training assets to grow the Advanced Transportation industry cluster
- Advocate for a legislative agenda and public policies that foster growth of the industry cluster
- Develop and implement industry cluster growth strategy

Since its establishment, the alliance has focused on bringing together stakeholders in the rapidly growing ridesharing market, to identify procurement and project opportunities.[130] Also, the alliance has focused on the LA region bus network and how it can be redesigned. By engaging the region's bus manufacturers, infrastructure developers, and bus-parts suppliers, the alliance helped

129 *Los Angeles County, Los Angeles County Economic Development Corporation E4 Mobility Alliance*, 2018, Los Angeles, Available at: https://laedc.org/our-services/initiatives/e4-mobility-alliance/.
130 Los Angeles County, *Next Wave of Ridesharing Platforms, Related Business, Explored by e4 Mobility Alliance*, 2018, Los Angeles, Available at: https://laedc.org/2018/02/01/ridesharing-industry-los-angeles-e4-laedc/.

update LA's stakeholders on innovative technologies, bus business trends, and regional transportation needs.[131] During 2018, the alliance also helped implement the SmartMatch service,[132] a supplier matchmaking platform that supports the advanced transportation industry.

3.3 Electric Vehicle Market Development Actions

The development of the electric vehicle charging infrastructure for the City of Los Angeles is based on analysis of EV market developments and EV market support actions. Market development includes actions to increase the volume of EVs on LA roads, which directly drives the need for charging infrastructure. In addition, these actions can help increase awareness about the value of transitioning to low-carbon mobility via electric vehicles. Market support actions include the initiatives taken to deploy, or facilitate the deployment of, EV charging infrastructure, thus directly supporting EV market development. Moreover, market support actions can include initiatives that contribute to process- and administrative-related adjustments to facilitate and enable charging infrastructure availability.

3.3.1 City of Los Angeles Fleet Expansion

As part of the City of Los Angeles sustainability plan, a short-term target to expand the city's light-duty vehicle fleet was set, for 50% of its purchases to comprise EVs by 2017 (City of Los Angeles, 2015). At the time, it was considered one of the most ambitious targets, spurring the City of Los Angeles to implement an EV task force engaging 13 city departments in monthly meetings to reach this EV fleet expansion goal. Since the implementation of this goal in 2015, 475 EVs have been added to the city's fleet and are being used by the following city departments:[133]

- General Services
- Los Angeles Police Department (LAPD)
- Los Angeles Fire Department (LAFD)

---

131 Los Angeles County, *e4 Mobility Quarterly Meeting*, June 2018, Los Angeles, Available at: https://laedc.org/event/e4-mobility-quarterly-meeting/.

132 Los Angeles County, *California SmartMatch: Helping OEMs Find LA-based Suppliers*, 2018, Los Angeles, Available at: https://laedc.org/2018/06/11/california-smartmatch/.

133 City of Los Angeles, *Los Angeles Sustainable City Plan 3rd annual report 2017– 2018*, 2018, Los Angeles, Available at: http://plan.lamayor.org/wp-content/uploads/2018/04/2018-pLAn-3rd-annual-report.pdf.

- Los Angeles World Airports (LAWA)
- Port of Los Angeles (POLA); and Los Angeles Department of Water and Power (LADWP)

3.3.2 EV Car Sharing—BlueLA

Beyond directly supporting the purchase of EVs for individual use, car-sharing programs can be used to expand electric mobility to users who do not need to own a vehicle, or otherwise can't afford one, as is often the case in low-income communities. The City of Los Angeles has implemented an EV car-sharing program, BlueLA, whose mission is to deliver the benefits of electric Mobility-as-a-Service (MaaS), replacing the need for significant upfront investment through per-ride usage fees.

This program was implemented in 2015, when the City of Los Angeles was awarded funding from the California Air Resources Board through California Climate Investments. As background, in 2014, the California legislature passed and Governor Brown signed into law Senate Bill 1275, establishing the state's goal of putting 1 million electric vehicles on California's roads by the end of 2023, while making sure that low- and moderate-income Californians benefit from and have access to electric vehicles. This law directed CARB to establish a suite of pilot projects designed to put equity at the forefront of the state's EV transition. Funding for low-income car-sharing pilots was established as part of this suite, and the City of Los Angeles received the bulk of the funding for the BlueLA program. This program is an example of the focus on equity present in California's EV policies—at the state, regional and local levels.

BlueLA consists of a 100% EV car-sharing service, which is part of the City of Los Angeles's mobility strategy. Users of this electric mobility service have access to a network of shared electric vehicles at self-service locations across neighborhoods. BlueLA stations are on-street, consisting of a self-service kiosk and five parking spots, each with an electric charger, where users collect and drop off vehicles. BlueLA is designed as a point-to-point mobility solution, with no need to return the car to the starting point.[134] Figure 3.7 provides an overview of the current available space for the service kiosks.

---

134 BlueLA, *About BlueLA*, 2018, Available at: https://www.bluela.com/about-bluela.

FIGURE 3.7 BlueLA EV Station Availability Map[135]

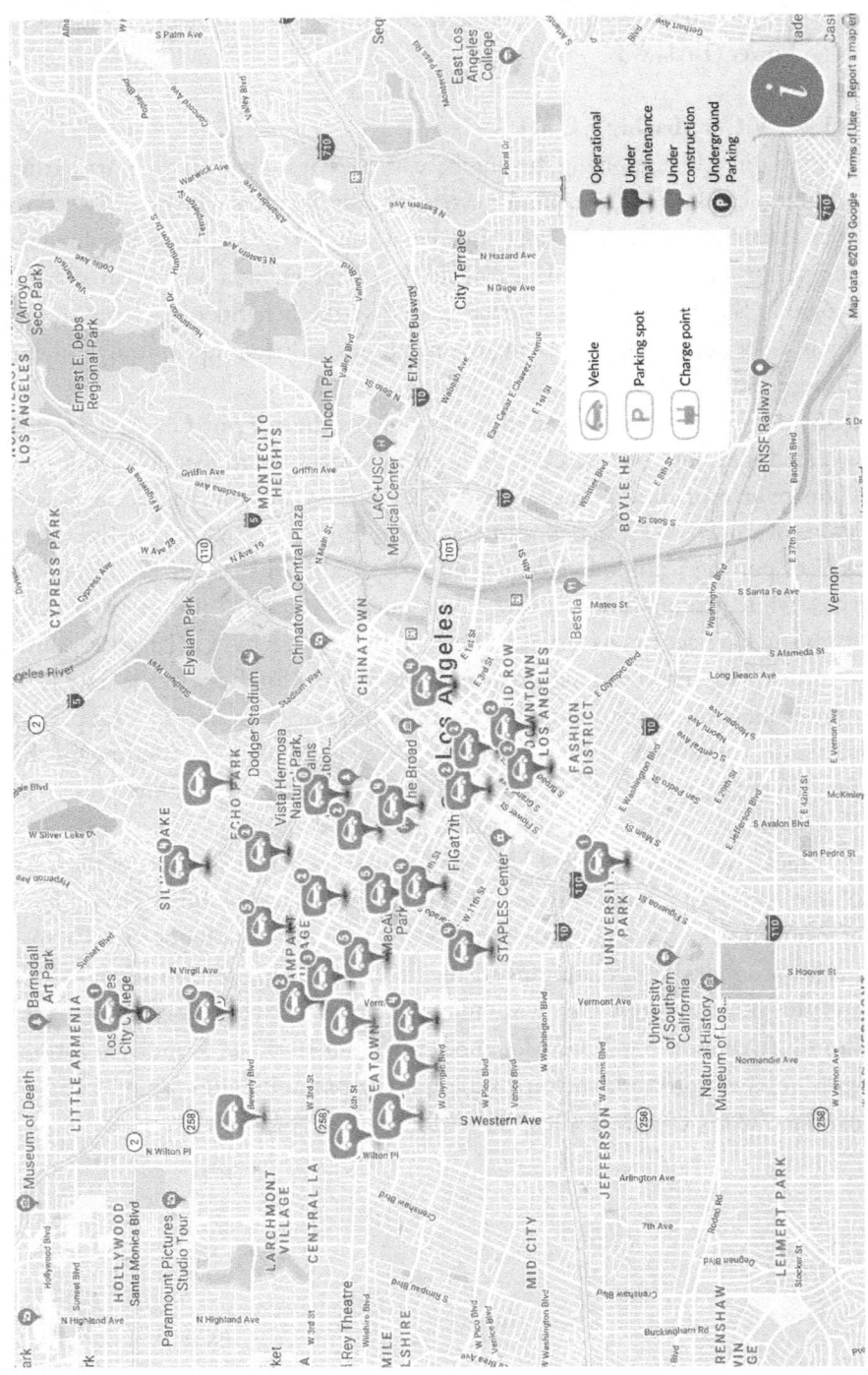

135 BlueLA, *Station Locator*, 2018, Available at: https://www.bluela.com/stations-map.

The communities served through this program include Westlake, Koreatown, Pico-Union, Downtown, Echo Park, Boyle Heights, and Chinatown. The service consists of 100 cars and 200 charging points. This program has been designed to benefit low-income residents in particular, with stations installed in densely populated low-income communities, and a pricing system adjusted according to income.[136] BlueLA operates this service in collaboration with the Los Angeles Department of Transportation (LADOT).

3.3.3 City of Los Angeles—Charge Up LA!

The City of Los Angeles has implemented Charge Up LA!, an EV charge rebate program, through the Los Angeles Department of Water and Power (LADWP), a public utility serving the city. The program is designed to help LADWP customers offset the costs of EV charge equipment. Under this program, residential and commercial customers have access to a specific rebate.[137]

Residential customers interested in applying for the rebate must be LADWP customers or live in the same household as an LADWP customer. The charger for which the rebate is being sought must be wall or pedestal mounted at a residential building also within the LADWP service area, and the EV that will use the charger must be registered at the same address. For residential customers, the rebate covers Level 2 chargers. The rebate targeting residential customers is designed to support the evolution to EV-ready residential building stock. The rebate available under this scheme is for up to $500 for a qualified EV charger. In addition to the rebate for the charger, customers can receive a $250 bonus if they install a dedicated meter for their EV charging needs, through which tailored time-of-use rates are applied. Customers installing TOU meters for their EV are also eligible for a discount of 2.5 cents per kilowatt-hour off the TOU rate.[138]

Commercial customers seeking the rebate must also be LADWP customers. The rebate applies to Level 2 chargers, which must be installed by a licensed contractor. In addition, commercial customers have to install a dedicated meter to measure the power delivered through the charging infrastructure. The rebate available for commercial customers is up to $5,000 for each hardwired EV charger, with an additional incentive of up to $750 per charge port (for lo-

136 Ibid., Miller, A., and Morris, T.
137 LADWP, Charge up L.A.! EV charger rebate program, 2018, Los Angeles, Available at:https://ladwp.com/ladwp/faces/ladwp/residential/r-gogreen/r-gg-driveelectric/r-gg-de-evncentives?_adf.ctrl-state=14ajmp7ep4_4&_afrLoop=208942704788049.
138 LADWP, *Residential Electric Vehicle Charger Rebate Application*, 2018, Los Angeles, Available at: https://www.ladwp.com/ladwp/faces/wcnav_externalId/r-sm-rp-ev?_adf.ctrl-state=a8l2lgq1e_4.

cations with more than one charging station). For this rebate, customers must have at least three parking spaces available to qualify for one charger rebate. An additional Level 2 charger rebate is available for each additional 10 parking spaces at the same location, with a cap of 20 rebates per location.[139]

3.4 Processes Enabling Charging Infrastructure

In California, state legislation significantly enables market support for EV adoption. Recent state enactments provide tax incentives for EV purchases and certain benefits for EV users, such as access to HOV lanes. City-level support is relevant because it can expand to state-level initiatives. For instance, in California, cities have the power to modify their building codes to require building owners to include EV chargers for tenants and the public. These policies are put into place by city councils and mayors. In this section, initiatives in the City of Los Angeles are discussed.

3.4.1 Building Regulations and EV in the LA Municipal Code

Building characteristics can affect the deployment process. For instance, parking space availability can be a barrier to charger installation for creating designated EV charging spaces because dedicated charging spaces shrink the availability of parking for ICE vehicles. Charging installations requested by tenants can result in additional facilities management costs for building owners. In addition, the interaction between building managers and owners slows decision-making.

Building regulations in the City of Los Angeles Municipal Code have been adjusted to include provisions that directly affect the availability of charging infrastructure.[140] As a result, the green building code now includes specific measures addressing EV infrastructure for both residential and nonresidential buildings. The implemented measures are described in this section.

Residential Mandatory Measures. In new multifamily dwellings and residential occupancies, 5% of the total number of parking spaces must be for EV charging and capable of supporting future EV charging infrastructure, with a minimum of 1 EV charge per dedicated space. For buildings with 17 or more

139 LADWP, *Commercial Electric Vehicle Charger Rebate Application*, 2018, Los Angeles, Available at: https://www.ladwp.com/ladwp/faces/wcnav_externalId/c-sm-rp-ev?_adf. ctrl-state=a8l2lgq1e_4&_afrLoop=1264369309958.
140 Rubin, B., Chester, M., and Mankey, J., *Zero Emission Vehicles in California: Community Readiness Guidebook*, 2013, Available at: http://opr.ca.gov/docs/ZEV_Guidebook.pdf.

dwelling units, at least one of the required EV spaces must be placed in a common-use area, equipped with an EV charging station and available for use by all residents. Those are the mandates for EV-charge-dedicated spaces in new buildings. Further specifics about implementing EV charge infrastructure follow.

An EV charger installation must comply with at least one of the following:

- The EV space must be adjacent to an accessible parking space meeting the requirements of the Los Angeles Building Code, allowing the EV charger to be used from that space.
- The EV space must be on an accessible route to the building, as defined in the Los Angeles Building Code.[141]

Nonresidential Mandatory Measures. For nonresidential buildings, the Los Angeles Municipal Code provides a detailed table specifying requirements for EV spaces depending on the number of parking spaces. See Table 3.3.

TABLE 3.3   Nonresidential Buildings' Mandatory EV Spaces and Stations[142]

Total number of parking spaces	Number of required EV charging spaces	Number of required EV charging stations
0–9	0	0
10–25	10	0
26–50	2	0
51–75	4	1
76–100	5	2
101–150	7	3
151–200	10	4
201 and over	6% of total	4 + (1 for every additional 500 spaces after the first 200)

141 These requirements are consistent with state level codes, noted earlier in this chapter.
142 City of Los Angeles, *Los Angeles Municipal Code*, 2018, Available at: http://library.amlegal.com/nxt/gateway.dll/California/lamc/municipalcode?f=templates$fn=default.htm$3.0$vid=amlegal:losangeles_ca_mc.

If a building requires only a single charging space, a raceway is required.[143] If a building requires multiple charging spaces, the raceways must be installed at the time of construction. The mandatory measures for nonresidential EV infrastructure may be waived by the municipal-code enforcing agency if evidence suggests that on-site electrical supply is inefficient, and/or if evidence suggests that additional local utility infrastructure design requirements may adversely affect the project's construction cost.

3.4.2 Traffic Regulations and EV in the Los Angeles Municipal Code

The deployment of public charging spaces in the city raises the issue of ensuring that new EV-dedicated spaces are used for charging purposes, not for general parking. ICE vehicles using EV-dedicated parking spaces impact charging access and availability. New parking procedures and penalties may be required to discourage ICE vehicles from using EV-designated spaces until habits change and more EVs are adopted. As a result, in early 2018, the Los Angeles Department of Transport (LADOT) proposed amendments to the Los Angeles Municipal Code (LAMC). Proposals include issuing citations and towing vehicles if they are illegally parked, at either on-street or off-street publicly owned charging station spaces.[144]

3.4.3 Permitting Process Development

Permitting processes affect the rollout of charging points. Permitting includes everything from applying for a permit to inspection after a job is completed. Delays sometimes occur, but it is unclear is whether permitting processes could be accelerated if the need for EV public charging infrastructure were to spike. The adaptability of EV infrastructure permitting calls for a guideline to address this point.

LADWP, in cooperation with the City of Los Angeles Department of Building and Safety (LADBS), has streamlined the process of providing EV home-charger permitting approval and expedited charger inspection and meter installation. Given this, the City of Los Angeles is compliant with California Legislation AB 1236 of 2016, which requires all local jurisdictions to adopt permitting standards that allow for timely and cost-effective installation of EV charging equipment.

---

143 A Raceway is a covered conduit through which an electrical cable travels from junction box to EV charger.
144 City of Los Angeles, *Los Angeles Department of Transport LAMC amendment request for parking at EV spaces*, 2018, City of Los Angeles, Available at: http://clkrep.lacity.org/onlinedocs/2014/14-0079-S3_rpt_tran_1-24-18.pdf.

From beginning to end, installation is structured around eight steps, described in Table 4. The city is committed to a seven-day approval process for infrastructure installation, if the customer's electrical system has sufficient capacity for the charger.[145]

The charger installation process in the City of Los Angeles requires contacting and scheduling with different city-level and external stakeholders. To respond more quickly to new charger installation requests, the LADBS included an express-permit option for new chargers. After the permit is obtained, the inspection process is also expedited, and the LADBS inspection can normally be scheduled for the business day after the request is made.[146] To make timely inspections, the LADBS created a dedicated EV charging infrastructure inspections team. LADBS' commitment to delivering chargers quickly will affect the implementation of infrastructure, because the entire city falls under its jurisdiction.[147]

The process described above applies to property owners as well. Property owners who are residents subject to homeowner association rules, living in multifamily dwelling units or rental apartments, must follow additional requirements when installing an EV charger. Before a final installation approval can be made, an EV owner interested in obtaining a charger must inform property owners and the homeowners association regarding a charger installation. These cases must follow a specific process prior to starting installation, as described in Table 3.4.[148]

Streamlining permitting and installation processes and stakeholder interactions, particularly in smaller towns where processes are outsourced to third parties, is a priority as numbers of EVs rise. Permitting and inspection is a critical link between plans and implementation. Permitting and inspection officers will have to consider expanding their capabilities to respond to requests for charging infrastructure. Infrastructure implementation can face barriers if capabilities are lacking.

145 Rubin, B., Chester, M. and Mankey, J., *Zero Emission Vehicles in California: Community Readiness Guidebook*, 2013, Available at: http://opr.ca.gov/docs/ZEV_Guidebook.pdf.
146 LADWP, *Charger installation: Los Angeles*, 2018, Available at: https://www.ladwp. com/ladwp/faces/ladwp/residential/r-gogreen/r-gg-driveelectric;jsessionid=j3zS cLzSmjvzFYKKYS5yNDLGR2nR9hHPWHgzvJt7MVppy8wf YSsl!-1447983279?_ afrLoop=1164395202703&_afrWindowMode=0&_afrWindowId=null#%40%3F_ afrWindowId%3Dnull%26_afrLoop%3D1164395202703%26_ afrWindowMode%3D0%26_adf.ctrl-state%3Da8l2lgq1e_4.
147 U.S. Department of Energy, *Los Angeles Sets the Stage for Plug-In Electric Vehicles*, 2014, Available at: http://www.afdc.energy.gov/case/1002.
148 Ibid., LADWP.

TABLE 3.4   City of Los Angeles EV Charger Installation Permitting Process[149]

Step	Necessary actions
1. Consult with car dealer	The EV dealership advises customer to contact an electrician and the LADWP to determine if the home or business is ready for a Level 2 charger.
2. Contact LADWP	Customer contacts LADWP for consultation on rate and meter options. The customer considers cost versus benefits of each option after researching EV information on the LADWP website.
3. Contact an electrician	Electrician inspects service wiring to determine if it has adequate capacity to supply the Level 2 charging station. Electrician advises customer about feasibility of the preferred meter option.
4. Charging station request	Customer completes the online EV Charging Station Request form. An LADWP electric service representative (ESR) is automatically dispatched within five business days.
5. LADWP site visit	LADWP ESR assesses service for possible system upgrades. ESR advises customer about LADWP meter options and provides a written report.
6. Obtain electrical permit	Electrician confirms meter and rate options with the customer and then obtains an electrical permit. Electrician completes the installation and calls for the inspection.[a]
7. LADBS inspection	The Los Angeles Department of Building and Safety (LADBS) inspects the installation. Approval of work is transmitted to LADWP when the installation passes inspection.
8. LADWP Installation	LADWP receives approval from the LADBS. Crew is dispatched to install meter and perform system work as needed.[b]

a   For jobs that involve a service panel upgrade or a separate Time-of-Use (TOU) meter, the ESR must also be called for the inspection.
b   A meter change to a TOU meter takes approximately 5 to 10 business days after LADBS approval if no panel upgrade is needed. Jobs with new panel work or LADWP system work may take longer.

149 LADWP, *Electric Vehicle Charger Installation Steps*, 2013, City of Los Angeles, Available at: https://www.ladwp.com/ladwp/faces/ladwp/residential/r-gogreen/r-gg-driveelectric;jsessionid=j3zScLzSmjvzFYKKYS5yNDLGR2nR 9hHPWHgzvJt7MVppy8wf YSsl!-1447983279?_afrLoop=1164395202703&_ afrWindowMode=0&_afrWindowId=null#%40%3F_afrWindowId%3Dnull%26_ afrLoop%3D1164395202703%26_afrWindowMode%3D0%26_adf.ctrl-state%3Da8l2lgq1e_4.

One LA stakeholder reported to the author an example involving a city in a county where a permitting official took four months to grant a permit. In this case, the charging equipment permitting request was issued by a shopping mall that fell outside of the scope of normal requests, requiring new equipment, new use of electricity, and new placement of electrical systems. This example illustrates that at this point in the evolution of EV adoption, capability development is, in some cases, more important than possible grid infrastructure capacity constraints.

3.5   Charging Infrastructure Implementation

As part of the City of Los Angeles's strategy to support the ongoing development of the EV market in 2017, $7.5 million in funding was approved for installing charging infrastructure. $2.6 million will be used for charging stations exclusively for the Los Angeles Police Department, and $4.8 million will be put toward citywide deployment of charging stations.[150] Also in 2017, $1.1 million was approved to continue the roll out of charging infrastructure, as well as public street lights.[151]

Every city has unique challenges in integrating electric chargers into roadways, parking areas, and other locales. In Brookline, Massachusetts, township officials considered using street lighting as hubs for EV chargers to use for on-street charging. This approach would integrate street lighting, on-street parking fees, and charging devices. However, Brookline discovered that the power supplied to street lights was insufficient for EV charging, and that upgrading street lights to provide Level 1 through Level 3 charge points alone would be too costly.

Los Angeles is also pursuing a strategy that aims to leverage existing lighting infrastructure to deploy electric vehicle charges. The experience, approach, and potential of this initiative are described next.

3.5.1 Public Infrastructure Coupled with Lighting Infrastructure

The City of Los Angeles has approximately 219,000 street lights, designated as a strategic network for future EV charger deployment plans. The city's EV Task Force considers street lighting to be a leverageable platform for EV infrastructure given the successful roll out of LED lighting technology throughout

---

150 City of Los Angeles, *City capital projects 2017–2018*, 2017, City of Los Angeles, Available at: http://clkrep.lacity.org/onlinedocs/2017/17-0924_rpt_CAO_08-16-2017.pdf.
151 Ibid., Miller, A., and Morris, T.

the city's street lighting network.[152] The City of Los Angeles, through the Bureau of Street Lighting, already is engaged in rolling out public chargers in its street light infrastructure. Coupling street lighting with charging infrastructure makes sense when the electrical system for public lighting can be adjusted to power EV chargers. At present, the Bureau of Street Lighting has deployed 82 charging stations. See Figure 3.8.[153]

The roll out of charging infrastructure in street lights started with an initiative spearheaded by the Bureau of Street Lighting between 2015 and 2016, through which 30 chargers were implemented. Based on the insights gained through the pilot program, 52 additional chargers were deployed between 2017 and 2018. Currently, the funding for the pilot and additional chargers deployed has to be reimbursed from the City's Unappropriated Balance, because the Bureau of Street Lighting is not allowed to allocate funds beyond operation and maintenance of the street lights. This approach to EV charging infrastructure has been implemented in collaboration with the Los Angeles Department of Water and Power and the Los Angeles Department of Transportation. The chargers implemented have a fixed fee ranging from $1 to $3 per hour of charging, depending on the location.

Increasing the installation of public chargers across the city's street lights can help position the City of Los Angeles as a leader in supporting the growing diffusion of EVs. Additionally, this can contribute to expanding EV usage in the region, further driving progress toward adoption of Zero Emission Vehicles.[154]

3.5.2 Public Charging in Downtown Los Angeles
To support the electrification of the city government vehicle fleet, the City of Los Angeles is installing 84 new charging stations in City Hall and City Hall East. These chargers will be made accessible to both city employees and public users and contribute to raising awareness of EVs.[155]

---

152 City of Los Angeles, *Citywide plan for electric vehicle charging infrastructure*, 2017, Los Angeles, Available at: http://clkrep.lacity.org/onlinedocs/2014/14-0079-s2_rpt_GSD_03-10-2017.pdf.
153 Ibid., City of Los Angeles.
154 Ibid., City of Los Angeles.
155 Ibid., Miller, A., and Morris, T. Note also, a similar awareness development approach was applied in Oslo several years ago. See Chapter 5 for more information.

FIGURE 3.8 EV Charger Infrastructure Available[156]

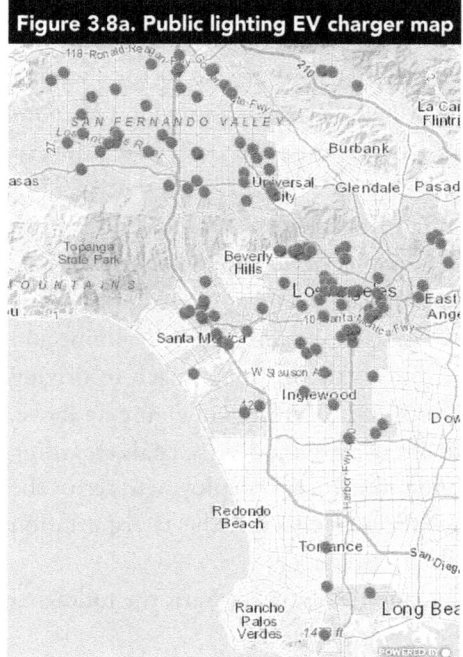

Figure 3.8a. Public lighting EV charger map

Figure 3.8b. EV chargers

3.6 Conclusions and Lessons Learned

This case study provided an up-to-date review of EV market development and support undertaken in the LA region. The insights gained by reviewing recent literature and from the interaction with stakeholders indicate that intergovernmental coordination is critical to successfully delivering EV charging infrastructure.

Los Angeles is a leader in EV adoption and has a track record of supporting electric mobility. Despite its record of innovation, the current availability of charging infrastructure could become a limiting factor affecting the volume and pace of EV adoption in upcoming years absent more amplified efforts to deploy more.

In Los Angeles, the availability of public charging infrastructure is low, and its development has been slow in spite of remarkably widespread efforts to increase deployment. As a result, EV owners rely significantly on private charge points, such as home charging or access to exclusive workplace charging.

156 City of Los Angeles. (2018a). EV Charging Stations. Available at: http://bsl.lacity.org/smartcity-ev-charging.html.

One of the most important challenges in deploying new EVSE infrastructure is determining how it will be funded. Up to the present time, funding has come from federal and state grants, utilities as directed by the California Public Utility Commission, some city-level support, and private sector charging service start-ups. These resources may not be sufficient if a surge in EV adoption occurs, where public charging infrastructure expansion will be required to support it.

Utilities have been active in charging infrastructure deployment as well. This is partly because private-sector charging service competitors are not able to find a business model that supports massive deployment of charging points.

Collaboration between government jurisdictions and specific planning and operations departments within jurisdictions is the main approach to driving EV infrastructure deployment in the LA region, as depicted in Figure 3.3 above. Collaborative efforts amongst jurisdictions occur with diverse goals regarding the what and the how of EV adoption and infrastructure deployment across the City and the region, which includes such regional efforts as the Transportation Electrification Partnership and E4 Mobility Alliance.

By analyzing ongoing EV market development and support, the following lessons can be gained from the LA region:

- **Public awareness.** The City of Los Angeles's effort to grow its EV fleet raises public awareness about the importance of electric mobility, while directly supporting long-term sustainability plans for its future.
- **Shared vision plus shared action.** Implementing a shared EV mobility initiative through the BlueLA program helps to present Mobility-as-a-Service (MaaS)—in this case, one designed to particularly benefit low-income communities that would otherwise face greater challenges to access.
- **Building and parking codes.** The adjustments to municipal building codes and parking codes that drive and support EVs at the city level promote a future in which EVs represent a large share of the vehicles market.
- **Streamlining permitting.** Creating smoother and faster permitting for installing public chargers by private users makes it easier for consumers to navigate a multi-stakeholder and multi-step process. But, while a defined process is helpful, further efforts are needed to ensure that process execution remains responsive as increased adoption occurs and more public charging infrastructure is needed.
- **Leverage existing infrastructure for EVs.** Public charging deployment coupled with street lights has been an ongoing effort in Los Angeles. It shows the possibilities for using existing infrastructure to expand charging availability. A better understanding is needed of street lights' ability

to accommodate rising demand. The matter has often been presented as a challenge, as discussed in the case of Brookline, Massachusetts (also in this volume). If street lighting can be leveraged to support EV charging deployment, there must be other opportunities, which may be identifiable if the street light example is used as a guide.

CHAPTER 4

Shanghai and Beijing, China:
An Unrelenting Sprint to Electrified Mobility

Z. Justin Ren, PhD, Boston University
Jie (Roger) Hao, Beijing EasytoFortune Tech Co.

4.1   The 1.4 Billion Person, $14 Trillion Journey

Disparate populations help illustrate the striking differences in the United States and China's transitions from ICE to EV platforms. The population of the People's Republic of China (henceforth referred to as "China," or PRC) was estimated at about 1.4 billion as of 2018,[157] representing nearly 20% of the world's population. Meanwhile, last year's US population, estimated by the US Census Bureau, was about 327 million,[158] or roughly four percent of the world's population. China's population is nearly five times the size of that of the United States.

A comparison of each country's Gross National Product (GNP) is also illustrative. The GNP of China was estimated to exceed $14 trillion USD in 2019,[159] while the 2018 estimate for the US GNP was about $20 trillion USD.[160] In other words, China's economy is about 60% the size of the United States, while its population is about five times larger. To serve China's growing population and rising wealth, the country has a colossal need for investment. However, such investment should not generate a carbon footprint like that created by the United States over the last 150 years, via industrialization and carbon-based wealth. While the United States must reorient, redirect, and rebuild to decarbonize, China must preempt, predetermine, and propel its

----

157 Demographics of China, Available at: https://en.wikipedia.org/wiki/Demographics_of_China.
158 Available at: https://www.census.gov/quickfacts/fact/table/US/PST045217.
159 Economy of China, Available at: https://en.wikipedia.org/wiki/Economy_of_China.
160 Economy of the United States, Available at: https://en.wikipedia.org/wiki/Economy_of_the_United_States.

development of sustainable energy, which the country committed to doing as part of the Paris Agreement.

Electrifying transportation is a priority in China, as it is in the United States. However, China's strategy must accommodate higher volumes, move much faster, and be more experimental than the current approach in most of the United States. Two of China's leading cities offer a window into the scale and velocity of change in electrifying mobility. A deeper look at Shanghai and Beijing can be instructive for the United States and the rest of the world.

Shanghai and Beijing are China's largest urban economies, led by Shanghai, with its annual Gross City Product (GCP) of $446 billion,[161] and Beijing, with $418 billion. Combined, Shanghai and Beijing contribute more than 7% of China's annual GDP. Both cities also lead the world in EV adoption. They have the highest number of EV sales in the world, and their EV market shares are also the highest. See Figure 4.1, from the International Council on Clean Transportation (ICCT).

In China, what in the United States are called "charge points" or "charging stations" are known as "charging piles." For this chapter, China's term will be used.

China has three charging pile classes:

- Public charging piles, which are open to all uses.
- Special charging piles, which are facilities not open to personal vehicles. They are open only to EVs such as buses, workplace piles exclusively available for employees, and logistics piles (e.g., shipping and delivery involving fleets).
- Private charging piles, which are equipped to serve vehicles for non-business uses only and are not connected to any communications networks.

Table 4.1 summarizes some basic facts about the cities' EV infrastructure.

161 List of Chinese prefecture-level cities by GDP, Available at: https://en.wikipedia.org/wiki/List_of_Chinese_prefecture-level_cities_by_GDP.

FIGURE 4.1 Global Cumulative EV Sales and Related Market Shares[162]

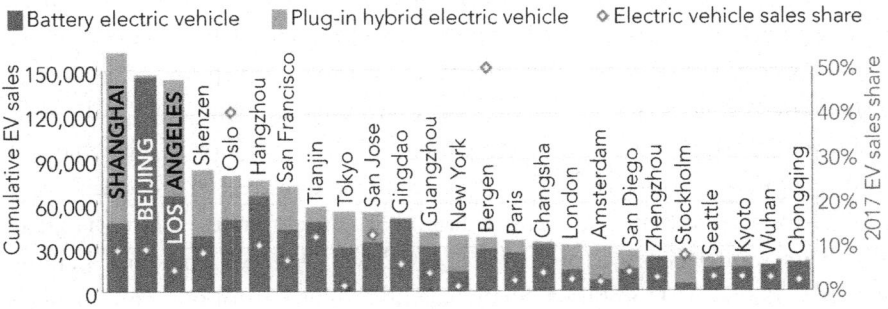

TABLE 4.1 Utilization Statistics of EV Charging Infrastructure as of 2018[163]

	Beijing	Shanghai
EV stock	219,000	231,000
Total EV charging piles	147,000	206,000
Private EV charging piles	108,000	138,000
Battery EV (BEV) proportion among all EVs sold in 2017	98.6%	23.8%
EV-to-charger ratio	1.49 : 1	1.12 : 1

As shown above, although both Beijing and Shanghai are leading the EV revolution, their approaches differ. Beijing heavily favors battery-only EV (BEV), whereas Shanghai leans toward plug-in hybrid EV (PHEV). The difference is largely due to "local characteristics": Beijing and Shanghai are where the two largest state-owned automakers are located (Beijing Automotive Industry Corporation, or BAIC,[164] and Shanghai Automotive Industry Corporation, or SAIC).[165] When it comes to developing new electric vehicles (NEVs), BAIC focuses on BEVs while SAIC leans toward PHEVs.

162 Source: International Council on Clean Transportation, *Electric vehicle capitols: Accelerating the global transition to electric drive*, 2018.
163 Data source: http://www.cscn.com.cn/news/show-701863.html.
164 BAIC Group, Available at: https://en.wikipedia.org/wiki/BAIC_Group.
165 SAIC Motor, Available at: https://en.wikipedia.org/wiki/SAIC_Motor.

4.2 EV Charging Infrastructure in Shanghai

As of July 2018, more than 40 operators of charging facilities were connected to a municipal data platform for public data collection and monitoring of power exchange facilities in Shanghai,[166] hereinafter referred to as the "city-level platform," which offers access to both public and special charging of the whole city.

A total of 61,411 power exchange facilities provide access to the public and special charging citywide, including 31,337 public charging piles and 30,074 special charging piles. Additionally, according to the Shanghai New Energy Automobile Promotion Office, the city includes 103,100 private charging piles. Finally, Shanghai has a total of 164,500 charging and battery replacement facilities, and about 186,000 new energy vehicles. Thus, the city's EV-to-pile ratio is about 1.1:1.[167] Figure 4.2 depicts the monthly rise in the number of new charging pile installations, demonstrating how quickly Shanghai is expanding its EV charging infrastructure.

Figure 4.2 Total Number of New Public and Special Pile Installations[168]

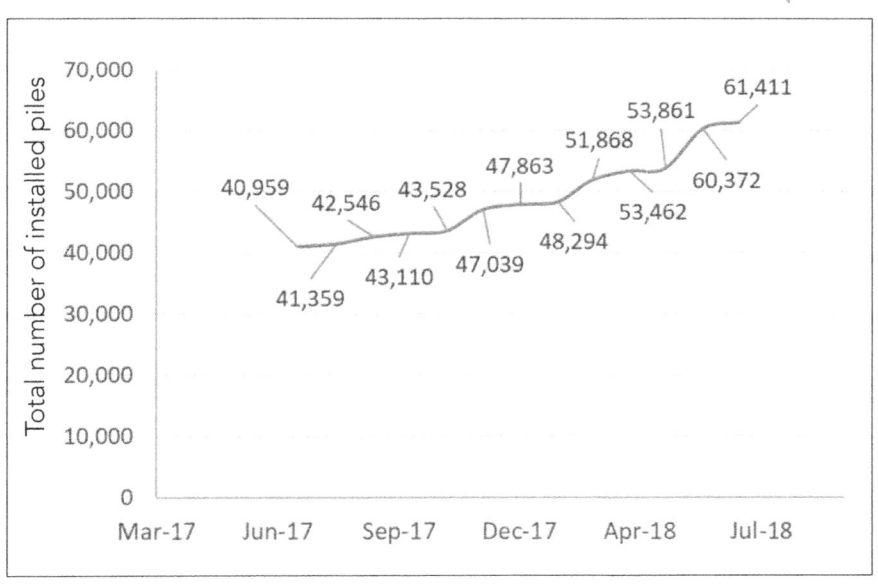

---

166 Available at: https://www.evchargeonline.com/.
167 Data source: Municipal data platform for public data collection and monitoring of Shanghai charging and replacing facilities, Data Statistics Monthly Bulletin No.12.
168 Ibid., Data Statistics Monthly Bulletin.

At the end of July 2018, AC charging piles accounted for about 84% (when rounded up), and DC charging piles accounted for about 16% (when rounded up). AC and DC integrated charging piles accounted for less than one percent of all charging piles. Growth for all categories of charging piles is high, reflecting China's successful EV infrastructure deployment efforts.

4.3 Coordination of Charging Infrastructure Development

There is significant heterogeneity across regions in China in the degree of coordination among the multiple parties involved in charging infrastructure development. There are multiple charging pile vendors each with their own charging networks that typically are not connected to each other. This creates inefficiencies in EV infrastructure deployment as well as inconveniences for consumers. Some cities in China are trying to solve this problem by aggregating charger information, but with varying degrees of success. For example, Beijing and Xi'an use a combination of websites[169] and downloadable apps, while Shenzhen heavily relies on the WeChat app, which is omnipresent in China, to help consumers find chargers. In this aspect, Shanghai stands out because it has a well-functioning public-private partnership to monitor and manage all the public charging infrastructure in the city.

4.3.1 Shanghai's Coordinating Platform

Shanghai Electric Vehicle Charging Infrastructure Enterprise Alliance (SEVCIEA) is a social group managed by the Shanghai Civil Affairs Bureau and the Shanghai Social Organization Administration. It was established to:

- Promote the exchange and cooperation of alliance members in constructing and operating charging facilities
- Promote the orderly construction and operation of charging facilities in Shanghai
- Realize the interconnection between charging facilities of all parties, to promote the innovation and implementation of the commercial operation of charging facilities
- Research and develop advanced charging technologies and develop technical standards and third-party certification and training

---

169 Available at: https://www.evehicle.cn/ for Beijing, and http://www.evxian.com/ for Xi'an, respectively.

- Create an intelligent, convenient, and standardized electric-vehicle charging service industry with domestic advanced level and Shanghai characteristics, thereby supporting the overall development of Shanghai's electric vehicles

SEVCIEA is a nonprofit organization based on voluntary, equal, cooperative, and mutually beneficial principles, jointly established by institutions including energy supply companies, charging facility manufacturers, charging operation service companies, electric vehicle manufacturers, charging technology research and development institutions, and certification organizations. Its participating members include China's State Grid EV Service, an EV charging subsidiary composed of major Chinese auto companies such as Shanghai Automobile Industry Corporation, and a host of private charging companies. A detailed list of members follows:

FIGURE 4.3 SEVCIEA Participants

Within this alliance of parties, a few charging pile providers stand out. Figure 4.4 summarizes.

FIGURE 4.4 The Number of Piles Owned by Charging Pile Enterprises (excluding private charge piles)

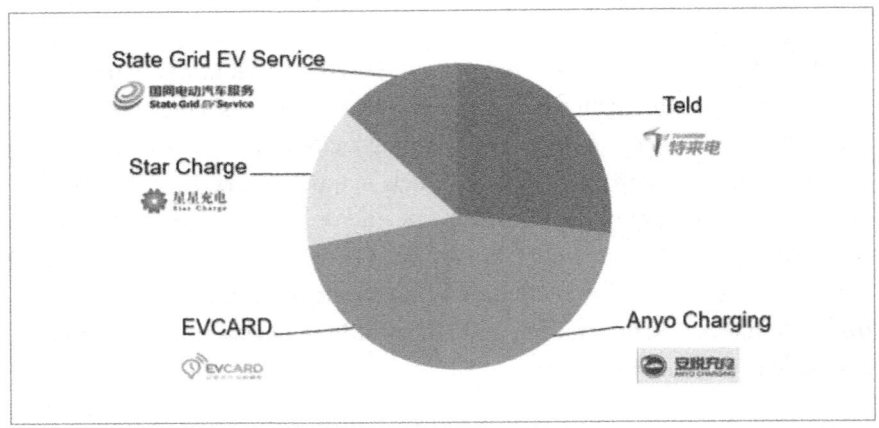

The top operators of charging piles are Teld (teld.cn, 27%), Anyo Charging (anyocharging.com, a subsidiary of SAIC, 25%), EVCARD (evard.com, a car-sharing company owned by SAIC, 20%), Starcharge (starcharge.com, 15%), and State Grid EV Service (13%). These companies operate different combinations of public and special-purpose charging piles.

4.3.2 National-Level Coordination

At the national level, there is the Chinese Electric Vehicle Charging Infrastructure Promotion Agency (EVCIPA),[170] an industry consortium that is dedicated to promoting EV adoption and EV charging infrastructure in China. The agency establishes hardware and software standards that are related to EV charging, and serves as a policy and data platform for China's EV and EVSE industries. It also publishes reports on EV infrastructure deployment at the national level.

To deepen coordination among different EV charging infrastructure providers, a group of four major EV infrastructure companies (State Grid EV Service, China Southern Power Grid Investment Limited, Star Charge, and Teld) formed a new alliance in December 2018 called "Xiong'An Lian Xing" to promote "Green and Smart" EV charging infrastructure. It has the potential of changing the landscape of China's EV charging industry by creating a nationwide information platform thanks to the participation of China's two largest state-owned utilities (State Grid, and China Southern Power Grid).

---

170 Available at: http://www.evcipa.org.cn/.

4.3.3 The Role of State Grid of China

State Grid Corporation of China (SGCC) is the largest of China's two monopoly, state-owned electric utilities, serving about four-fifths of the country. With revenue of $349 billion, it is also the largest utility company in the world; in 2018, it was the overall second-largest company in the world.

SGCC plays a leading role in China's EV adoption and deployment of EV charging infrastructure. First, SGCC is pushing to upgrade its power grid into a "smart grid" (defined as a system that can bidirectionally transmit electricity efficiently and allow for greater information and control). Such a smart grid system can have a large impact on how EVs are used and recharged. In managing electricity load for its EV charging network, for example, SGCC is experimenting with innovative charging methods such as Vehicle-to-Grid (V2G) to more efficiently charge EVs and manage its grid load.

SGCC has established standards for EV charging and is developing new fast-charging standards in anticipation of next-generation EVs. With a total of about 200,000 charging piles connected to its network throughput China, SGCC has the largest EV charging network in the world. Also, it has established a subsidiary called State Grid EV Service Company (SGEVSC) to build and service EV charging infrastructure. China plans to have 500,000 public charging piles by 2020, built mainly by the private sector, but SGEVSC alone plans to build about one-quarter of them. By building charging stations, the company aims to reduce the distance between charging stations to less than 5 kilometers (about 3.1 miles) in suburban areas, less than 3 kilometers (1.9 miles) in inner suburbs, and less than 1 kilometer (0.6 miles) in urban areas.

4.3.4 The Challenge of Low Charging Pile Utilization Rates

China's EV adoption moves with remarkably high volumes of EV adoption and nonstop high speed charging pile deployment in Shanghai. However, usage rates tell a different story. Table 4.2 shows usage rates that range from 1.6% to about 15% for different categories of charging facilities.

TABLE 4.2 Utilization of Charging Piles for Different Site Types in Shanghai (2018)

Site types	Accumulated charging time (hours/month)	Utilization rate
Bus charging	298,574	15.06%
Logistics charging	18,584	2.51%
Workplace charging	80,682	2.08%
Community charging	75,755	1.98%
Public charging	372,860	1.65%

Here, usage rates for DC chargers are about five times higher than those for AC chargers (6.54% versus 1.18%[171]). However, these rates seem unusually low given the scale of China's EV deployment and the significance of Shanghai as a mega city. In Beijing utilization rates are similarly in the single digit (a news article published in April 2019 reported that the overall charger utilization rate in Beijing is 7.26%, up from 4.63% in 2018).

The reasons behind such low rates are due to multiple factors such as:

- **High price of charging.** Unlike Europe or the United States, where free or heavily subsidized public charging is available, public EV charging in China is relatively costly. EV owners can pay an estimated three times more to use public charging stations than they pay at their residences.[172] The reasons for such a high cost are multiple: First, parking space in metropolitan areas in China is expensive, driven by land scarcity and the high number of vehicles. Hence, most charging pile operators put a high cost on parking for EV charging. For the same reason, many operators are not willing to exclude ICE vehicles from occupying EV charging spaces. In addition, most operators' fees for charging are relatively high, so as noted most EV owners charge at home, where rates are much lower. Private charging piles cost about 0.6 Yuan/kWh, and public charging piles cost at least two or three times that amount, in addition to parking fees (depending on localities).

---

171 Available at: https://finance.sina.com.cn/roll/2019-04-09/doc-ihvhiewr4209669.shtml.
172 Available at: https://about.bnef.com/blog/china-electric-vehicles-public-charging/.

- **Lack of coordination between operators.** Each vendor uses an app and/
  or a prepaid card to enable charging. Those apps do not always include
  correct information about other vendors' charging piles. There are multiple charging pile vendors, as noted above, each with distinct charging
  networks. To allow consumers to use most public chargers, vendors must
  install more than a dozen apps. In addition, apps require a cash deposit of
  varying amounts. As a result, EV owners are averse to installing chargers
  in public places. The result is a cumbersome and confusing interface between EV and charging pile.[173]
- **AC charging dominates.** Most public charging piles are AC and too
  slow to meet many EV owners' fast-charging needs. In addition, some
  charging piles are not properly maintained or are not usable, partly due to
  the lack of incentives for parking-space operators, who are compensated
  for parking but not charging.
- **Profitability challenges of charging operators.** Turning a profit with
  public charging piles is difficult, and no clear business model has emerged
  that promises consistent profitability for charging pile operators. The
  standard cost equation for public charging piles is electricity fee + service
  fee. The industrial electricity fee for public charging piles is 1.2 yuan/
  kWh[174] (which goes to the utilities), and the service fee is somewhere
  between 0.8 yuan/kWh and 1.6 yuan/kWh. Each AC charging pile costs
  about 3,000 yuan and each DC charging pile 30,000 yuan. With this cost
  and revenue structure, the simple payback period for an AC charger used
  around-the-clock is 78.1 days, even assuming the service fee at the high
  end of 1.6 yuan/kWh. But at the actual 2% utilization rate the payback
  period is 10.9 years.[175] Hundreds of charging-related companies across the
  country are operating at a loss. In 2019 only a few of the largest charging
  companies are slowly getting into profitability zones, after years of capital
  spending and operating loss.

---

173 Available at: https://www.citylab.com/transportation/2017/09/chinas-ban-on-gas-
power-cars-still-wont-solve-its-charging-challenge/539388/.
174 Before April 2018, charging fees in China were regulated to be fixed at 0.8 yuan/kWh.
After April 2018, prices were no longer regulated, and each municipality can decide on
their charging fee structures. For more details, see https://www.d1ev.com/kol/68252
175 The AC charging pile cost recovery period: cost / charging service fee =1875 hours=
78.1 days. The utilization rate is less than 2%, 24 * 0.02 = 0.48 hours, 24/0.48 = 50, 78 * 50
= 3,900 days = 10.9years.

- **Local protectionism.** Local EV manufacturers have decreased the accessibility of EVs to certain charging piles, thus reducing the accessible number of chargers for cars of other brands.[176]
- **Consumer lag.** Finally, utilization is affected by consumer willingness to replace conventional ICE vehicles, range anxiety and insufficient promotional solutions that spur acquisitions.[177]
- **Suboptimal location.** Many charging piles are sited without much planning or siting study. In fact, some piles were installed just to collect government subsidies, with no regard for EV charging demand.

The next two sections discuss government incentives that are in place for EVs, and for EV charging infrastructure.

4.4 EV Incentives: A Taxonomy and Comparison

EV-related incentives in China are varied, complex, and determined by each locality. To properly understand them, first consider a taxonomy to classify them. Then delving into details and comparing EV incentives between Beijing and Shanghai will make sense.

4.4.1 A Taxonomy of EV Incentives in China

Two levels of incentives exist: Those that the central government applies to the entire country; and those created by the local government for each locality. The exact form of incentives can be put in two broad categories: Monetary incentives, and nonmonetary ones (also called regulatory incentives). In addition, incentives are updated every year as situations change. The following taxonomy describes the structure of the recent rounds of EV incentives up to April 2019.

All subsidies are issued at the point of purchase. Once an EV manufacturer verifies that a buyer meets all the subsidy requirements—such as residency, good driving record, and no previous EV ownership—the manufacturer then sells the consumer the EV at the discounted price, meaning the original price minus all applicable subsidies (from both the central and local governments). After the sale, the car manufacturer applies for reimbursement from the government. Through this mechanism, EV manufacturers get paid the full price of the EV, while consumers enjoy subsidies when purchasing EVs.

---

176 Consulate General of the Kingdom of the Netherlands, Guangzhou, *China Top Sector E-Mobility: Opportunities for Dutch Companies*, 2014.

177 Wang, N., Tang, L. and Pan, H., *Analysis of public acceptance of electric vehicles: An empirical study in Shanghai*, Jan. 2018, Technological Forecasting and Social Change, vol. 126, pages 284–291.

TABLE 4.3   A Taxonomy of EV-Related Incentives[178]

	Central Government Incentives	Local Government Incentives
Monetary Incentives	(1) Cash subsidy. Amount depends on: (a) battery capacity; (b) battery energy density; and (c) energy saving relative to government benchmark (2) Waiving vehicle tax	Cash subsidy, typically pegged to central government incentives as a ratio (e.g., 1:0.5 means that for every RMB yuan of subsidy from the central government, local government adds another 0.5 RMB yuan). Starting March 2019, local cash incentives toward EV purchase are no longer permitted. Instead, local incentives are directed toward building EV charging infrastructure.
Nonmonetary Incentives	Delegate to local government	Depending on each locality, EV owners could be given priority on the issuance of license plates, the use for business of right-to-travel on roads under certain congestion, and traffic regulation situations.

Since 2018, the Chinese central government has been reducing subsidies for EVs with low-range and low battery energy-density while boosting EVs with long-range (over 300 km) and high battery density. This is to encourage EV manufactures to shift their resources toward designing and manufacturing more energy-efficient EVs. In addition, the central government now requires auto manufacturers to preset a portion of their sales as EV sales. Those who meet the requirement are given "positive credits" while those who do not are assigned "negative credits." Such credits (called "double points" in Chinese) can be in theory-traded among auto manufacturers.

4.4.2 Comparison of EV Incentives in Beijing and Shanghai

First of all, in China, fuel-cell EVs and BEVs are broadly called New Energy Vehicles (NEV). Subsidies are structured not just for BEVs but also for fuel-cell

---

178 Source: Compiled by authors from various sources.

EVs.[179] The first comparison concerns the monetary incentives of the two cities. Note that central government incentives are not included in the comparison because they are identical in both cities. A few highlights from Table 4.3:

- For BEVs, Beijing and Shanghai offer identical local incentives (a 1:0.5 ratio).
- But for PHEV, differences are dramatic: Shanghai continues to offer incentives (albeit at a lower ratio, of 1:0.3), while Beijing does not offer any subsidy. This partly explains why almost all EVs sold in Beijing are BEVs, while most EVs sold in Shanghai are PHEVs.
- Both cities limit how much money EV manufacturers can receive.
- Both cities intend to subsidize passenger EVs and restrict or exclude other vehicles such as buses.

179 While not widely emphasized in research literature, subsidies for BEV and fuel-cell EVs are equivalent. A deeper understanding of the investment risks and deployment implications of a multi-channeled "fueling system" for multiple EV technologies warrants more research.

TABLE 4.4 Shanghai–Beijing Financial Subsidies for New Energy Vehicles (NEV) 2018[180]

Financial Subsidy	Beijing	Shanghai
Battery Electric Vehicle (BEV)	Muncipal subsides are given according to the central and local ratio of 1:0.5 (i.e., for every RMB yuan of subsidy from the central government, local government adds another 0.5 RMB yuan). There is no operating mileage requirement for privately purchased new energy passenger cars. For other types of new energy vehicles, municipal subsidies will be given after the vehicle has traveled 20,000 km.	For eligible BEVs, the city's financial subsidies shall be given in accordance with the central- and local financial subsidy ratio of 1:0.5.
Fuel-cell vehicle		The city's financial subsidy is given no more than the central financial subsidy of 1:1 to the fuel-cell vehicles.
Plug-in Hybrid Electric Vehicle (PHEV)	NA	The city's financial subsides are given to eligible PHEVs with engine displacement no more than 1.6 liters, in accordance with the central financial subsidy ratio of 1:0.3 (1 national to 0.3 local).
Exclusion	New energy sanitation vehicles, new energy buses, and new energy vehicles purchased by administrative institutions using financial funds do not enjoy the city's financial subsides.	This implementation method is not applicable to new energy vehicles used in the bus industry.
Vehicle manufacturer	The total amount of financial subsidies automobile manufactures receive shall not exceed 60% of the sales price of the vehicle. If the total subsidy exceeds 60% of the sales price of the vehicle, the local subsidy shall be calculated after deducting the central government subsidy from 60% of the vehicle's sales price.	The total amount of financial subsides shall, in principle, not exceed 50% of the sales price of the vehicle. If the total subsidy exceeds 50% of the vehicle's sales price, the local subsidy of the city is calculated after deducting the central subsidy.

Note: Such subsidies have been retired in 2019

---

180 Data source: *Administrative Measures for the Promotion and Application of New Energy Vehicles in Beijing*, 2018, Jingkefa, No. 25; Data source: *Implementation Measures for Shanghai to Encourage the Purchase and Use of New Energy Vehicles*, 2018, Shanghai Office Regulations No. 7.

Nonmonetary incentives are available for EVs and are described in Table 4.5.

TABLE 4.5   Nonmonetary Policies for NEV in Effect in 2019[181]

Nonmonetary Preferential Policy	Beijing	Shanghai
License Plate Issuing	No restriction on issuing license plates for NEV (while those for ICE vehicles remain restricted). However, the total number of NEV plates issued is capped. Applications join a waiting list, and plates are allocated on a first-come, first-served basis.	No restriction on issuing license plates for personal use NEV for FREE (while those for ICE vehicle remain restricted and issued by a bidding process). However, the total number of plates issued is capped. Application join a waiting list, and plates are allocated on a first-come, first-served basis.
Business Use	NA	Consumers who purchase NEVs need to get business licenses from relevant departments, which will give priority to issuing permits.
Traffic Regulation	BEVs are exempt from travel restrictions on certain days of the week. (This policy was intended to limit the total number of vehicles on the road in Beijing.)	NEVs are given preferential treatment over ICE vehicles when travel restrictions are in place.

4.4.3 EV Incentives Are Transitional and Are Being Gradually Phased Out by 2020

Even though multiple EV incentives exist at the central government and local levels, the central government has decided incentives will be gradually phased out by 2020.

In fact, since China began its EV subsidy in 2009, incentives have declined steadily, starting in 2016. But another trend is emerging: *China is increasingly focused on building its EV charging infrastructure and is willing to put resources toward accelerating charging infrastructure buildout.* In effect, in the latest round

---

181 Data source: Ibid., Jingkefa. Data source: Ibid., Shanghai Office Regulations.

of policy revisions in March 2019, China completely eliminated local cash incentives toward EV purchases, and instead local incentives were to be directed toward building out charging infrastructure. The incentives and policies associated with China's EV charging infrastructure are detailed in Section 4.5.

4.5 EV Charging Infrastructure Incentives

4.5.1 Central Government Incentives for Infrastructure Buildout

China's central government has set specific targets for EV and EV charging infrastructure over the last few years.

In a five-year planning document issued in 2015, the government set a goal of installing 12,000 centralized charging stations and 480,000 distributed charging piles nationwide by 2020, in order to satisfy the expected charging needs of five million EVs. (That target has been surpassed – as of the end of 2018 there were 728,000 charging piles.)

To help achieve its goals, in 2016 the central government established stimulus packages to help each region pay for its EV charging infrastructure buildout. For example, in heavily polluted regions such as Beijing, the stimulus was for every additional 6,000 NEV adopted, a subsidy of RMB 1.1 million would be paid to the local government to help offset the cost of building EV chargers.

In addition, multiple ministries in China and governing bodies have issued goals and policies to accelerate deployment of charging facilities in residential communities and workplaces, and for public parking spaces.

In July 2018, additional ordinances focused on building centralized charging stations and fast-charging stations in large commercial spaces. In November 2018, China set a three-year agenda to further advance EV charging technology and improve service quality, network capability, and interoperability of charging equipment in order to achieve an EV:charger ratio of 1:1.

With initiatives and incentives in place, local governments have been coming up with matching incentives to add more stimulus for constructing EV charging infrastructure. *Such a policy priority was again reinforced when the Chinese central government updated its policy in March 2019, where local incentives budgeted toward EV adoption were redirected toward subsidizing charging infrastructure for buildings and at street level.*

4.5.2 Beijing Focuses on Increasing and Improving Charging Infrastructure

The Beijing government took a two-pronged approach to upgrading its EV charging infrastructure: quantity and quality.

Quantity-wise, Beijing has set an aggressive goal: By 2020, one charging pile will be available every 900 meters, in order to meet charging needs for its estimated 0.6 million EVs.[182]

Quality-wise, Beijing's government has been focusing on increasing the usage of installed charging infrastructure. In late 2018, Beijing issued a set of incentives to improve operations of public charging facilities.

Eligible chargers are evaluated quarterly as well as annually, and are ranked based on measures such as:

- Electricity rate
- Utilization rate
- Safety
- Data
- Certification

Vendors are then given grades of A, B, C, and D based on scores for each measure. Financial incentives of different amounts are based on grades. (Vendors graded A get the highest amount, while those graded D get zero.)

4.5.3 Shanghai Emphasizes Innovation, a Common Platform, and Provides Additional Incentives for Building EV Chargers

Shanghai's government has introduced a host of policies and incentives that apply to all chargers (public, private, and special purpose). In most iterations of citywide regulations in 2016, the guiding principles were:

- To establish a citywide platform with 50% of development cost shared by the city (the platform was successfully launched last year, and is shown in an earlier section of this chapter)
- To establish standards in building and operating charging facilities, and data sharing
- That the city would give charging facilities priority in land use and subsidize 30% of total cost of building EV chargers
- That the city would also subsidize the operating cost of public and special-purpose charging stations based on actual electricity usage
- That electricity would be provided free of charge (or at reduced rates) to centralized large-scale charging stations and special-purpose charging stations
- That service charges would be capped, to encourage usage, but caps may later be lifted, to transition to market-based pricing

---

[182] Available at: https://news.mydrivers.com/1/479/479222.htm.

- That a new business model will be encouraged, involving installing and operating charging facilities using financing from crowdfunding
- That businesses and other entities will be encouraged to open up their own chargers to the public

Under the latest directives from the Chinese central government in March 2019, both cities are expected to pour even more capital into making EV charging facilities more ubiquitous and EV charging more affordable and convenient. Each city may come up different policies with different parameters, which will range from reducing charging fees to subsidizing charging pile operators to incentivizing EV charging technology innovation and development. The intent of all efforts should be to build more EV chargers and to promote shared private chargers in residential communities. While paths to desired outcomes may vary by city, the government's expected results will be similar: there will be more EVs in both cities, and consumers in both cities are likely to find EV charging experiences less frustrating and more affordable.

4.6 Conclusion

China's innovative, end-to-end approach to EVs continues. With more new energy vehicles, confidence is high that more people will use public charging piles. Already, consumption of the overall charging pile infrastructure is increasing in Shanghai and Beijing. Annual growth in use of charging piles is 100%.[183]

Studying public infrastructure deployment in Shanghai and Beijing can inform the US and other countries about critical success factors, which could be adopted by other cities as further public charging infrastructure is deployed. Specifically:

- **National policies are essential in setting overall directions in EV infrastructure deployment.** But they do not ensure consistent local execution or effectively support desired outcomes. Local deployment requires local engagement and coordination. If local differentiation undermines national priorities, then greater national engagement will be required.
- **Efficient utilization of charging infrastructure clearly depends on sufficient numbers of EVs using them.** However, what constitutes a high utilization rate for a public charging pile still has to be determined; in other words, it is possible that high utilization will hover around 50%, at best. If so, pricing of public charging services will become important in increasing off-peak use and rationing on-peak use. While the issue is

183 Available at: http://www.pudongtv.en/pindaoguanli/ pudongxinwen/2018-04-03/41178.html.

seemingly simple, the randomness of vehicle movement adds an interesting dimension to planning.

- **Public charging infrastructure needs to be designed to enable private sector participation.** To maximize utilization, standards for hardware and data sharing are important. Establishing an interconnected platform to optimize the use and layout of charging piles will help improve access to—and therefore use of—public charging piles.

CHAPTER 5

EV Infrastructure in Oslo, Norway

David O. Jermain

5.1 Introduction

Nordic countries (Denmark, Finland, Iceland, Norway, Sweden) are aggressively driving EV adoption. Nearly 250,000 EVs have been sold and are in use across Scandinavia, which accounts for about eight percent of the world's electric vehicles and the highest ratio of EVs per person worldwide. This region is the third-largest EV market, with China and the United States the top two, respectively. Norway is the leader within the Nordic block of countries with about 40% of its vehicle market share composed of EVs as of 2018.[184]

Each Nordic country has distinctive policies that have driven comparatively rapid market share shifts between ICE vehicles and EVs. Types of policies used by all Nordic countries include a focus on reducing the purchase price of EVs, cutting circulation taxes,[185] and offering local incentives such as waivers or partial exemptions on road use charges, free parking, or use of bus lanes by EVs. Also, Nordic countries have emphasized the buildout of EV charging infrastructure; recognizing that while about 80% of EV charging occurs at home, publicly accessible charge points reduce range and wait anxiety, which can dampen interest in EV adoption.

----

184 From a summary of IEA's, *Nordic region offers valuable lessons for rapid EV deployment worldwide,* March 2018, Available at: https://www.iea.org/newsroom/news/2018/march/nordic-region-offers-valuable-lessons-for-rapid-ev-deployment-worldwide.html
185 A Circulation Tax is a fee charged to a vehicle based on its engine power, fuel efficiency, or engine displacement and CO_2 emissions, which varies country by country. See: Duer, H., Rosenhagen, C. and Ritnagel, P.O., *A comparative analysis of taxes and CO2 emissions from passenger cars in the Nordic countries,* 2011, Nordic Council of Ministers, Available at: https://read.nordic-ilibrary.org/environment/a-comparative-analysis-of-taxes-and-co2-emissions-from-passenger-cars-in-the-nordic-countries_tn2011-523, page 5, and https://www.cesifo-group.de/ifoHome/facts/DICE/Infrastructure/Transportation/General-Transport-Policy/overview-vehicle-taxation-scheme/fileBinary/Overview-vehicle-taxation-schemes.pdf.

Norway's success in achieving an EV market share of about 40% in 2018 tops other Nordic countries as well as the rest of the world. Its stated national policy of selling only zero-emission vehicles by 2025 puts it on center stage for other countries and their cities to study and to follow best practices emanating from Norway's efforts.

Norway's national policies drive EV adoption and infrastructure buildout. Cities in Norway enhance national policies with complimentary local incentives. Priorities for appropriately balancing EV adoption with EV charging infrastructure deployment vary city by city based on EV adoption rates, trip patterns, and other distinctive local factors.

Oslo is the capitol of Norway, as well as its most populated city. Thus, to learn from Oslo requires not only understanding Norway's national EV policy priorities but also how Norway's cities are implementing and enhancing those policies.

5.2   Norway's EV Policies

5.2.1   National Market Characteristics

By June 2017, battery electric vehicles (BEVs) comprised about 19% of the vehicle market in Norway, with plug-in hybrid electric vehicles (PHEVs) capturing about 16% of the overall vehicle market. Combined BEV and PHEV sales captured about 35% of the overall vehicle market.[186] By October 2018, EV market share of total new vehicle sales in Norway was 57%.[187]

BEV market share growth and PHEV market share shrinkage can be explained in part by changes in EV incentives that reward BEV adoption over PHEVs.[188] Norway's EV incentives include support for EV purchases, EV use and circulation tax forgiveness, as well as waivers on road access. Table 5.1 summarizes.

186 Lorentzen, E., Haugneland, R., Bu, C., and Hauge, E., *Charging infrastructure experiences in Norway—the world's most advanced EV market*, Oct. 9–11, 2017, EVS30 Symposium Stuttgart, Germany.
187 Interview with staff person, City of Oslo.
188 IEA, *Nordic EV Outlook 2018*, page 17.

TABLE 5.1 Overview of Support Policies for electric vehicles in Norway, 2017[189]

EV Purchase Incentives	EV Use and Circulation Incentives	Waivers on Access Restrictions
• Registration tax/sale rebates • Registration tax (excel VAT) exemption • VAT exemption	• Circulation tax rebates	• Local registration tax/sale rebates • Local free/dedicated parking

The primary incentive options motivating Norway's EV buyers include exemption from vehicle registration taxes, VAT sales taxes for BEVs, and additional local waivers.[190] In fact, the effect of Norway's incentive programs have exceeded expectations. The EV adoption goal for 2020 (a target of 500,000 vehicles), set in 2011, was met by 2017. It prompted Norway to reset its 2020 EV adoption target to a goal of two million vehicles.[191]

The road to two million vehicles appears to be on schedule. Norway's cities and EV partners are addressing a host of related challenges, including rising congestion at charge points, charge-point queues that increase the length of time spent to "refuel" batteries, and the need for widespread, easy access to varying levels of charging.[192] Questions concerning the adequacy of EVSE infrastructure are of particular interest in cities where EV adoption impacts are the most significant. When attention turns to Oslo, the above noted concerns will be further explored.

189 Ibid., IEA, page 19. Graph is adapted from the original by the author.
190 References throughout this chapter support this assertion beginning with, IEA, 2018, Ibid.
191 Centre for public impact, *The rise of electric vehicles in Norway*, April 8, 2016, Available at: https://www.centreforpublicimpact.org/case-study/electric-cars-norway/.
192 Ibid., Centre for Public Impact.

5.2.2 Adjusting National Policy to Support Evolving EV Adoption Patterns and Infrastructure Needs

Figenbaum[193] argues that relationships between policy, markets, and technology change define distinct EV policy phases in Norway's path to be a global leader in EV adoption. Figenbaum marked four main policy phases:[194]

- **Experimentation**, 1989–1998: activities focused on creating niches and industrial development to allow experimentation to see if BEVs could be viable.
- **Stalled progress**, 1999–2002: attempts to expand market niches failed, which led to new incentives to drive adoption.
- **Sustained EV market niches**, 2003 to the end of 2009: successful niches kept the BEV option alive even though overall market expansion faltered.
- **Adoption tipping point**, 2014 to the start of 2016: BEV market advanced, transforming regional niche markets into a national market with significant growth in EV adoption.

Now, a fifth phase is in flight. This new phase seems focused on downsizing incentives while putting greater emphasis on Level 3 charging in urban areas, developing commercial fleets, and supporting home charging.

However, not all incentives are being downsized. Some are standing as they are for the near-term while others remain intact with modified terms. Specifically:

Sustained (unmodified) incentives:
- No import taxes on purchased EVs
- Exemption from 25% VAT on purchase or leasing
- No annual road taxes

Modified incentives:
- No charges on toll roads or ferries (however, in 2018, charges were introduced on ferries, with a maximum fee of 50% of full price; and in 2019, toll road fees were reinstated, also with a maximum fee of 50% of full price)
- Free municipal parking (terminated in 2017, but in 2018, parking fees of no more than 50% of full price were put in place)
- Access to bus lanes (as of 2016, local authorities can allow EVs access)
- From 2000 to 2018, company car tax reduction of 50% (in 2018, it was reduced to 40%)

---

193 Figenbaum, E., *Perspectives on Norway's supercharged electric vehicle policy*, 2017, Environmental Innovation and Societal Transition, 25, pages 14–34. Note that the chapter author, not Figenbaum, named the phases to help differentiate one phase from others.
194 Ibid., Figenbaum, page 19.

- Fiscal compensation for scrapping of fossil-fuel vans when converting to zero-emission vans (effective 2018)

Thus far, no incentives have been terminated, and many of them will continue until the end of 2021. After 2021, incentives will be revised and adjusted to reflect further market development.[195]

Norway focused its incentives policy on home charging early into the 21st Century. For example, household electricity sockets were tailored for EV needs as one of the nation's first moves. About 1,800 such sockets were dispersed throughout the country, but they had high maintenance costs, and in a few cases the first generation of sockets caused electrical fires. As international standards developed, these first-generation sockets were replaced to meet new standards. For homes, Level 1 chargers remain dominant and by June 2017 the estimated number of household sockets was about 4,400 with the number of publicly accessible Level 2 chargers reaching about 2,700.[196]

While the lion's share of public EVSE infrastructure is composed of Level 1 and Level 2 chargers, Level 3 fast-charging is deemed increasingly important. Several fast-charge operators in Norway are building out charging stations without public support, especially in Norway's larger cities and along major highways in response to EV owners preferring widespread charging access, even though home charging dominates.[197] Figure 5.1 summarizes vendor deployment patterns from 2014 to 2017.

195 Ibid., Figenbaum.
196 Lorentzen, E., Haugneland, P., Bu, C., and Hauge, E., *Charging infrastructure experiences in Norway—the world's most advanced EV Market*, Oct. 9–11, 2017, EVS30 Symposium, Stuttgart, Germany. Lorentzen is Senior Advisor to the Norwegian EV Association. The other authors work for the Norwegian EV Association as well; Hauge is the President of the Association. Lorentzen is responsible for projects and issues related to charging infrastructure. He has several years of experience working with climate and transport related issues for the Norwegian Ministry of the Environment, the public funding agency Transnova and for the Directorate of Public Roads. Note that for the remainder of Section 5.3, Lorentzen, et al., is the primary reference, as this paper is a benchmark for EV adoption progress and mapping deployment issues as of 2017.
197 Ibid., Lorentzen, E., Haugneland, P., Bu, C., and Hauge, E.

FIGURE 5.1 Pattern of Fast-Charger VENDOR Deployment in Norway[198]

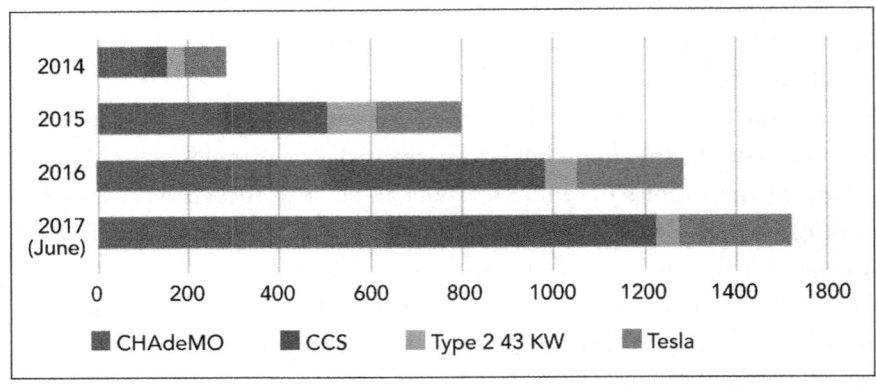

As of June 2017, the fast-charging infrastructure in Norway totaled:[199]

- 648 CHAdeMO[200] points
- 595 CCS points
- 47 AC Type 2 43 kW points
- 246 Tesla Super-chargers

Norway's road to incrementally evolving EV incentives has experienced bumps along the way. One recent pothole was a tax exemption for Tesla vehicles, which was proposed for elimination in 2018. The debate about the Tesla exemption questioned why incentives should be given to people who could afford expensive vehicles. The counter argument contended that Tesla vehicle incentives attracted buyers interested in larger passenger cars. The Jaguar I-Pace BEV SUV was used as an example.[201] Nevertheless, in October 2018, the Tesla tax exemption was terminated by the Norwegian government.

As EV adoption increased in Norway, innovations in public charging infrastructure *pricing policy* began to be more important. Currently, two national charging operators, Fortum Charge & Drive and Gronn Kontakt, have a pay-

198 Ibid., Lorentzen, E., Haugneland, P., Bu, C., and Hauge, E.

199 Ibid., Lorentzen, E., Haugneland, P., Bu, C., and Hauge, E.

200 CHAdeMO is the trade name of a quick charging method for battery electric vehicles delivering up to 62.5 kW by 500 V, 125 A direct current via a special electrical connector. A revised CHAdeMO 2.0 specification allows for up to 400 kW by 1000 V, 400 A direct current. CHAdeMO is an abbreviation of "CHArge de MOve", equivalent to "move using charge" or "move by charge" or "charge 'n' go", a reference to the fact that it is a fast charger.

201 Vanghan, A., *Norway leads way on electric cars: 'it's part of a green taxation shift'*, Dec. 25, 2017, The Guardian, Available at: https://www.theguardian.com/environment/2017/dec/25/norway-leads-way-electric-cars-green-taxation-shift.

ment model for fast charging whereby customers *pay per minute of charging*, regardless of how many kWh the car receives. Lorentzen et al. found that many users preferred *paying per kWh* rather than per minute because EV charging effects differ based on state of charge, battery temperature, and the on-board charger of different BEV models.

Contrary to this approach is the argument that payment per kWh will increase the risk of queues at charging stations, in part because users of chargers will not have a reason to move their vehicles when charging is slow. Lorentzen et al. argue that a market for different charging speeds with different pricing structures will emerge as more BEVs penetrate Norwegian markets.[202] In other words, incentives policies may shift toward a greater emphasis on pricing as EV adoption continues to take market share from ICE vehicles.

While pricing public charging may grow in significance as a top policy priority, the prevailing focus of EV infrastructure planning is focused on shifting deployment efforts to additional fast-charging EVSEs, even though it is still not a primary factor for prospective EV buyers. Lorentzen, et.al., write:

"When it comes to BEV adoption, there is often a discussion about the chicken and the egg regarding BEVs and charging infrastructure. The Norwegian experience shows that there is a substantial number of potential early users that will buy BEVs even without a comprehensive fast-charging network. In for instance neighboring Denmark, there is a quite well-developed charging infrastructure network, but the BEV sale is sluggish, and even more so after a weakening of the tax incentives when buying the car. This implies that other incentives are more important than a charging network on its own." [Further,] "A well-developed charging infrastructure is appreciated by EV users, but it is not on its own enough to convince consumers to buy BEVs. The Norwegian case shows that the tax breaks/incentives at time of purchase still are vital to the BEV development. However, it should be noted that as we are moving to a mass market adoption of BEVs, there is an obvious need for a large-scale fast-charging network as new user groups are preparing to move into the world of BEVs, and as a growing number of BEV owners don't rely on conventional cars as backup."[203]

5.2.3 National EVSE Infrastructure and Charging Patterns

Norway's success with EV adoption brings with it new challenges in planning for and managing rising market penetration of EVs.

Nordic-wide market surveys show publicly accessible fast chargers are used more frequently than slow chargers. This suggests that wider coverage of fast

---

202 Ibid., Lorentzen, E., Haugneland, P., Bu, C., and Hauge, E.
203 Ibid., Lorentzen, E., Haugneland, P., Bu, C., and Hauge, E.

chargers simplifies the choice between fast chargers and Level 1 or 2 chargers, given the time trade-off between fast and slow chargers. Some research suggests that increased battery capacity and reduced range anxieties make fast chargers a favored choice.[204]

Table 5.2 shows the allocation of charging activity of Norwegian BEV owners, with special attention on whether charging occurs in detached housing or apartment buildings. The table is based on 12,000 surveys of BEV owners and illustrates the charge pattern differences that are a function of dwelling type. This particular table provides an important perspective for countries that haven't yet experienced significant market penetration of EVs, and BEVs in particular. It shows that:

- Detached-home owners rarely "refuel" using public charge points
- Apartment dwellers charge at public charging stations and use fast charging more frequently because they have no viable "home charging" options

Table 5.2   How Often Do You Charge?[205]

	Detached Housing	Apartment Buildings
At home, daily or weekly	97%	64%
At home, monthly or never	3%	36%
At work, daily or weekly	36%	38%
At work, monthly or never	64%	62%
At public charging stations, daily or weekly	11%	28%
At public charging stations, monthly or never	89%	72%
At fast-charging stations, daily or weekly	12%	18%
At fast-charging stations, monthly or never	88%	82%

204 Neaimeh, M., Salisbury, S.D., Hill, G.A., Blythe, P.T., Scoffield, D.R. and Francfort, J.E., *Analysing the usage and evidencing the importance of fast chargers for the adoption of battery electric vehicles*, 2017, Energy Policy, 108, pages 474–486.
205 Ibid., Lorentzen, E., Haugneland, P., Bu, C., and Hauge, E., page 7. Table prepared by the authors and replicates table in the paper.

In Norway, the ratio of apartment dwellers to detached-housing dwellers is skewed significantly to the former. EV use for apartment dwellers must be easy and cost-effective (two principles Norway, in particular, has consistently applied as EV adoption has increased).

Even if EV owners charge at home and can manage without daily fast charging, Norwegian market research shows that EV owners prefer to have the option to fast charge when needed wherever they may be. Moreover, consumers are willing to pay more for fast charging—on average, three times more than they pay for home charging.[206]

A Nordic-wide survey that reflects what is happening in Norway is consistent with research findings from other areas, which also shows that publicly accessible fast chargers are used more frequently than slow chargers, when public use is required. The conclusion drawn from this research is that wider coverage of fast-chargers simplifies the choice of which charge level is best, given the time trade-off between fast and slow chargers. Some research suggests that increased battery capacity and reduced range anxiety make fast-chargers the favored choice.[207]

One barrier to effective and efficient use of public EVSE has to do with the complications EV owners face when accessing privately owned public charging infrastructure. Each public charging vendor requires a special account for EV users to access specific charge points. This leads to EV users having several accounts and charging process requirements that vary by vendor.

In addition to the account complexities noted above, several methods are used in Norway for executing transactions: RFID-tags, SMS or phone apps, and closed transaction systems such as Tesla's. BEV owners prefer RFID-tags to other platforms. Figure 5.2 summarizes.

---

206 *Norway is leading the way for a transition to zero emission in transport*, n.d., Available at: https://elbil.no/english/norwegian-ev-policy/ Note also that all Level 2 and Level 3 charging stations in Norway are owned and/ or operated by charging operator enterprises. In discussions between authors and Oslo city staff, it was noted that free electricity for EV adopters using public charging was used by some municipalities to stimulate demand. EV owners always have paid for electricity for home charging and for fast chargers located on highways, as noted above.
207 Ibid., Neaimeh, M., Salisbury, S.D., Hill, G.A., Blythe, P.T., Scoffield, D.R. and Francfort, J.E.

FIGURE 5.2 Transaction Options for Fast Charging in Norway, 2017[208]

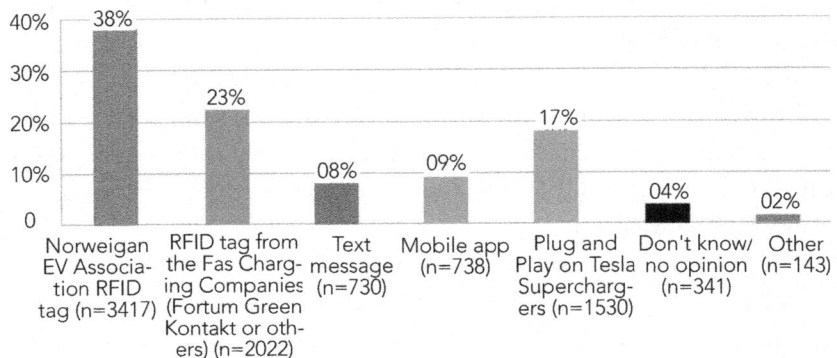

As part of Norway's EV infrastructure deployment efforts, its state-owned enterprise, ENOVA, and the Norwegian EV Association created a joint enterprise, NOBIL, which is the online database of EV charging stations throughout Norway. The EV Association manages NOBIL and works with national and local authorities to promote use of EVs. Each locality has distinct incentives (e.g., city-level incentives offering free parking), which are consistent with national options. Through these services, the aim is to take the noise out of efficient EV use, including transaction execution.

Social and cultural shifts that alter markets may influence adoption and use patterns as well. In Norway, studies indicate that the generation beginning to enter the workforce and take on public leadership roles for the first time imagines vehicle-sharing models superseding conventional EV ownership.[209] The effects of widespread vehicle sharing on pricing models and use patterns merits ongoing evaluation to keep the type and scope of incentives aligned with market dynamics. Also, it points to the need for ongoing policy evaluations, adjustments to present and future policies, and a practice of keeping an open door for innovations that can make EV adoption and use easier.

208 Ibid., Lorentzen, E., Haugneland, P., Bu, C. and Hauge, E.
209 Elliott, C., *The War Between Car Sharing and Rental Companies Just Escalated. Here's Why You Should Care.*, Oct. 18, Forbes, Available at: https://www.forbes.com/sites/christopherelliott/2018/10/13/the-war-between-car-sharing-and-rental-companies-just-escalated-heres-why-you-should-care/#6eb17baf757c; Also, Spurlock, C.A., Sears, J., Parodic, G.W., Walker, V., Jin, L., Taylor, M., Duvalld, A., Gopala, A. and Todda, A., *Describing the users: Understanding adoption of and interest in shared, electrified, and automated transportation in the San Francisco Bay Area*, Jan. 31, 2019, Transportation Research Part D—Transport and Environment; And, Ferreroc, F., Perbolibd, G., Rosanob, M. and Vescoa, A., *Car Sharing Services: An Annotated Review*, Feb. 2018, Sustainable Cities and Society, vol. 37, pages 501–518.

5.3 EVs in Oslo

Oslo is the economic and governmental center of Norway, with a population of about 650,000 and progressive policies that have made it the leader in EV adoption. The city focuses on urban development through the planning of urban areas and their related public transportation. Within this framework, the city of Oslo is:

- Building new EV public charging infrastructure for BEVs
- Doing the same for hydrogen and biofuels, which serve the needs of fuel-cell vehicles and ICE vehicles combusting clean fuels
- Designing systems to support freight, public, and private transport
- Prompting more people to use bicycles
- Favoring local energy resources for heating and electricity, including sharp emphasis on energy-efficiency measures in all sectors[210]

Indicative of its leadership within Norway, the City of Oslo deployed 400 chargers before any EVs hit the Norwegian market in 2010.[211] Until recently, the Oslo ratio of EVs to public charge points was two EVs per charge point. One measure of success is the spread of EVs to public charge points is widening. Accordingly, a new phase is unfolding in the effort to achieve a zero-emissions vehicle rolling stock. But before diving into present and emerging policy and investment issues, a brief profile of Oslo and its EV profile is presented.

5.3.1 EVs in Oslo by the Numbers (Trends, Marketing Messages, and Benefits)

In 2016, EVs accounted for 52% of new car sales, and for 2018 (as of September) the share of new car sales was about 50%. Norway closed 2018 with 7,171 new passenger plug-in EVs. While that is nearly 11% lower than in 2017, the overall market share for EVs for 2018 was 57.5%. BEV sales (5,140 units) were up 16.2% year-over-year and held a 41% share of the EV market. Five hundred seventy-four used EVs were sold and 203 EV vans (196 new and seven used) were sold. Seven fuel-cell vehicles were sold, with 2,031 PHEVs sold, down by

---

210 The above bullet points and notation on Oslo as an active C40 partner sourced from: Espegren, K., *The use of energy system models for analyzing the transition to low-carbon cities: The case of Oslo*, 2017, Energy Strategy Reviews 15, pages 44–56.

211 See Szcepanek, A., and Botsford, C., *Electric Vehicle Infrastructure Development; An Enabler for Electric Vehicle Adoption*, May 13–16, 2009, EVS24, Stavanger, Norway, for perspective on the early planning for EV adoption in Norway.

nearly 44% year-over-year.[212] Overall, EVs accounted for 49% of the total new vehicle registrations in Norway (i.e., 72,638, up 17% from 2027[213]). For the first time in history, ICE vehicles comprise less than 50% of new vehicle sales in one location of the world.

In 2017, the EVs more often purchased in Norway included the Volkswagen Golf, BMWi3, Toyota RAV4, and Tesla Model X.[214] According to city staff, the Norwegian government, and published literature, three factors encourage EV adoption:

- **Cheap to buy.** The national government made EVs cheap to buy.
- **Cheap to use.** EVs became cheap to use thanks to perks such as free parking, free entrance to toll roads, and free ferry and tunnel access.
- **Easy charging access.** EVs were given easy access to charging infrastructure through concerted public investment and the facilitation of private charging vendor deployments.

Oslo's success has led to significant reductions in CO_2 emissions from the total vehicle rolling stock within the city. The city's aim is to reduce CO_2 emissions by 36% from 1990 levels by 2020, and to be a zero-carbon-emission city by 2030.[215] It should be noted that Norway's goal is to achieve sales of only zero-emission vehicles by 2025. Oslo's ambition to achieve significant reductions in CO_2 is a broader goal requiring deeper decarbonization across other economic sectors in addition to meeting national goals for electrifying mobility.

Recent research on EV adoption, as noted, has focused on a simple metric to guide public infrastructure planning: the ratio of charge points to EVs on the road. Of course, this is by no means the only metric or analytic focus used for EV infrastructure planning purposes by cities worldwide.

As noted above, Oslo's early strategy for spurring EV adoption began with deployment of public charge points before the first EVs hit the streets, in 2010.

---

212 The author suggests that one reason for a drop in new car sales may be the uptick in used EV sales. A forthcoming area of research might be analysis of how increasing volumes of used EVs affect not only new vehicle sales, but also uses of public charging infrastructure. Subjects might include effects of older vehicles on charge times, frequency of charging needs, compatibility with fast charging, whether older vehicles require retention of "legacy Level 1" public charging, dealer service impacts, and life-of-vehicle effects of new EV buyer decision-making.

213 Kane, M., *Almost 50% of passenger cars Sold in Norway in 2018 Plugged In*, Jan. 2, 2019, InsideEVs, Available at: https://insideevs.com/half-passenger-cars-norway-2018-evs/.

214 Knudsen, C., and Doyle, A., *Norway powers ahead (electrically): over half new car sales now electric or hybrid*, Jan. 3, 2018, REUTERS, Available at: https://www.reuters.com/article/us-environment-norway-autos/norway-powers-ahead-over-half-new-car-sales-now-electric-or-hybrid-idUSKBN1ES0WC.

215 City of Oslo, Municipality of Oslo, Climate Budget 2018, Preliminaries, Climate Budget, Technical Report.

The thinking was that visibly accessible chargers would reduce range anxiety, which was considered a key adoption barrier for consumers.

Oslo's EV adoption, once it reached a tipping point, has quickly accelerated, as Figures 5.3, 5.4, and 5.5 on the next two pages illustrate. In this chapter, Norway's EV adoption patterns are used as a proxy for Oslo, since Oslo is the largest city in Norway.

- Figure 5.3 shows the Norwegian Public Roads Administration data on EV adoption patterns with significant growth accelerating from 2014 to 2018, with BEVs taking the lion's share of EV growth from 2015 through 2018, but with PHEVs continuing to have a meaningful share of aggregated EV market growth.
- Figure 5.4 shows aggregated EV sales growth from 2010 to 2018, bringing into greater contrast the acceleration of EV adoption from 2014 to 2018.
- Figure 5.5 shows a more granular picture of EV adoption from 2016 to 2018 by plotting month-to-month EV sales. Also, Figure 5.5 shows that 2017 and 2018 exhibited steady growth despite midyear slumps in sales.

FIGURE 5.3 EV Fleet in Norway 2010–2018[216]

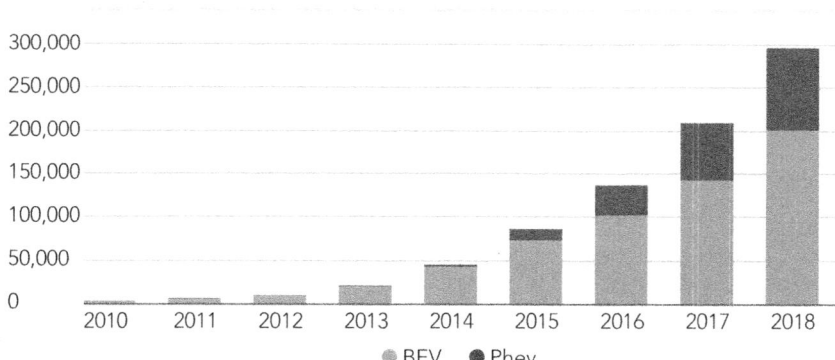

Number of registered electric passenger vehicles and light commercial vehicles in Norway from 2010.

---

216 The Norweigan Public Roads Administration, updated December 31, 2018, Available at: https://elbil.no/english/norwegian-ev-market/.

FIGURE 5.4 Annual EV Sales in Norway 2010–2018[217]

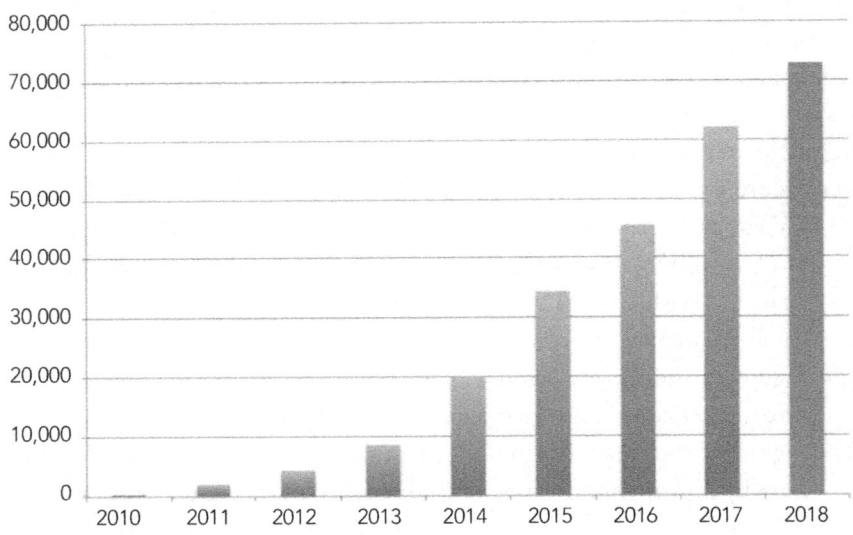

FIGURE 5.5 Monthly EV Sales in Norway 2016–2018[218]

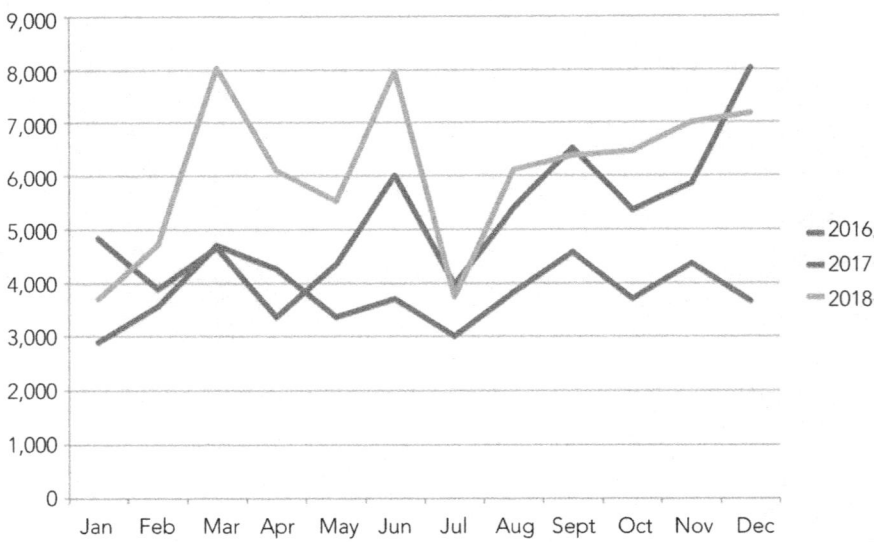

217 Available at: https://wattev2buy.com/global-ev-sales/norway-ev-sales/.
218 Available at: https://wattev2buy.com/global-ev-sales/norway-ev-sales/.

Even with Norway's and Oslo's increased emphasis on home charging, the EV sales growth trajectories of the last few years indicate a need for additional public charging infrastructure. The city is focused on realigning public infrastructure with accelerating EV adoption by adding 400 new semi-fast (Type 2)[219] chargers and six fast chargers (Type 3). Also, Oslo intends to subsidize up to 8,000 charge points in multifamily dwellings. Even so, a prevailing concern is that the city may be approaching a circumstance that involves running out of places to deploy chargers.[220]

In Oslo, city streets are narrow, as are sidewalks in many areas, which can thwart charging infrastructure deployment. On-street charging is considered important to meeting public EV infrastructure needs because so many multi-family dwellings do not have off-street parking. For EV owners living in such dwellings, charging at workplaces or elsewhere is definitely necessary.

Oslo's current concerns about public charging infrastructure include charging capabilities for electric buses as the city attempts to quickly replace its ICE and hybrid bus fleets with all electric buses. The goal is having 60% of the bus fleet composed of EVs by 2025. Electric freight vehicles also are on the checklist of charging infrastructure support requirements, and electric taxi charging is in the works, with pilot programs already operating.[221] Oslo recently announced that the city's taxi fleet will be zero-emission only by 2023, using wireless BEV charging.[222]

The city seems to understand its power and importance in driving EV adoption through its role in EV infrastructure deployment. After all, the city literally owns its roads. One innovative possible solution mentioned to the

---

219 Note that the Norwegian term "type" for designating charger voltage is synonymous with the US term "level."

220 The answer is not self-evident, because it depends on a series of factors from types of chargers deployed to pricing of charging services. One study of fast-charger infrastructure needs developed a model for prioritizing charger infrastructure based on EVs to charger point ratios derived from a mix of variables, which could be applied along with indexing tools presented in Chapter 7. Of course, this is not the only such methodology. The point is that clear policy is needed for each city to guide its approach to meeting public infrastructure charging needs by location and type. The article referenced here is: Gnann, T., Funke, S., Jakobsson, N., Plotz, P., Sprei, F. and Bennehag, A., *Fast-charging infrastructure for electric vehicles: Today's situation and future needs*, 2018, Transportation Research Part D, 62, pages 314–329.

221 Berg, L., *How did Oslo become the electric vehicle capital of the world?*, March 7, 2018, Available at: http://news.trust.org/item/20180307114110-a0cqx. Note that the author's interview with City of Oslo staff corroborates published statements.

222 Frangoul, A., *Electric taxis in Oslo to be charged using wireless technology*, March 22, 2019, CNBC, Available at: https://www.cnbc.com/2019/03/22/electric-taxis-in-oslo-to-be-charged-using-wireless-technology.html.

author for addressing the challenges of crowded streets and narrow sidewalks is to adopt wireless EV (induction) charging, placing induction plates in roads, and/or curbside. Existing EVs can be adapted to enable induction charging, and new "induction ready" vehicles are coming to Oslo in the foreseeable future.[223] Oslo's move to use wireless charging on the city's taxi fleet also points to an interest in wireless charging solutions as possible best fits given city road, sidewalk, and parking characteristics.

In keeping up with demand, it is important to understand demand patterns and their geographic impact as much as, if not more than, consumer characteristics. For example, Mersky, et al., found that EV owners charge their vehicles most frequently at home or at their workplaces, but use of fast chargers is rising, while the use of Level 1 public chargers is dropping.[224] Also, recent Norwegian research on BEV adoption and charging infrastructure found that chargers within or adjacent to major cities had more influence over demand than do incomes of BEV buyers. Also, short-range vehicles showed more correlation to income and unemployment than sales of longer-range vehicles (which cost more).[225]

Barriers related to range anxiety and charging access appear to be declining in Norway. Only four percent of EV owners have experienced an empty battery and less than 25% have experienced a "close call." Nevertheless, declining concerns over range anxiety have not led to declining concerns over how long it takes to recharge an EV.[226]

Discussion with Oslo city staff acknowledged an ongoing shift in consumption whereby "top-off" tactics are being used to ease range anxiety as well as

---

223 For a timely review and analysis of the path forward on EV charging infrastructure adoption of wireless charging, see Philip Machura and Quan Li, *A critical review on wireless charging for electric vehicles*, 2019, Renewable and Sustainable Energy Reviews, 104, pages 209–214. Note also, auto manufacturers have been working on this solution for at least 10 years. Stewart, B., *2014 Infiniti EV to Debut Wireless Inductive Charging System*, Nov. 29, 2011, Available at: https://www.popularmechanics.com/cars/hybrid-electric/ a7331/2014-infiniti-ev-to-debut-wireless-inductive-charging-system/; Wernel, B., *Wireless Charging Unleashed: Cord cutting will be key to EV adoption and autonomous cars*, Oct. 3, 2016, Automotive News, October 3, 2016, Available at: https://www. autonews.com/ article/20161003/OEM06/310039948/wireless-charging-unleashed.
224 Mersky, A.C., Sprei, F., Samaras, C., and Qian, Z., *Effectiveness of incentives on electric vehicle adoption in Norway*, 2016, Transportation Research, Part D, 46, pages 56–68. Ibid., Mersky, A.C., Sprei, F., Samaras, C., and Qian, Z.
225 Ibid., Mersky, A.C., Sprei, F., Samaras, C., and Qian, Z.
226 Figenbaum, E., Kolbenstvedt, M. and Elvebakk, B., Electric vehicles—environmental, economic and practical aspects. *As seen by current and potential users, Institute for Transportation Economics*, Norwegian Center for Transportation Research, 2014.

reduce the time required to charge a vehicle (sometimes referred to as "charging anxiety"). More public infrastructure may be needed if the trend continues. Also, it is important because nearly 20% of EV owners refuse to drive into locations with limited or no public charging infrastructure access. Finally, a perceived lack of charging infrastructure at home, work, or while driving is the single largest reason consumers continue to shy away from EV purchases in Oslo and Norway overall. In other words, keeping public infrastructure deployment on pace with EV adoption spurs continued adoption of EVs with attendant shrinkage in ICE vehicle market share.[227]

A typical barrier in Oslo, as with many cities worldwide, to EV adoption is whether building owners have discretion to install EV charge points, or whether they are required by cities to do so. On the one hand, throughout Norway, installation of charge points in existing buildings can occur without the consent of housing-unit boards. On the other hand, no national building regulations require charging infrastructure. However, adoption rates of EVs have pressured building owners, especially apartment building owners, to provide charge points for all parking spaces.

In 2014, a manual for housing associations on how to establish a charging station for residents was issued jointly by the City of Oslo, OBOS (the large cooperative building association), and Transnova, a solutions provider for transportation management systems. Since 2017, OBOS has been working on EV charging systems for apartment buildings. Finally, in 2017 Oslo mandated that at least 50% of new buildings' parking spaces must be equipped with EV chargers.[228]

Lorentzen et al. note that new shared apartment buildings need to be "charging ready" (i.e., the building should provide basic infrastructure for every owner of an EV). Also, owner-installed equipment should be mandatory to allow individual owners to install charging stations of their own on demand.[229]

Finally, car owners using on-street parking daily, without access to charging at work, will remain a challenge for Oslo and other Norwegian cities for the foreseeable future. The solutions may not be found in conventional EV charging models. Instead, new smart charging solutions, autonomous vehicles,

---

227 Ibid., Figenbaum, E., Kolbenstvedt, M. and Elvebakk, B.
228 This paragraph summarizes Q&A with Oslo city staff, which thusly characterized the challenges of deploying chargers in buildings. For a current state assessment of challenges in multifamily dwellings with EV charging, see Behar, D.L., Tran, M., Froese, T., Mayaud, J.R., Herrera, O.E., and Merida, W., *Charging infrastructure for electric vehicles in Multi-Unit Residential Buildings: Mapping feedbacks and policy*," March 2019, Energy Policy, 126.
229 Ibid., Lorentzen, E., Haugneland, R., Bu, C., and Hauge, E.

car sharing, and other innovations may crack the code for designing workable charging solutions for on-street EV charging needs.[230]

5.4 Lessons Learned

The city of Oslo, as the leading city for EV adoption, has frontline experience that may be helpful to other cities.

- **Anticipate EV owner needs.** While aggressively driving EV adoption through incentives and leadership from public officials, anticipating the needs of EV owners as EV buying accelerates will help mitigate the need to catch up as surging demand overtakes early-stage public infrastructure deployment.
- **Plan for more public infrastructure.** More public infrastructure than originally planned may be needed, depending on the way that EV owners use their vehicles (e.g., high frequency short trip uses versus lower frequency highway trips, or short trips orbiting a residential location where home charging always is available).
- **Home charging should be a priority.** But, greater attention should be put on multifamily and large apartment dwellings, especially if on-street parking may be needed, because many older buildings do not have sufficient parking spaces for all tenants.
- **Plan for more fast chargers.** Increasing volumes and concentrations of EVs may require more Level 3 chargers to minimize wait time and congestion around chargers or charging stations.

Ruoff concludes that four actionable Norwegian priorities can be learned from early deployment of EV charging infrastructure.[231]

- **Multi-sourced guidance.** Develop great user guides and 24/7 hotlines to support EV owners and users.
- **Mitigate queuing anxiety.** The fear of having to wait in line to use a public charging station leads to EV-user adaptive tactics (e.g., regular users avoid sites with just one charge point, which suggests a policy that cities can adopt, i.e., a multi-charge point requirement at every charging location, to the extent possible).
- **High-quality charging hardware is critical.** Low quality raises costs because it requires more maintenance. Upfront costs may be higher, but

230 Ibid., Lorentzen, E., Haugneland, R., Bu, C., and Hauge, E.
231 Ruoff, C., *6 EV infrastructure lessons we can learn from Norway*, March 14, 2016, Charged, electric vehicles magazine.

long-run O&M costs will be lower while charging assets will have longer life cycles.

- **Keep good fault logs**. It helps when root cause analysis is required to define and dissect a problem.

If home charging remains the dominant platform, staying up to date on the differences within the public charging category is important as EV markets evolve. For instance:

- **Highway configurations.** Fast DC charging on highways may constitute a different form of fueling supply-chain symbiosis with electricity service. For example, more chargers clustered within reach of each other based on average miles per charge, or other design metrics that help ensure optimal highway spacing.
- **Older building configurations.** Electricity service changes may be required for concentrations of older buildings in downtown areas of cities with limited parking availability. This may drive the investment focus to (a) induction charging for on-street and public parking facilities, and/or (b) induction charging built into downtown streets, which may serve to reduce the need for some public charging.

Finally, the pricing of charging services and payment systems used for them can significantly influence EV adoption and use patterns, as previously noted. For instance, Norwegian EV users are willing to pay higher kWh prices for the convenience of fast charging. Norwegians are willing to do so because most drivers in the country charge their EVs at home.

Payment systems for charging stations in Norway have been improving with the introduction of a universal charging tag by the Norwegian EV Association. Rapid adoption of app-based solutions has increased the accuracy and reliability of payment systems as well.[232]

---

232 Ibid., Lorentzen, E., Haugneland, R., Bu, C., and Hauge, E.

CHAPTER 6

Brookline, Massachusetts:
A Small Town Seeking to Lead in a
Broader EV Charging Network

Jennifer Hatch and John Helveston, PhD

6.1 Background and Overview

Brookline is a small township within the Boston Metropolitan Statistical Area (MSA). In 2016, Brookline was one of the top five towns and cities for total electric vehicle registrations in Massachusetts, behind only its neighbors Boston, Newton, Cambridge, and Lexington. The town is much smaller than those in this volume's other case studies, each of which has large populations and large total numbers of electric vehicles. But examining Brookline provides an opportunity to dive more deeply into processes, opportunities, and challenges for EV adoption in moderately sized cities.

Despite the town's campaign to prioritize electric vehicles, it still struggles to put its vehicle charging policies into motion. Brookline's privileged position within one of the most EV-forward states and municipal areas in the country illustrates the challenges to EV infrastructure adoption in the United States. At the same time, the successes of Brookline's adoption efforts provide some insight into the benefits of a regional EV infrastructure ecosystem and the creative ways in which a smaller town can build momentum around EV infrastructure and adoption.

6.2 State and Regional Enabling Environment

The policy and infrastructure of Brookline cannot be considered in a vacuum; the town both benefits from and is hindered by regional and state infrastructure, incentives, and policies. On that front, examining Brookline provides insight into the broader mechanisms of the region—especially for less-resourced, smaller towns as opposed to major hubs such as Boston.

In Massachusetts, the number of EVs grew from under 100 in 2011 to 5,610 in January 2016, with a high percentage (39%) of battery electric vehicles (2,193), or BEVs. There is a somewhat higher EV registration per capita in smaller communities, with most EVs in communities with 5,000 to 50,000 people. Also, consistent with researchers' findings worldwide, the correlation between where EVs are registered and where they publicly charge is meaningful.

The number of public EV charging stations (Level 2 electric vehicle supply equipment and direct current fast chargers) in Massachusetts grew from 33 in 2011 to 596 by July 2016 at a variety of charging venues, including retail, parking (short term and long term), workplaces, dealerships, hotels, schools, recreational facilities, and medical facilities. The vast majority of the charging venues contain Level 2 electric vehicle supply equipment (EVSE) solely or combined with Level 1 EVSE or direct-current fast chargers (Level 3). Well over half of the charging locations in Massachusetts offer free charging. For those that require payment, different pricing models are employed: hourly; by energy transferred based on kWh drawn from the EVSE; adjustable hourly and monthly; and flat fee.

Neighboring towns. The neighboring city of Boston is meeting challenges similar to those faced by Brookline and examined below. For example, the statewide zoning challenges discussed below require creative solutions particular to each town and city in the state. The city has required that five percent (5%) of parking be equipped with EVSE equipment and that new or substantially renovated parking areas and an additional 10% of spaces must be EV-ready.[233] This rule is enforced not by statewide zoning laws but by the City of Boston's Transportation Access Plan and the Environment Department.

Incentives. In 2012, Massachusetts committed to a goal of putting 300,000 EVs on the road by 2025. Since that time, several pieces of climate change legislation and EV incentives have been put into place.

In late 2017, the Massachusetts Department of Public Utilities (DPU) laid the foundation for greater EV growth by approving a $45 million charging station program put forth by Eversource—a utility serving 1.4 million electric customers in the state. The program is the largest of its kind approved outside of California, and it sparks the Commonwealth's zero-emissions vehicle (ZEV) initiative and climate commitments by deploying charging stations necessary to support EV adoption. This program is expected to deploy over 400 EV chargers across the state.[234]

---

233 *EV-Boston: Electric Vehicle Resources*, Available at: https://www.boston.gov/departments/environment/ev-boston-electric-vehicle-resources.
234 Kinney, J., *Eversource begins rollout of 400 electric car chargers across Massachusetts; 'range anxiety' seen as enemy to emissions progress*, Aug. 29, 2018, Available at: https://www.masslive.com/business-news/index.ssf/2018/08/eversource_rolls_out_electric_car_charge.html.

In addition to the significant expansion of EVSE installations, since June 2014 Massachusetts has spent over $24 million on a vehicle incentive and rebate program called MOR-EV, which, to date, has prompted the purchase of over 11,000 electric vehicles. The program started as a $2,500 rebate for the purchase of electric vehicles and has since been extended into 2019 as a rebate of $1,500.

6.3   Brookline: A Small Boston Suburb

6.3.1 Overview

Compared to neighboring Boston, Brookline, Massachusetts, is a small town with limited resources for initiating a comprehensive EV charging plan. It has roughly 60,000 residents, one-tenth Boston's number. Brookline's population is generally wealthier than that of Boston, with median incomes and property values 50%–60% greater than those in Boston. Car ownership is slightly higher than it is in Boston, with roughly 80% of Brookline households owning one or more cars, while the same figure is 76% in Boston. Table 6.1 compares Brookline's demographics to Boston's and the state of Massachusetts.

TABLE 6.1   Comparative Profile of Brookline and Boston[235]

Category	Brookline	Boston	MA
Population	59,180	672,840	6,810,000
Median household income	$102,175	$63,621	$75,294
Median property value	$758,400	$495,400	$366,900
Average car ownership	1 car per household	1 car per household	2 car per household
Commute-drive alone	35.5%	39.4%	70.1%
Commute: public transit or walking	48%	46%	10%
Average commute time (minutes)	27.2	29	28.1
Own one or more vehicles	80.3%	77.0%	94.1%
Homeownership rate	49.2%	34.1%	62.1%
Poverty rate	12.4%	21.0%	10.4%
Median age	34	32	40
White population	71.6%	45.4%	72.4%

235 Available at: Sourdatausa.io 2016.

Analysis of Massachusetts' MOR-EV incentive program indicates the most likely customers for the EV incentives program: From 2013 to 2017, households with incomes between $100,000 and $199,000 comprised 43% of the MOR-EV program; furthermore, 82% of MOR-EV recipients were white. Given Brookline's high median income, it is no surprise that Brookline has among the highest absolute EV adoption numbers in Massachusetts.

Other indicators that Brookline is a promising target for EV adoption include its regionally high vehicle ownership and home ownership rates, as well as its low poverty rate. The town is characterized by well-educated citizens with relatively high incomes, two factors associated with higher EV adoption.

6.3.2 Brookline Governance and Organization

Brookline is distinct from neighboring Boston and other cities not only in its demographics, but also in its governance structure. The Township of Brookline has a well-organized local government covering typical city services. It is governed by an elected representative Town Meeting, which is the legislative body of the town, and a five-person Select Board serving as the executive branch of the township.

FIGURE 6.1 Organization of Brookline Township Governance[236]

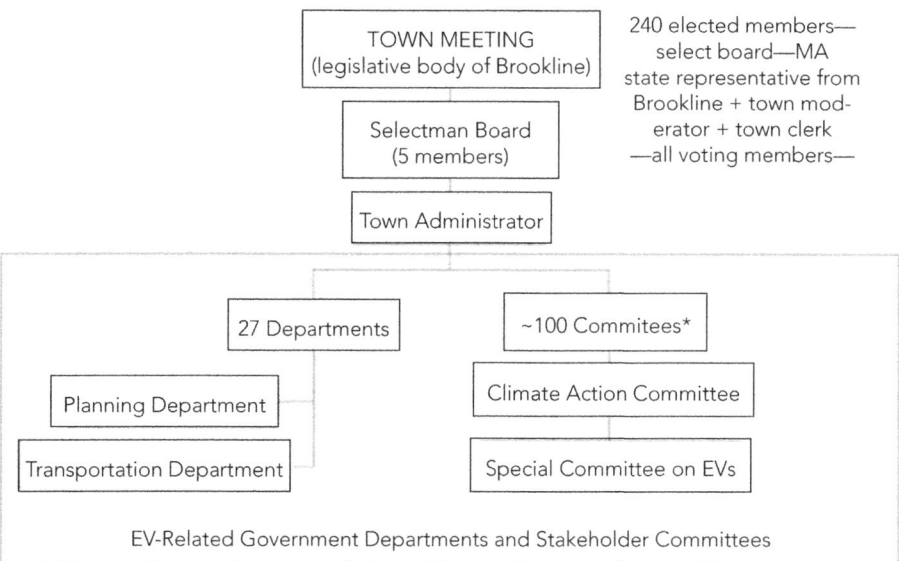

* Committees are composed of staff from the Township, elected members, and stakeholders/citizens.

236 Diagram source: Editors.

Compared to other cases in this work, Brookline's governance structure is relatively straightforward. Given the smaller population of the town and the lack of an elected executive, implementing climate action appears to be more bottom-up than the process in larger and more complex governing institutions and regions.

Bottom-up processes can have positive and negative implications for the buildout of EV infrastructure. On the one hand, it provides opportunity for citizen committees and nonprofit organizations to engage more closely and frequently with town-level government. On the other, smaller governments may have fewer resources and be less likely to attract the attention of major EV and EVSE incentive initiatives offered by state, federal, nongovernmental organizations (NGOs), philanthropies, or possibly private charging infrastructure providers, meaning that such a town must exert more effort to establish EVSE related programs.

6.3.3 Brookline Current EV Demographics

Brookline's EV population. In the town of Brookline, 263 vehicles participated in the state EV incentive program as of October 2017. This is likely a low measure since it reflects 2017 data. A more contemporary estimate for the Brookline population of EVs is about 485 vehicles as of the beginning of 2019.[237] While other cities in the Boston suburbs claim among the highest EV adoption rates in Massachusetts based on their 2016 per capita vehicle adoption, Brookline had the state's fifth-highest absolute EV population, further solidifying the township as a leader in EV adoption.

The public charging mix in Brookline is principally Level 2. Since visibility into Level 1 at-home charging is unavailable, the true ratio of chargers to vehicles is unclear. However, an estimation of 24 chargers for 430 electric vehicles is likely to be low for available charging within the township's borders.

Surrounding accessible charging. Brookline township's EV adoption rate benefits from its residents' ability to take advantage of the surrounding charging infrastructure and the state incentives available to its residents. If nearby Boston-based chargers are included, access to charging stations increases. In Figure 6.2, note that in Brookline, nodes at "G," "H," "E," and "J" are within about one mile of Brookline township boundaries.

---

237 This estimate is based on extrapolation from October 2017 data using an estimated in-state Massachusetts growth rate in EV adoption of about 87% year on year. See https://evadoption.com/ev-market-share/ev-market-share-state/. Also, authors have discussed present Brookline EV numbers with CSE staff in November 2017, which corroborates data used from the website included in this footnote.

Further, an estimated 506 EV charging stations are within a 30-mile radius of Brookline. This radius informs less about chargers enabling direct at-home (or nearby) charging and more about the ability of EV drivers to use their vehicles for regional trips. For instance, even for BEVs with 200- to 300-mile charge capacity, a multi-mile trip to recharge would be taken only if the vehicle's power supply was very low. However, the broader radius of charging stations may help to address range anxiety, one of the primary barriers to electric vehicle adoption cited in EV literature. The top towns for per capita EV adoption are also all located within Boston's suburbs—not only adding to the supportive infrastructure environment, but also to a reinforcing social environment.

FIGURE 6.2 Charging Locations in Brookline[238]

Babook Street Parking Lot
Brookline, MA
Level 2: 2 outlets
J1772 connections

41 Fuller St.
Brookline, MA
Level 2: 2 outlets
J1772 connections

1181 C entre St.
Brookline, MA
Level 2: 2 outlets
J1772 connections

1498 Pierce St.
Brookline, MA
Level 2: 2 outlets
J1772 connections
TOWN HALL LOT

2399 Webster Pl
Brookline, MA
Level 2: 2 outlets
J1772 connections
Lot at Kent/Webster

1 Brookline Place
Brookline, MA
Level 2: 14 outlets
J1772 connections

238 This is a map of the areas where EVSE charging stations operate. The map is intentionally blurred to enable more focus on the location of charging stations. Key landmarks are labeled for ease of geographic reference The text above Figure 6.2 notes that nodes G, H, E, and J are placed at the edge of Brookline's geographic boundaries.

6.3.4 Brookline's EV Initiatives

Deploying EV infrastructure in Brookline is a multilayered process. Once a charging station is approved for installation, procurement cannot go forward until its specifications are mapped and included in procurement processes to select contractors. New "greenfield" charge points require different actions than upgrading or expanding existing charge points. Furthermore, township maintenance obligations must be specified and funding for ongoing maintenance must be confirmed before proceeding. When private enterprises are engaged in EV charging infrastructure, clarity regarding which entity is responsible for what maintenance obligations must be affirmed before proceeding with construction. Once these specifications are made, contractors and the EVSE must be procured, then installation can proceed following timelines specified in contracts. Figure 6.3 depicts the decision and execution that staff from the township must navigate to install EV public charging infrastructure.

FIGURE 6.3 EV Deployment Pathways in the Township of Brookline[239]

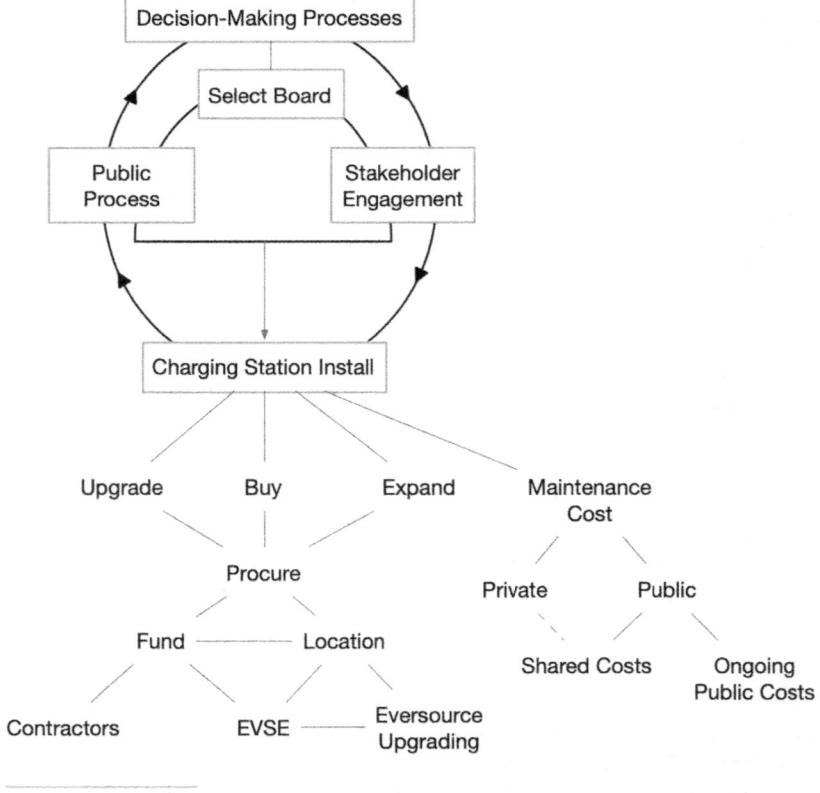

239 Developed by editors.

In the Brookline EV subcommittee's exploration into opportunities and barriers to deployment, two categories of barriers came to light: legal and regulatory barriers, and financial barriers.

6.3.5 Legal and Regulatory Barriers

Aligning public and private interests is a challenge. Brookline is a town with narrow streets and a diverse mix of buildings. As noted earlier, many multifamily dwellings do not have parking spaces for tenants. Moreover, the township has had an overnight parking ban for several years, leaving car owners to park their cars in parking lots, where they pay daily or monthly fees. Some buildings have parking garages, and there are some standalone garages for private vehicles. Surface lots with leased parking spaces are ample. The challenge is for parking lot owners to reconcile the cost of EV charge point deployment with attendant revenue to cover such costs and provide a meaningful increase in parking profits.

State regulations as barriers to expanded EV infrastructure deployment. According to some town officials, many towns want to do more with EV infrastructure, but their hands are tied by state regulations. In particular, state building codes do not enable nor require EV infrastructure to be part of new building construction. This makes deploying chargers in new buildings without infringing on building code rules very difficult. The town has no authority to order private landholders to install EV charge points, leaving the town limited to inserting EVSE suggestions in developer guidelines for new developments.

Moreover, changing building codes at the state level takes time and is itself very difficult, since such changes require legislative, not administrative, action. The principal blockers to building code changes have to do with single-family homes. To require new home construction to be EV-ready increases building costs.

This also means that there can be no sweeping requirement for the installation of EVSE—the town must work with every single new development to ensure new charging infrastructure is installed. If state building codes were updated, the township could require EV charging infrastructure installations. In the absence of such changes, Brookline staff faces the complex and daunting challenge of coordinating with all affected parties to gain approvals to add charge points.

At the multifamily dwelling level, this workaround is challenging but not impossible. Brookline staff and the Select Board recommended a change to Brookline's Transportation Access Plan (TAP) so that any major projects trigger a requirement to review transportation activity around the building location. Where possible, the township can require some chargers when housing projects are big enough. But it is not possible to place a blanket requirement for single-family home charging infrastructure. Instead, home charging infrastructure must be required case-by-case, making single-family homes particularly complicated. One staffer said, "It's just impossible."

The Devil can be in the Details. Even if the EVSE have standard components, installation projects are not trivial, and execution is even slower with less standardization. But equipment problems are often the less substantial hurdles on EVSE projects. For instance, in one project, the township installed five ChargePoint chargers in multiple public spaces. Staff worked with an install vendor from a DOE-approved contractor list, and all chargers were Level 2. At two locations, electrical cabinets had to be upgraded, which required a separate grant. Brookline competed with over 200 other communities and won a "green communities" grant from the state. Thereafter, a contractor had to be hired to deal with the cabinet upgrading issues and a DOE contractor had to be hired to build the charge points. Afterward, ChargePoint did an inspection, the DOE did an inspection, and finally the five chargers were deployed. The entire process took one year, even though the equipment itself was relatively standard.

6.3.6 Financial Barriers

Funding processes are important because the township does not have funds in its budget to expand EV public charging infrastructure. Even if a private-sector entity, such as a charging station provider, invests in the infrastructure, there are public sector costs that cannot be avoided. For example, ongoing maintenance of public area spaces surrounding a privately-owned charging station accessible to the public represents an added cost to township operations. Without state help with expedited requests and approval processes, Brookline's ability (or any town or city in Massachusetts) to expand EV infrastructure beyond incremental additions as resources permit is limited at best.

Funding issues complicate deployment in terms of funding sources, access, bidding processes, and dispersal. Funding is complicated in several ways:

- Identifying and selecting appropriate funding sources
- Competing in a bidding process
- Accepting funds and dispersing them according to schedule requirements of grants
- Accounting for funds dispersed and ensuring work products meet inspection standards

Typically, publicly funded building projects for roads and highways get federal and state money for capital costs and local entities pay for ongoing operation and maintenance. Often, these "unfunded liabilities" lead to requirements that fall outside of reasonable budgeting for towns and cities. Consequently, either decisions are made to not undertake projects, or built facilities are neglected due to funding limitations. In one deployment case, the Township of Brookline had to buy long-term maintenance plans associated with the charging station build because the administrative staff lacked the know-how and capacity to handle maintenance. Staff said that past experiences had exposed an important problem. If a charger failed and nobody knew how to fix it, and no money was available to pay for its repair, the asset was stranded—not used and not useful. To prevent that from happening in the future, long-term maintenance plans are a workable, albeit costly, solution.

Apart from stitching together funding sources for EV charging infrastructure, the larger challenge is how decision-makers allocate funds within city budgets. Arguably, schools take precedence over building infrastructure for still-emerging vehicle-market transitions. For example, Brookline is designing two new schools with the goal that they are both net zero carbon emissions schools. This is a significant step for a small township when the planned costs are about $200 million.

EV charging point revenue. Private enterprises providing public charging services are currently recovering costs only by charging for the parking spaces they provide. Eventually, consumers will be expected to pay for electricity services for their EVs. As the situation unfolds, the township will have the option of capturing revenue through some form of tax, or through a sharing agreement with vendors.

Building retrofits as special challenges. Retrofits can take several forms: remodeling, which does not affect the building footprint; renovations and modernizations, which can include reworking parking garages and amenities—such as surface parking lots—surrounding a building; and, finally, retrofitting multiple buildings on one or more streets. Brookline, like many cities, has experienced significant renewal and transformation, with new construction and renovation of existing structures occurring simultaneously.

Brookline township staff have tried to connect owners with the local utility (Eversource) to engage the utility in building EV infrastructure as part of the electric system upgrades retrofitting and renovation often require. Often, funding is available to support EV infrastructure construction through grants. The barrier to accessing such funds lies in having to work with all affected landowners to garner their commitment to install EV charge points, should grants be obtained.

Even if multiple landowners agree to support EV charge point installations, timing of deployment hinges on landowner schedules for renovations. Often the timing of grants being awarded and landowner schedules for construction are misaligned, so no action is taken because landowners, for many reasons, are reluctant to—or simply cannot—alter schedules to fit grant award timelines.

Challenges in scaling EV public charging infrastructure. One proposal under consideration by the township is to place 25 chargers along Beacon Street, one of the main streets in Brookline. Such a project would cost about $500,000, including equipment, electric system upgrading, and ongoing maintenance. One option for realizing this project would be to contract with Electrify America, which would own and operate the chargers, leasing public land from the township.

EV advisory and management functions. Brookline has taken significant steps toward climate emissions reductions and has had discussions specifically about mitigating transportation emissions since climate-change action started in the town. Two functional departments and one main advisory committee have oversight and actionable authority regarding EVs. The Planning Department is responsible for incorporating climate-related activities into town plans and the Transportation Department is responsible for all EV implementation matters.

Climate-action committee and EV subcommittee. Starting in 2000, the Board of Selectmen voted unanimously to join the "Cities for Climate Protection" program of the International Council for Local Environmental Initiatives (ICLEI). That May, the Board organized a public forum on climate change. Shortly thereafter, the first official meeting of Climate Action Brookline, a citizen's group dedicated to emissions reductions in Brookline, took place.

Two years later, the town created a dedicated selectmen's Climate Action Committee. The advisory group's purview is all climate-action-related projects in the township. In its inaugural year, the committee issued its first climate action plan, which was updated in 2012. The updated plan mentions EVs several times and addresses significant behavior and mode-shift efforts toward incentivizing bicycles and regulating taxi fleets and other non-car alternatives.

In 2016, a citizen filed a citizens' petition warrant article to request that the town require Level 1 and Level 2 charging stations. In response, an EV subcommittee was formed to examine the feasibility of such a requirement, and to explore further barriers and opportunities for EV infrastructure and incentives.

The EV subcommittee is composed of elected officials and township staff, with three independent members. One independent member is the original warrant articles petitioner, who was motivated by an interest in installing private charging services on township lands and proposed several policy changes to enable it.

The EV subcommittee worked to prepare a comprehensive study of issues related to EV deployment, including recommendations for policy and zoning changes. Mapping deployment pathways for electric vehicles in Brookline was the first consideration.

The subcommittee report. The report included guidelines for encouraging EVSE installation, pursuit of funding sources, recommendations for building and permit planning processes, and various emphases on specific projects throughout the township. A full list of the recommendations can be seen in appendix 1.

The transportation plan. The Township of Brookline's transportation plan included providing 50 charging station ports in the public way to support an additional 300 EVs on the road. In part due to the recommendations of the subcommittee, the town has updated its transportation access plan (as of January 2018) to request that major-impact projects have charging equipment installed for at least 2% of parking spaces and that another 15% of spaces be EVSE ready.

Multifamily dwellings are not the only buildings that come under the new TAP rules. New parking garages, such as at the Brookline Village T-stop, can be required to install EV chargers. In the Brookline Village T-stop case, six new chargers were required for the project to be approved.

6.4 Current EVSE Plans

After submitting their recommendations for further work on EV charging infrastructure, the subcommittee effectively disbanded. Efforts to expand EV infrastructure are now in the hands of the township staff and Climate Action Committee. Both groups have a longer-term view of EV deployment, recognizing the need for increased EV public charging infrastructure. Brookline has the advantage of its longer-term focus, as well as its location, nestled within the larger Boston MSA. Proximity to EV charge points in the City of Boston allows the township to lean on its geographic position, should expected growth in EVs within Brookline turn out to be underestimated.

However, given the already-low EV to charger ratio in Brookline, if plans to expand EV use in Brookline are to succeed, the EV public charging infrastructure must expand significantly. While the risk that the ratio of EVs to charge points will drop is minimal (thanks to available chargers nearby in Boston), compared to in other districts with similar constraints, charging infrastructure must remain integral to the EV adoption plan.

Given the existing legal and financial barriers Brookline faces to accelerating at-home charging, in fall 2018, the town determined that fighting to require charging stations is not the best use of the town's limited funds and resources.

Instead, Maria Morelli, senior planner for Brookline, indicated that the town is focusing on influencing new commercial development.

For the fiscal year 2018–2019, the city's transportation plans included several suggested improvements for EV charging infrastructure, but there is a notable focus on upgrading a two-mile stretch of the Beacon Street median with 50 charging ports. After suggesting all possible updates and changes given the regulatory limitations of the state, and investigating the current financial limitations of charging stations, Brookline staff came up with creative ways to incentivize EV infrastructure. Under the leadership of Senior Planner Morelli, in the last year, the town has dedicated an "investment corridor" to change perceptions of EV charging stations.

This focus was inspired by the challenges and investigations the EV subcommittee encountered over the last two years. At this point in the development of EVSE, staff realized two things: 1) EVSE is not financially self-supporting; and 2) there is not enough funding to install EVSE widely. Therefore, staff, and particularly planner Morelli, decided to reframe the promotion of EVSE in Brookline. Focusing on the Beacon Street corridor, the staff framed charging infrastructure as an amenity to local businesses, not as a money maker in and of itself. In doing so, Morelli hopes to accomplish several things:

- First, she has already begun to attract investment from utilities such as Eversource as well as local businesses
- Second, she and the local businesses in the corridor hope to attract further economic activity as EV owners wait for their vehicles to charge along the corridor
- Finally, she hopes that the momentum from the corridor will generate further enthusiasm from other business districts, which will in turn create more charging availability and incite more EV purchases

These "investment corridor" ideas are still in early stages, so their success is still undetermined. Yet Morelli is optimistic—she believes this type of corridor will have a multiplier effect that will create an environment for further investment. "Once the public gets used to it," she says, "they will definitely ask for more."

Brookline's approach differs from other cities—in particular, its focus on an investment corridor demonstrates the creative thinking necessary to overcome its small-city barriers. The smaller city size and participatory governance structure are uniquely suited to concentrate resources on one specific investment zone. While larger cities may have to triage among several priorities, Brookline is in a stronger position to build consensus for specific, and effective, flagship projects. Importantly, efforts are largely the result of a dedicated group of people who overcame legal and financial barriers to promote charging infrastructure in their town.

Clearly, Brookline is well on its way to creating a welcoming EV adoption ecosystem. Still, roughly 25,000 light duty vehicles are registered in Brookline; roughly 1.6% of those vehicles are electric. Gathering the investment and political will to push adoption from a miniscule 1.6% market share to the 80%–90% necessary to combat global climate change remains a steep uphill climb—even in one of the most forward-looking towns and states in the United States.

Brookline is remarkable for the community commitment to EVs and the bottom-up process used to frame a township EV strategy. The initiatives began with a citizen's action committee for climate change in 2000, proceeded through citizen pressure to install further charging infrastructure, and continues with a dedicated staff working to fundraise, problem solve, and conduct significant stakeholder engagement in order to ensure that momentum builds for electric vehicles in Brookline.

Still, Brookline faces challenges on two fronts: (1) there is limited funding available to continue increasing available EV charging infrastructure, and (2) township building codes and zoning ordinances may require changing, which will lead to a collision with state-controlled policies and approval processes. So far, the town is making progress in spite of these constraints. Yet, in order for charging infrastructure to spread to other cities, even in a progressive state like Massachusetts, significant changes in law and financing need to take place.

APPENDIX TO CHAPTER 6

Subcommittee Report Recommendations

The EV subcommittee issued the following recommendations as part of their final report:

- Guidelines to encourage EVSE installation so that major projects better meet the parking needs of users and occupants
- Utilizing one of several possible alternative approaches (explained in detail in the report)
- Pursuing all available funding sources and mechanisms for public and private EV charging infrastructure
- Encouraging the Building Department and Planning Department staff to ask for EV charging infrastructure within their review of buildings plans and permits
- Pursuing an assessment of Brookline's need for additional EV charging and recommending locations, types, and funding sources for future EV charging expansion
- Advocating for adding a detailed definition of EV charging readiness to the State Building Code
- Advocating for robust funding and support for EVSE in Eversource's 17-05 rate filing
- Advocating for EV charging infrastructure funding and Zero-Emission Vehicle standards at the state legislative level
- Further analyzing the potential for EV charging at open-air parking facilities licensed by the Board of Selectmen

PART III

TRANSITION AVENUE

CHAPTER 7

Measuring Electric Vehicle Infrastructure Among Cities: A Multidimensional Approach

Z. Justin Ren, PhD and John P. Helveston, PhD

7.1 Introduction

Urban areas across the world are leading Electric Vehicle (EV) adoption, with over 40% of the world's EVs concentrated in just 20 cities. EV adoption is transforming cities' mobility and energy systems, and in particular EV charging infrastructure. While earlier literature considered the effects and implications of national- and state-level EV policies, few studies have focused on helping city-level decision-makers prepare for future EV adoption. This chapter quantifies the various dimensions of a city's readiness in meeting demand for EV charging infrastructure. A multidimensional framework is proposed, comparing what influences infrastructure investment decisions in different cities around the world. That index then prompts a discussion about what policymakers can learn from such a framework to contribute to better EV infrastructure decisions by cities.

Along with much other evidence, the case studies in this volume indicate that accelerated adoption of electric vehicles (EVs) will require a substantial increase in the buildout of EV charging infrastructure.[240] However, EV adoption rates vary substantially among different cities around the world, due to idiosyncrasies that support varying EV adoption rates and levels of available charging

---

240 National Renewable Energy Laboratory (NREL), *National Plug-In Electric Vehicle Infrastructure Analysis*, 2017, Available at: https://www.nrel.gov/docs/fy17osti/69031.pdf; China's National Development and Reform Commission (NDRC), *Guidelines for accelerating the plug-in electric vehicle charging infrastructure deployment*, 2015, Available at: http://www.ndrc.gov.cn/zcfb/zcfbtz/201511/W020151117576336784393.pdf.

infrastructure. For example, greater levels of public charging infrastructure will be required to support greater EV adoption in cities like Beijing, where most residents live in high-rise apartments with limited dedicated parking. By contrast, in cities like Austin, Texas, most residents have at least one dedicated parking space at their home, where charging can occur.[241]

In addition, while EV adoption is frequently studied at the national level[242] and state level,[243] cities remain the spearhead for large portions of global EV adoption. As of November 2017, 40% of all EVs in the world were concentrated in just 20 cities.[244] The advent of increased EV adoption in urban centers is requiring city policymakers to consider important structural changes to city infrastructure systems, particularly in EV charging infrastructure. Indeed, examining city-level adoption rather than national or regional adoption has important implications for ensuring adequate infrastructure planning and implementation.

This chapter uses the metropolitan area as a unit of analysis in order to characterize how different factors are associated with EV adoption in select cities. By focusing on the city level, we aim to help city planners and policymakers understand what drives EV infrastructure needs in their own localities and devise appropriate policies accordingly. In particular, we identify a series of city-specific drivers underlying residents' decision to adopt EVs. Then we propose a multivariate framework that incorporates those drivers in order to measure a city's readiness to adopt an EV public charging infrastructure. The framework can be depicted visually and possibly aggregated into a single number. Therefore, the framework has the potential to help city policymakers look at peer

241 Hall, D., Cui, H. and Lutsey, N., *Electric vehicle capitals of the world: What markets are leading the transition to electric?*, 2018, ICCT, Available at: https://www.theicct.org/sites/default/files/publications/EV_Capitals_2018_final_20181029.pdf.

242 Helveston, J. P., Liu, Y., Feit, E. M., Fuchs, E. R. H., Klampfl, E. and Michalek, J. J., *Will subsides drive electric vehicle adoption? Measuring consumer preferences in the U.S. and China*, 2015, Transportation Research Part A: Policy and Practice, 73, 96–112, Available at: https://www.sciencedirect.com/science/article/pii/S0965856415000038; Rietmann, N., and Lieven, T., *How policy measures succeeded to promote electric mobility—Worldwide review and outlook*, 2019, Journal of Cleaner Production, 206, 66–75, Available at: https://www.sciencedirect.com/science/article/pii/S0959652618328415.

243 Jenn, A., Azevedo, I. L., & Ferreira, P., *The impact of federal incentives on the adoption of hybrid electric vehicles in the United States*, 2013, Energy Economics, 40, 936–342, Available at: https://www.sciencedirect.com/science/article/pii/S0140988313001709; Jenn, A., Springel, K., and Gopal, A. R., *Effectiveness of electric vehicle incentives in the United States*, July 2017, Energy Policy, 119, 349–356, Available at: https://www.sciencedirect.com/science/article/pii/S0301421518302891.

244 Ibid., Hall, D., Cui, H., & Lutsey, N.

cities to better understand their own barriers to accelerating the electrification of their transportation sector.

The rest of the chapter is organized as follows: First, relevant background information is discussed. Then we present a multifaceted framework that measures a city's EV public infrastructure readiness by analyzing the real-world data that have been collected and compiled. A discussion of findings from this application follows. The chapter concludes with suggestions to practitioners and thoughts on future directions for research.

7.2 Background

The transportation sector is now the largest contributor to anthropogenic carbon (CO_2) emissions in the United States.[245] As a result, vehicle electrification is perceived as one of the most significant ways to reduce air pollution and CO_2 emissions in the United States.[246] Accelerated EV adoption is also perceived as one of the most significant sources of new electricity demand for the energy sector.[247]

Meeting this electricity demand will require substantial increases in charging infrastructure. A study by the National Renewable Energy Laboratory (NREL) estimates that approximately 600,000 nonresidential Level 2 chargers (240 V and 12–80 A) and 25,000 DC fast chargers (up to 500 V and 125 A) would be necessary to satisfy charging demand from an anticipated 15 million EVs on the road in 2030, which would make up just 5% of the total number of vehicles in the United States.[248] China's National Development and Reform Commission (NDRC) issued similarly large estimates of increased vehicle electrification in China with its plan to build 12,000 charging stations and more than 4.8 million chargers nationwide by 2020.[249] In Norway—the world leader in EV adoption by percentage of new vehicle sales—approximately 100,000 EVs (3% of all vehicles) in operation are supported by a network of 4,400 Level

---

245 US EPA, *Fast Facts on Transportation Greenhouse Gas Emissions*, 2018, Available at: https://www.epa.gov/greenvehicles/fast-facts-transportation-greenhouse-gas-emissions.

246 Sperling, D., *Three Revolutions: Steering Automated, Shared, and Electric Vehicles to a Better Future*, 2018, (Washington DC: Island Press).

247 Fox-Penner, P., Gorman, W. and Hatch, J., *Long-term U.S. transportation electricity use considering the effect of autonomous-vehicles: Estimates & policy observations*, Feb. 2018, *Energy Policy*, 122, 203–213.

248 NREL, *National Plug-In Electric Vehicle Infrastructure Analysis*, 2017.

249 NDRC, *Guidelines for accelerating the plug-in electric vehicle charging infrastructure deployment*, 2015.

1 chargers (120 V and 16 A) and 2,700 Level 2 chargers,[250] which is roughly 14 EVs per Level 1 and Level 2 charger combined.

Based on national-level data and analyses, increased charging infrastructure will clearly be necessary even for modest increases in the number of EVs on the road. However, prior work also shows high levels of heterogeneity in city-level rates of EV adoption. While many cities across the world have virtually no EVs on the road, other cities, such as Oslo and Bergen in Norway, are rapidly adopting EVs, which represented more than 33% of vehicle sales in 2016.[251] In larger cities such as Los Angeles and Shanghai, EV sales made up just 4% and 6% of 2016 sales, respectively. However, given the size of their markets, both Los Angeles and Shanghai already have approximately 100,000 EVs on the road—close to the total number in all of Norway.[252] As an illustration of this variation in EV adoption, consider the EV adoption rates in the United States shown in Figure 7.1.[253]

State-level EV policies that incentivize EV adoption are clearly visible in the Figure. For example, many cities in California have higher adoption than cities in other states, and California has had comparatively stronger policies to support greater EV adoption, such as the "Zero-Emission Vehicle" (ZEV) mandate, which requires that a minimal percentage of an automaker's state-wide sales must be vehicles that produce no tailpipe emissions. However, the large variance in EV adoption across cities cannot be explained solely by national- or state-level policies or incentives. For example, EV shares across different metropolitan areas within the state of California are quite different even though, as a whole, the state accounts for the largest portion of EV sales in the United States. These trends suggest that cities play an important role in EV adoption around the world; also, that different cities may require different quantities and types of EV infrastructure to support their respective rates of EV adoption. (Refer to Chapter 8 and 9 in this work for more discussion on cities' role in EV adoption.)

---

250 Ibid., Lorentzen, E., Haugneland, P., Bu, C., and Hauge, E.
251 Ibid., Hall, D., Cui, H., & Lutsey, N.
252 Ibid., Hall, D., Cui, H., & Lutsey, N.
253 Slowik, P., and Lutsey, N., *The Continued Transition to Electric Vehicles in U.S. Cities*, 2018, ICCT, Available at: https://www.theicct.org/sites/default/files/publications/Transition_EV_US_Cities_20180724.pdf.

FIGURE 7.1 Electric Vehicle Share of New 2017 Vehicle Registrations by Metropolitan Area[254]

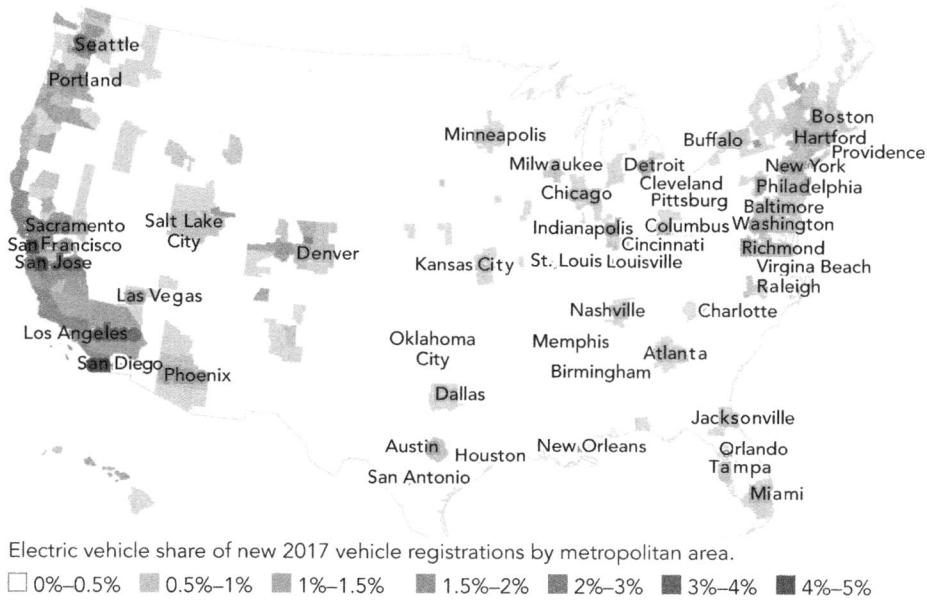

Electric vehicle share of new 2017 vehicle registrations by metropolitan area.

☐ 0%–0.5%   ▨ 0.5%–1%   ▨ 1%–1.5%   ▨ 1.5%–2%   ▨ 2%–3%   ▨ 3%–4%   ■ 4%–5%

While prior literature has examined ways different policies spur increased EV adoption at the national level[255] and state level,[256] less work has been done comparing features associated with city-level EV adoption. In this chapter, we compare important characteristics of different cities around the world that support the infrastructure needs of increased EV adoption. Given the idiosyncrasies of cities worldwide, cities might need vastly different charging infrastructures to support a given number or percentage of EVs. The framework proposed here highlights the various influencing factors of a city, such as its EV-related incen-

254 *The Continued Transition to Electric Vehicles in US Cities*, 2018, ICCT. New Vehicle registration data from IHS Automotive.
255 Helveston, J. P., Liu, Y., Feit, E. M., Fuchs, E. R. H., Klampfl, E. and Michalek, J. J., *Will subsides drive electric vehicle adoption? Measuring consumer preferences in the U.S. and China*, 2015, Transportation Research Part A: Policy and Practice, 73, 96–112; and Rietmann, N., and Lieven, T., *How policy measures succeeded to promote electric mobility— Worldwide review and outlook*, 2019, Journal of Cleaner Production, 206, pages 66–75.
256 Jenn, A., Azevedo, I. L. and Ferreira, P., *The impact of federal incentives on the adoption of hybrid electric vehicles in the United States*, 2013, Energy Economics, 40, 936–342, Available at: https://www.sciencedirect.com/science/article/pii/S0140988313001709; Jenn, A., Springel, K., and Gopal, A. R., *Effectiveness of electric vehicle incentives in the United States*, 2018, Energy Policy, 119, 349–356, Available at: https://www.sciencedirect.com/science/article/pii/S0301421518302891.

tives, public transit, traveling distance, housing types, workplace charging, and air pollution. By comparing those factors side-by-side across cities, city planners can benefit from:

1. Gaining a global look at the various dimensions of a city's ecosystem that relate to EV adoption, such as housing, commuter behavior, and air quality. For example, a city with particularly poor air quality caused by heavy use of Internal Combustion Engine (ICE) vehicles may have an added incentive to deploy more EV infrastructure in order to encourage faster EV adoption.

2. Learning how their own cities stack up against peer cities, but more important, what causes the difference. A city can also identify its peer-comparable cities to deepen its comparison and learning.

3. Helping guide their investment decisions related to EV public infrastructure based on their local environment. For example, a city that finds itself low on both home charging and workplace charging may start to think of ways to increase public infrastructure deployment to increase its EV impact.

Next, the framework to measure a city's EV impact as a system is presented.

7.3 Framework

The goal is to develop a quantitative and visual framework to measure and compare major factors related to EV infrastructure on different cities. The framework is referred to as a city's "EV Infrastructure Graph" (EVIG) 1.0.

In measuring the EVIG of a city, it is important to take a holistic view and consider a variety of factors that affect the city's EV adoption rate and the associated public charging needs, keeping in mind that the same adoption rate in two different cities may require vastly different infrastructure needs. EVs are part of a complex urban ecosystem with multiple subsystems, each of which EV would interact with. The following figure provides a simple illustration.

FIGURE 7.2 EV as Part of a City Ecosystem[257]

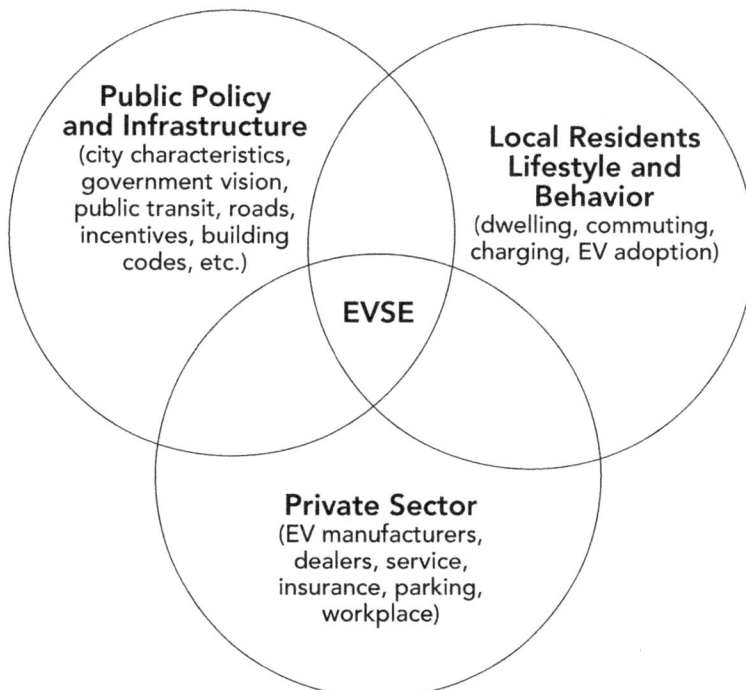

As shown in the figure, EV is at the intersection of multiple systems: EV supply chains, public policy and infrastructure, and consumers. Therefore, any meaningful attempt to measure a city's EV infrastructure must incorporate major factors in those systems. The figure makes it clear that, for a city planner, deepening the impact of EVs is not only about installing more public chargers. Instead, it should be viewed in the context of a city's inherent characteristics, linked to its history, infrastructure, culture, demographics, and people.

Summarizing how all the variables above relate to a city's EV impact is not easy. Ahead, some major factors included in the multidimensional framework are discussed.

257 Source: Authors.

7.3.1 EV Incentives and EV Market Share

Incentives related to EV ownership are probably the most direct driver of EV adoption, as well as the most deeply researched aspect of EV adoption literature.[258] There are two main types of incentives:

- **Monetary incentives offered to a city's residents for owning an EV.** These include rebates, deductions in taxes, tolls, and fees at all levels (national, state, and local). The stronger such monetary incentives are for a city, the greater EV demand there will be, and consequently, the greater the needs for public charging infrastructure. Various nations have implemented such direct financial incentives, from the $7,500 tax credit in the United States to the 50% exemption from value added tax (VAT) and purchase tax in Norway. In addition, many states or local municipalities adopt their own incentives to encourage EV purchase.

- **Traffic regulation and nonmonetary incentives offered for owning an EV.** This category includes HOV lane access (e.g, Norway, and California in the United States), priority registration (or restriction on ICE vehicles, which is being implemented in major cities in China). Similar to monetary incentives, they are expected to spur EV demand and, in turn, public charging infrastructure. Following Rietmann and Lieve,[259] this category is called Traffic Regulation and Incentives.

- **Local EV market share.** An EV market share measure is included in the framework because market ownership of EVs provides a baseline to measure the potential impact of EV charging infrastructure. The dynamics between EV market share and charging infrastructure are bidirectional and subject to other factors. However, given a fixed amount of EV charging infrastructure, the higher a city's EV market share is, the higher the use of charging infrastructure and overall impact.

7.3.2 EV Charging Infrastructure: Home Charging and Workplace Charging

Imagine an EV that has been purchased by a typical consumer. In its whole lifespan of use, where would this EV spend its time, and how long? Of course, a precise answer will depend on the lifestyle of its owners, but assume a typical consumer is one who drives to work, where he/she spends 40 hours a week, goes to home every night, and does most leisure activities on weekends. In that case, it is not farfetched to conclude that this owner's EV will spend about half

---

258 Ibid., Jenn, A., Azevedo, I. L. and Ferreira, P.; Ibid, Jenn, A., Springel, K., & Gopal, A. R.; Ibid., Slowik, P., and Lutsey, N., 2017.
259 Ibid., Rietmann, N., and Lieven, T.

of its time in its owner's home (roughly 12 hours a day, or 84 hours a week). The rest of the time (about 168 hours a week – 84 hours at a week at home – 40 hours at work = 44 hours a week) this EV will be somewhere traveling or parked elsewhere (sometimes public roads or in parking facilities). Public charging needs are derived from this last bucket of time. This EV's time is divided as shown in Figure 7.3.

FIGURE 7.3 Where Does an EV Spend Its Time? A Typical EV Driven to Work Five Days a Week and Spending Every Night at Home

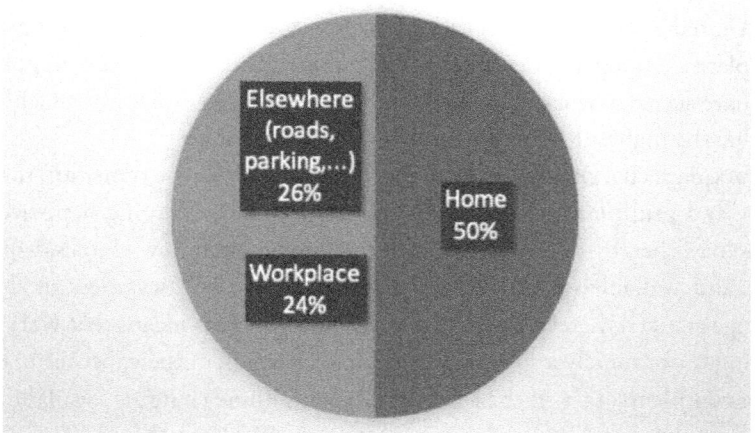

Figure 7.3 highlights the fact that there are three major destinations for EV charging: home, workplace, and other parking facilities. Public charging infrastructure falls into the last category. Note that such infrastructure concerns are unique to EVs. Refueling for ICE vehicles happens at one type of facility: gas stations. EVs need electricity, so it matters where they can get recharged.

If total charging needs are constant, public charging needs can be viewed as a substitute to home and workplace charging. (In the longer run, however, higher availability of home charging can spur more EV adoption, which creates total higher charging needs and, in turn, higher demand for public charging. So, home charging complements public charging in the long term.) A city that has a very strong home charging base or workplace charging infrastructure may not need as many pubic charging facilities as a comparable city that has the same total EV battery volume but less access to charging at home or at a workplace. The reverse is also true: a city with extremely accessible public charging can focus less on private charging demand, whether it be for charging at home or at work. Therefore, it is measured as follows:

- **Availability of home charging.** Home charging is an important part of EV infrastructure, as most privately owned EVs will spend the majority of their time in private homes and/or garages. When an EV owner is able to charge his/her EV at home, it reduces need for public charging facilities. However, a city that has 100% home charging for EV owners will still need some public charging. But a city or town with less home charging infrastructure for EV owners (a densely populated urban center versus a town dominated by single-family houses, for example) will face more demand pressure for EV chargers on public roads and at other facilities.
- **Availability of workplace charging.** Similar to home charging, workplace charging provides another important base for EVs. A few states in the United States and some cities are making great strides in expanding workplace charging. For example, in California almost 50% of all EVs reportedly have access to workplace charging, which may help explain why California has the highest EV adoption rate in the United States.[260]

Workplace charging is also strategically important in the transition to clean energy and grid planning. After all, most workplace charging happens during the day, thereby taking advantage of abundant solar, low wholesale power prices, and available system capacity. It can also raise EV awareness and alleviate range anxiety, thereby boosting EV adoption.[261] This means that workplace charging is not merely a substitute to public charging in the short term, but it can be complementary in the long run. As with home charging, availability of workplace charging may have a positive effect on EV ownership. That is, people may be more likely to consider buying an EV if they can actually charge their EVs at work. But again, the focus here is on the effects of substituting workplace charging with public charging by fixing total EV demand as constant.

7.3.3 Mobility Behavior of Residents

EV adoption and EV charging needs are a direct function of how their owners use their vehicles, so the extent of vehicle usage in a city must be measured. A city with a greater distance driven by EV calls for more public charging infrastructure, compared to one in which driving distances are shorter with less driving, *ceteris paribus*. We view two factors as having the largest effect on a

---

260 California Air Resources Board (CARB), *California's Advanced Clean Cars Midterm Review: Appendix B: Consumer Acceptance of ZEVs and PHEVs*, 2017, Available at: https://www.arb.ca.gov/msprog/acc/mtr/appendix_b.pdf.
261 O'Connor, P. and Jacobs, M., *Charging Smart: Drivers and Utilities Can Both Benefit from Well-Integrated Electric Vehicles and Clean Energy*, 2017, Available at: https://www.ucsusa.org/clean-vehicles/electric-vehicles/smart-charging.

locality's public charging needs: average daily driving distance and availability of public transportation.

- **Travel distance.** To measure the impact of EV and EV infrastructures across cities, a benchmark for vehicle usage should be established for the following reasons. First of all, a city whose residents drive more miles each day has a higher potential for EV adoption than a comparable one in which driving is less routine. Second, an EV's charging frequency is linked to its usage. The farther an EV travels on a regular basis, the more frequently it needs to be charged. On a city level, the farther the distances its residents drive their EVs, the more public charging infrastructure the city needs.

- **Availability of public transportation.** The link between public transportation and public EV infrastructure may not be obvious, but it is actually a strong one. If a city has very comprehensive and readily available public transportation, then its residents are less likely to need to own private cars, including EVs, and the demand for EV public charging infrastructure is reduced. Put another way, consider two cities, one of which has a strong public transportation network while the other does not; otherwise, they are similar in every aspect. This framework will assign a higher value to the latter (the city with less public transportation), and a lower value to the former (the city with more public transportation).

It should be noted that some cities are actively pursuing electrifying their public transportation fleets such as buses or trams. Since the focus here is on personal EV ownership, our definition of public charging infrastructure does not include charging stations built specifically for those public transportation vehicles.

7.3.4 Environment Impact

The focus here is on measuring a locality's potential relation between its EV infrastructure and its local environment. The connection is not direct—installing EV charging infrastructure will not directly improve the environment. In addition, from a value chain perspective, just replacing ICEs with EVs does not necessarily reduce a city's carbon footprint or pollution because generating electricity or producing the EV can cause carbon emission and pollution elsewhere in the supply chain.[262] However, we would like to establish a link between the EV infrastructure and the environment for two reasons.

First, as discussed in the section on home and workplace charging, EV public infrastructure can stimulate EV demand, which in turn can reduce gasoline

---

262 Nealer, R. and Hendrickson, T. P., *Review of Recent Lifecycle Assessments of Energy and Greenhouse Gas Emissions for Electric Vehicles*, 2015, Current Sustainable/Renewable Energy Reports, 2(3), 66–73, Available at: https://link.springer.com/article/10.1007/s40518-015-0033-x.

consumption and greenhouse gas and other pollutants. Second, building an environment benchmark in the framework can reflect how urgently a city wants to increase its decarbonization efforts. A city with heavy pollution from transportation has a greater need for EV adoption. For these reasons, we include an air-quality measure in our framework.

7.4 Data and Measurement

In this section, the multiple aforementioned measures are incorporated into an operational framework. Here, the measurement of each dimension, and where such data were obtained, is discussed. Next, the multiple dimensions of data were converted into one common scale. Last, the results are presented in a multidimensional matrix and methods to aggregate into a single-number index are proposed.

7.4.1 Measurement and Data Sources

Measuring each of the dimensions depends on state-of-the-art research literature as well as our own primary research and data collection. Below, we detail how we measure and collect data on each dimension.

Monetary incentives offered to a city's residents for owning an EV. Because monetary incentives are quantifiable, it is relatively straightforward to summarize all the incentives available in a locality. Some difficulty does arise when such incentives depend on vehicle characteristics such as battery type, capacity, weight, or value. One could take averages or pick their modal values. Another issue is how to compare incentives in different currency denominations. Here, most research literature converts them to US dollars. Such an approach is valid because EV manufacturers in general align their EV out-of-factory prices across different markets (excluding tariffs and taxes). Data were compiled from various public sources on monetary incentives given to EVs in each market.

The last issue to consider is which statistics should be used in across-city comparisons: ratios themselves, rank data, or percentile. However, to provide a uniformed numeric scale across all dimensions, we adopt decile measurement. Decile information is convenient and easy to understand: A data point of smallest value that falls into the first decile would get a value of 1, while the largest value would belong to the 10th decile and get a value of 10.

Using decile information also implies that a city's ranking is a relative measure that will depend on which other cities it is being compared to. It is appropriate in this setting because our goal is to compare side-by-side how cities differ in their potential to meet their EV demand. Table 7.1 shows incentive ratios at selected cities around the world.

TABLE 7.1 Incentive Ratios

	Monetary Incentives (USD)	Decile
Beijing, China	6,000	1
Oslo, Norway	25,000	10
Los Angeles, USA	12,000	6
Portland, USA	10,500	3
Boston, USA	12,500	8

Traffic regulation and nonmonetary incentives offered to own an EV. Compared to monetary incentives, nonmonetary incentives are more difficult to gauge and compare. However, prior research has demonstrated that it is possible and such comparison can generate meaningful results (e.g., Slowik and Lutsey 2017, Rietmann et al. 2018).[263] Similar to the evaluation scheme proposed by Rietmann et al. 2018, each cities' nonmonetary incentives are reviewed and a three-point weighting method that maps the strength of each locality's nonmonetary incentives is put into a numeric scale from 1 to 3, with 1 being nonexistent and 3 being the strongest. Finally, this is converted into deciles, which is the common numeric scale for all measures. Table 7.2 contains numeric mapping of nonmonetary incentives at selected cities around the world.

TABLE 7.2 Nonmonetary Incentives

	Nonmonetary Incentives (USD)	Decile
Beijing, China	2	8
Oslo, Norway	3	10
Los Angeles, USA	3	6
Portland, USA	1	3
Boston, USA	1	3

---

263 Ibid., Hall, D., Cui, H., and Lutsey, N.; Ibid, Rietmann, N., and Lieven, T.

Home charging potential. As a first step, the percentage of a city's households with private parking space is used to gauge the potential of home charging. Such data can be obtained from the US census for US cities, and through various other sources for international cities (for example, for Norway cities we obtain information through data published on Statistics Norway website[264]). This percentage is an upper bound on how much private charging a city can contain. As an example, if 63% of a city's dwellings have a garage or carport, private charging can be installed in at most 63% of its houses or apartments. Then, the above percentages are converted into deciles. Table 7.3 summarizes such a metric for selected cities.

TABLE 7.3 Home Charging Potential

	Home Charging Potential	Decile
Beijing, China	30%	2
Oslo, Norway	52%	6
Los Angeles, USA	80%	10
Portland, USA	72%	8
Boston, USA	43%	3

Workplace charging. For workplace charging, a different approach is used because no data are available on workplace parking across all cities to gauge its potential for charging. Instead, the status quo is looked at by obtaining the number of workplace-charging-points per million population in a city. Such information for major cities is available from research by third-party sources such as International Center for Clean Transportation (ICCT). For other cities, data were obtained through ad hoc researches. In a few cases, estimates are relied upon, and these are clearly marked as such. Table 7.4 shows these metrics for selected cities.

---

264 Statistics Norway website: https://www.ssb.no/en/statbank/.

TABLE 7.4 Workplace Charging

	Home Charging Potential	Decile
Beijing, China	325	10
Oslo, Norway	206*	8
Los Angeles, USA	33	3
Portland, USA	90	6
Boston, USA	25	1

*Unable to obtain data on workplace chargers in Oslo so it is assumed that 25% of all chargers in the city are workplace chargers.

Vehicle usage. Total Daily Vehicle Miles of Travel (DVMT) is used to capture vehicle usage. For that, first the DVMT per capita that has been consistently measured for major US urbanized area is used. In particular, a dataset maintained by the US Department of Transportation, which can be found at https://www.transportation.gov/mission/health/transportation-and-health-tool-data-excel, contains vehicle miles traveled per capita for major urban areas in the United States. For cities outside the United States, ad hoc searches were conducted and compiled into the same scale. Then, the resulting data were multiplied by city population to obtain the total DVMT of each city. Finally, these numbers were used to compute deciles for each city in the sample.

Table 7.5 contains these metrics for selected cities.

Substitutability of public transportation. Multiple measures can gauge a city's public transportation infrastructure, such as public transportation miles per capita, or coverage area of public transportation. But the preferred measure is percentage of commuters who use public transit, because it is an outcome measure (i.e., commuter choice) which is a function of the state of public transportation infrastructure. In other words, if a city has a high percentage of public transit users, it has less need for private cars, including EVs. In turn, that city has less demand for public charging for EVs than does another city that has a lower percentage of public transit users, ceteris paribus.

Such commuter choice data are available for most cities from multiple organizations (for example, https://alltransit.cnt.org/metrics/), Or, for US cities, the aforementioned Transportation and Health Tool dataset is available from the US Department of Transportation. After obtaining those data for cities, the complementary percentages are taken, and their deciles are computed. Table 7.6 contains these metrics for selected cities.

TABLE 7.5 Vehicle Usage[265]

	DVMT Per Capita	City Population (metro area)	Total DVMT (in million miles)	Decile
Beijing, China	325	40,000,000	1,600,000,000	10
Oslo, Norway	206*	1,710,000	16,758,000	1
Los Angeles, USA	33	13,000,000	289,900,000	8
Portland, USA	90	2,389,228	44,917,486	6
Boston, USA	25	4,628,910	103,687,584	3

TABLE 7.6 Substitutability of Public Transportation

	Substitutability of Public Transportation	Decile
Beijing, China	35%	1
Oslo, Norway	65%	6
Los Angeles, USA	88%	10
Portland, USA	87%	8
Boston, USA	65%	3

Environmental impact. In order to measure the potential effect of EV adoption on a city's environment, air quality was selected, since it is the effect most closely related to cities and transportation. In particular, the internationally-adopted PM2.5 measure was used, which describes concentration of fine inhalable particles with diameters that are 2.5 micrometers and smaller. Such data are available for practically all major cities around the world.

---

265 In the DVMT per capital column, reference for Beijing is Wang, M. and He, D., *Projection of Chinese Motor Vehicle Growth, Oil Demand, and CO2 Emissions through 2050*, 2006, Argonne National Laboratory. For DVMT per capital for Oslo, see country level data from http://internationalcomparisons.org/environment/transportation.html.

However, not all city air pollution is caused by transportation. Other major sources include industry and residential use of fuels of various sources. Also, cities around the world differ in the proportion of transportation in their total energy consumption. To control for such differences, the PM2.5 measure is multiplied by the percentage of transportation in a locality's total energy consumption. Table 7.7 provides these metrics for selected cities.

TABLE 7.7 ENVIRONMENTAL IMPACT

	Environmental Impact	Decile
Beijing, China	12.8%	10
Oslo, Norway	2.5%	6
Los Angeles, USA	4.5%	8
Portland, USA	2.5%	3
Boston, USA	2.5%	3

7.5 Application of a Multidimensional Comparison Framework

Having collected data for all the above variables, the next step is to assemble them into a visual framework.

The key idea is to present all the dimensions on one single graph. The tool chosen is called a radar chart. Using the data compiled for Beijing, Oslo, Los Angeles, Portland, and Boston, their EV public infrastructure impact comparison is as follows:

FIGURE 7.4 Multidimensional EV Infrastructure Graph (EVIG) 1.0: An Application[266]

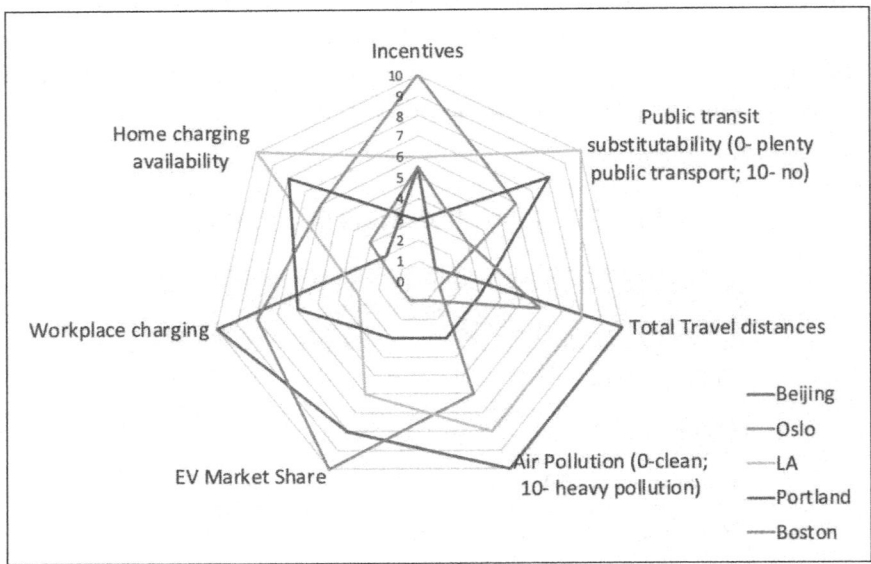

In the radar chart, each city is represented by a polygon with colored sides. Each polygon has seven vertices, each representing one dimension of impact measurement. The position of each vertex is determined by the decile value of each dimension that we have compiled above. The higher the value, the farther the vertex is from the center. For example, the city of Oslo has a value of 10 in the incentives dimension. Hence, its vertex on that dimension is the highest and farthest from the center.

As we can see, each city has a unique shape due to differences in each of those dimensions. This is important because the graph tells us that even though each city would like to have maximum impact from additional EVSE, it should follow its own path, in keeping with its unique infrastructure, people, and economic conditions.

As an aggregate measure, the overall impact from additional EVSE in each city could be measured by the total area of each polygon. The larger area of a polygon, the greater the overall impact of more EVSE of the city the polygon represents. We can visually see that polygons for Beijing and Los Angeles have the greatest area, the one for Oslo is in the middle, while the polygons for Portland and Boston are smallest. (It is also important to note that this

---

266 Source: By authors.

comparison is entirely relative because all statistics are deciles, and thus highly dependent upon data from the underlying comparison cities.) Based on this metric, three groups of potential impact seem to exist: high-impact cities (Beijing and Los Angeles), medium-impact cities (Oslo), and low-impact cities (Portland and Boston).

Beijing. Even though it is somewhat unsurprising that Beijing scores high on the overall impact, it is interesting to see what the specific underlying main drivers are: air quality, travel distances, workplace charging, and EV market share. The connection between air quality and EV adoption is obvious. Beijing has the worst air quality among all cities. More EV infrastructure will encourage EV adoption, which could meaningfully reduce pollution from driving gasoline-powered cars and improve air quality. In addition, daily driving distances in Beijing are the highest in the world. To alleviate range anxiety, which has been identified as one of the main obstacles of EV adoption in Beijing, it is critical that the city deploy more public chargers along main commuter routes. (See Chapter 4 for details on how Beijing is aggressively embarking on such an initiative.)

Compared to other cities, Beijing does not have plentiful home charging infrastructure, but its city government has installed many workplace chargers. This suggests that the city could expand its EV impact if it can find creative ways to increase home charging availability.

Beijing's EV incentives are only average among its peers, suggesting that it could amplify EV impact by increasing its incentives. Finally, it is worth noting that Beijing has a good public transportation system, which serves as an effective substitute for personal vehicles.

Los Angeles. Compared to Beijing, Los Angeles ranks almost as high on overall EV impact but its profile is somewhat different.

Los Angeles has significant air pollution, which calls for more EV use and less ICE use. LA residents also drive longer distances than residents of most other cities, such as Portland or Oslo, which further necessitates public charging infrastructure deployment. But what really makes LA stand out from Beijing in this index is its lack of an extensive public transportation system. Therefore, aside from huge capital expenditure to develop a public transit system, one sensible policy recommendation would be to spend more on EV charging infrastructure.

Los Angeles has a high home charging potential because almost 80% of single-family dwellings have parking, but it has fewer workplace chargers. So, to increase the impact of EVs, one strategy might be to push for city regulations regarding EV charging readiness in single-family homes as well as at workplaces.

Another interesting point that is not so apparent in the EVIG graph is that research has shown that HOV access has been a quite powerful incentive for LA residents to buy EVs.[267] The City of Los Angeles has very high traffic congestion,[268] but the State of California allows advanced clean energy vehicle to use HOV lane as an incentive. In fact this incentive turns out to be working too well: clean energy vehicles are clogging some HOV lanes, and the State of California had to revoke access for a number of EV owners.[269]

Oslo. Despite the fact Oslo has the most incentives for EVs, our framework puts Oslo behind Beijing and Los Angeles for several reasons. First of all, its residents do not drive as far each day as the residents of other cities (in fact, its daily driving distances are the shortest among the five in our comparison group). Also, it boasts an extensive and convenient public transportation system. Last, its air quality is relatively good. For all of those reasons, the impact of further EV infrastructure deployment is limited. Nevertheless, Oslo is still relatively high on EV impact because it has a high EV market share and high charging availability at homes and workplaces. However, the workplace charging estimate may not be accurate.

Boston. Our framework puts Boston among the low-impact cities. Its EV penetration is low, but so is its air pollution. It also has a heavily used public transit system. Boston residents actually drive farther than residents of other cities (Boston's distances are second only to Beijing's, and even higher than Los Angeles's). However, because its population is medium-sized, its total driving distances fall into the medium range among cities in our sample. In addition, its home charging infrastructure is relatively scarce because the city is small and densely populated, and many of its residents do not have dedicated parking.

Currently, Boston requires that five percent of its parking be equipped with EV chargers, and an additional 10% be EV-ready for new buildings in parts of the city. To accelerate its EV impact, the city could, among other things, consider more aggressive pubic charging infrastructure deployment and more progressive construction codes on residential and commercial building. Doing so would increase EV adoption and charging infrastructure in all homes, workplaces, and public places.

---

267 Tal, G. and Nicholas, M.A., *Evaluating the Impact of High Occupancy Vehicle Lane Access on Plug-in Vehicles in California*, n.d., UC Davis Institute of Transportation Studies, Available at: https://policyinstitute.ucdavis.edu/files/HOV_April_2014_Final3.pdf.
268 See various city rankings. For example: https://www.tomtom.com/en_gb/trafficindex/list?citySize=LARGE&continent=ALL&country=ALL.
269 Newberry, L., *Anger in California's carpool lanes as more than 200,000 drivers are set to lose decals*, Sept. 17, 2018, Los Angeles Times, Available at: https://www.latimes.com/local/california/la-me-ln-clean-air-car-decals-20180917-story.html.

Portland. Portland is considered medium to low in terms of EV impact. Its EV incentives are not as strong as those of other cities, but it has ample workplace and home charging capabilities. It has good air quality, and its residents do not drive as far as residents of other cities.

Portland is an interesting case because it has a comprehensive public transit system. However, that system's usage is low, suggesting that it has potential to increase ridership. City planners should consider that when they seek to reduce Portland's dependence on ICE vehicles.

7.6 Extension and Conclusions

Cities play a pivotal role in reducing carbon emissions and global warming. In that role, EVs are at the center of efforts to decarbonize transportation and reduce cities' carbon footprint.

This chapter proposed a system-wide framework for cities to evaluate ways their infrastructure, economic conditions, and residents' behavior relate to EV adoption and EV usage. We use a multidimensional chart to provide visuals of the overall impact EVs could have on a city based on identified factors such as EV incentives, home charging potential, workplace charging, public transportation, total driving distance, and air pollution. Ideally, city planners can use this to form ideas about how their cities can most effectively reduce carbon emission caused by transportation.

Future work will focus on refining and extending this framework in several directions. For one, those factors that we identify are interconnected and their dynamics are complex. For example, public transportation is directly linked to EV adoption, but it is also indirectly related through total driving distance. Similarly, EV incentives may directly affect purchase decisions but may also affect home or workplace charging, depending on incentives. The framework can be further extended to model such interactions. With available data, quantitative assessment of the impact of each factor could be done. Collaborating with cities to further implement and test this work is of particular interest.

CHAPTER 8

Applying a Systems Approach to Practice

David O. Jermain

8.1 Introduction

This chapter builds on the preceding one. While Chapter 7 focused on developing and using an indexing tool, this chapter is written for practitioners who will focus on details regarding related processes and practices. It begins by mapping key guideposts for city planners and administrators. Then, it explores metrics that may be helpful to city planners as they hone EV infrastructure deployment priorities using the index tool. Examples of where the index tool may be useful include prioritizing charge point congestion mitigation, engaging with utilities on electrical infrastructure support, and managing Operations and Maintenance (O&M) requirements of deployed charge points. Together, Chapter 7 and this chapter emphasize the value of applying a systems approach to deploying and managing EV infrastructure.[270]

8.2 Guideposts for City Planners and Administrators

Through case studies in this work and analysis from Chapter 7, an actionable framework for planning and managing EV deployment emerges. The main steps include the following:

1. Define the EV infrastructure deployment situation as cities having vital responsibility for enabling EV adoption. Of course, each city's EV planning and management efforts take place in a distinct context. Still, underlying the unique characteristics of individual cities are commonalities

---

270 This chapter focuses planning and management practices for city planners and operations staff. Attention is skewed toward US application of tools presented in Chapter 7 and this chapter. However, learning from Chinese and European case studies is a significant part of the framework presented in this chapter. Accordingly, the systems approach presented should be reviewed and applied to fit specific city needs, regardless of location worldwide.

such as deploying EVs to leverage the existing ICE-based system, to support the emerging new EV supply chain, and to exploit complementary existing transportation-related infrastructure.

2. Accelerate adoption (which may occur due to market pull or public policy push, or both), using a systems approach to driving infrastructure deployment.

Figure 8.1 visually depicts the interdependencies among key EV infrastructure deployment success factors.

FIGURE 8.1 The Importance of a Systems Approach to Public EV Infrastructure[271]

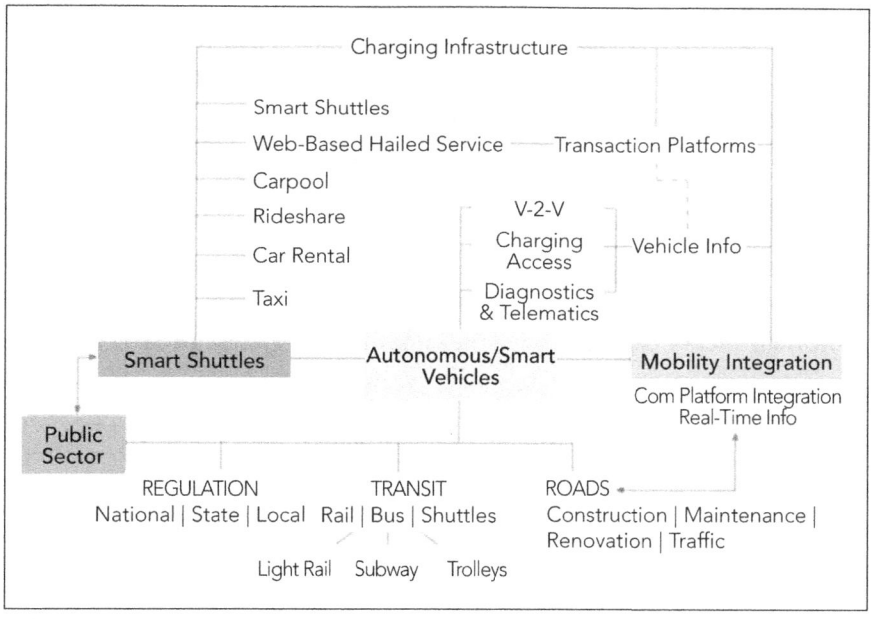

From Figure 8.1, it can be seen that there are three main elements interacting with each other.

Mobility services are composed of the various transportation options available to city residents. These include conventional taxis, car rentals, rideshare offerings, and carpooling. Recent additions include web-based hailing services such as Uber or Lyft, smart shuttles (a still-emerging autonomous route-based service) and evolving public charging infrastructure for EVs.

Most mobility services have well-established transaction platforms. For instance, cash and credit cards for taxis, credit and debit cards for rental cars,

---

271 Source: Chapter author.

cost-sharing for rideshare and carpooling, and smart shuttles, which may be either complimentary or fee-based using conventional credit and/or debit cards.

Web-based hailing services use web-based transaction platforms such as conventional credit cards, Apple Pay, and similar applications for Android smartphones, as well as other apps. Private network charging vendors use tools similar to those used by web-based hailing services.

Mobility integration. Mobility services depend on communication platforms; and platform integration seems to be naturally coevolving with mobility service innovations.[272] Mobility integration involves using transaction platforms and real-time vehicle information to inform users of the pre-arrival status of services requested and guidance to the best in-transit pathways, as well as progress of a trip.[273] It also uses online mapping and location services and confirms ride completion using web-based apps. These patterns now apply to conventional services like taxis and car rentals as seamlessly as they apply to hailing services or accessing EVSE infrastructure.

As autonomous vehicles (AVs) begin to penetrate mobility markets, real-time information will become vital to their effective, efficient, and safe operation. For electric AVs, automated access to charging stations will be key, as will real-time diagnostic systems reporting vehicle integrity and/or problems.[274] Further, vehicle-to-vehicle communications will be necessary to ensure that more than one AV can function in the same highway space without colliding or affecting pedestrians or passengers.[275]

Even present-day, real-time communications will require more processing speed and capacity as EV adoption expands and new mobility services emerge.

---

272 Lin, K., Xia, F. and Fortino, G., *Data-driven clustering for multimedia communication in Internet of vehicles*, May 2019, Future Generation Computer Systems, vol. 94, Pages 610-619.
273 This is a modeled analysis of demand driven mobility services, which exemplifies the importance of integrating diverse data sources in real-time and offers a broad discussion of the benefits and costs of demand information for key stakeholders in a mobility integrated ecosystem, including users, operators, and society. Wen, J., Nassir, N., and Zhao, J., *Value of demand information in autonomous mobility-on-demand systems*, March 2019, Transportation Research Part A: Policy and Practice, vol. 121, pages 346-359; Mia Yamauchi, M., *How will autonomous vehicles charge themselves?*, 2018, Plugless Power, Available at: https://www.pluglesspower.com/learn/solve-last-mile-vehicle-autonomy/.
274 Ibid., Yamauchi, M.
275 Elliott, D., Keen, W. and Miao, L., *Recent advances in connected and automated vehicles*, Jan. 2019, Journal of Traffic and Transportation Engineering (English Edition).

Forthcoming 5G wireless communications are likely to be essential to fully real-ize the decarbonization potential in electric mobility transformations.[276]

Public sector policy and processes. The interplay between mobility ser-vices and mobility integration also requires interaction between public sector policy and processes. Regulation at the national, state, and local level will con-tinue to ensure safety, reliable transportation flows within and between cities, and that conventional transit options—from heavy rail to city trolleys—re-main available to people.

Finally, part of the public sector contribution (and necessary to engage consumers, vendors, manufacturers and others in the mobility space) is road management, including road construction, maintenance, renovation (and ex-pansion), and traffic controls.

Each element is partially correlated in a complex and rapidly evolving sys-tem. New mobility solutions, such as EVs, promise disruption while creating remarkable new or enhanced benefits. Examples of benefits include increased driver and pedestrian safety, lower cost and more efficient one-way trip op-tions, cleaner air, fewer vehicle accidents and consequently lower insurance costs, as well as (with the advance of autonomous EVs) less need for parking despite a highly mobile urban-based society.

A systems approach involves integrating institutional organizations and their functional structures, processes to deliver services to city residents, and technologies that enable, facilitate, and assure service delivery. Social and cul-tural circumstances and collective behavior influence city mobility flows, as do city decision-makers and administrators who must manage mobility services. The economies of cities and the underlying (and overriding) dependence on information and communications platforms make cyber security vital to the complex mobility ecosystems taking shape as new technologies and decarbon-ization needs propel change.[277]

Engage outside groups to gain national and regional financial and policy support. Doing so will help with anticipating infrastructure requirements and

---

276 *Ericsson Mobility Report*, Nov. 2018, available at: https://www.ericsson.com/assets/ local/mobility-report/documents/2018/ericsson-mobility-report-november-2018.pdf ; Posawatz, T., *Victory in the Electric Car Market Will Go to Whoever Creates a Smartphone-Like Ecosystem*, Oct. 1, 2018, Forbes, Available at: https://www.forbes.com/sites/ tonyposawatz/2018/10/01/it-takes-an-ecosystem-electric-vehicles-need-to-build-a-smartphone-ecosystem/#797c66f66e89.
277 Loukas, G., Karapistoli, E., Panaousis, E., Sarigiannidis, P., Bezemskija, A., and Vuong, T., *A taxonomy and survey of cyber-physical intrusion detection approaches for vehicles*, March 2019, Ad Hoc Networks, vol. 84, 1, Pages 124–147. See also, Dairi, A.A. and Tawalbeh, L., *Cyber Security Attacks on Smart Cities and Associated Mobile Technologies*, 2017, Procedia Computer Science, vol. 109, pages 1086–1091.

meeting those requirements in a timely manner. This can be done in many ways but working with existing EV-related trade and advocacy organizations is one important pathway for cities, individually and collectively, to press national and regional governments to support cities both financially and with other types of incentives. The LA case study illustrates how to do this and why it is important.

Figure 8.2 summarizes main advocacy organizations with whom cities can and do work. Importantly, organizations involved in commercial deployment of EVSE or other related construction are not included in the diagram because their main purpose is not advocacy per se.

As EV adoption accelerates, advocacy-related organizations may press to expedite city adoption plans and actions including broadening the scope of EV infrastructure deployment.

Adopt and own the focal point of change for a specific city, which will enable each city's efforts to center on continuous improvement within a systems approach. Each city is unique, but cities, especially large cities, are driving the EV transition, which puts EV adoption at the heart of efforts to drive the electrification of mobility. For example, some cities require less support for public charging infrastructure and more for installing charging systems in homes, while other cities have a greater need for public infrastructure because many residences are constrained by roads and sidewalks, as noted in Chapter 7.

Share information on operational details among cities. Sharing operational details within and between cities is key to continuously improving the efficiency and effectiveness of infrastructure buildout. Figure 8.3 depicts these points. Discussion follows.

Sharing operational details within and between cities is key to continuously improving the efficiency and effectiveness of infrastructure buildout. Figure 8.3 depicts these points. Discussion follows.

FIGURE 8.2 EV Advocacy and Knowledge-Sharing Associations

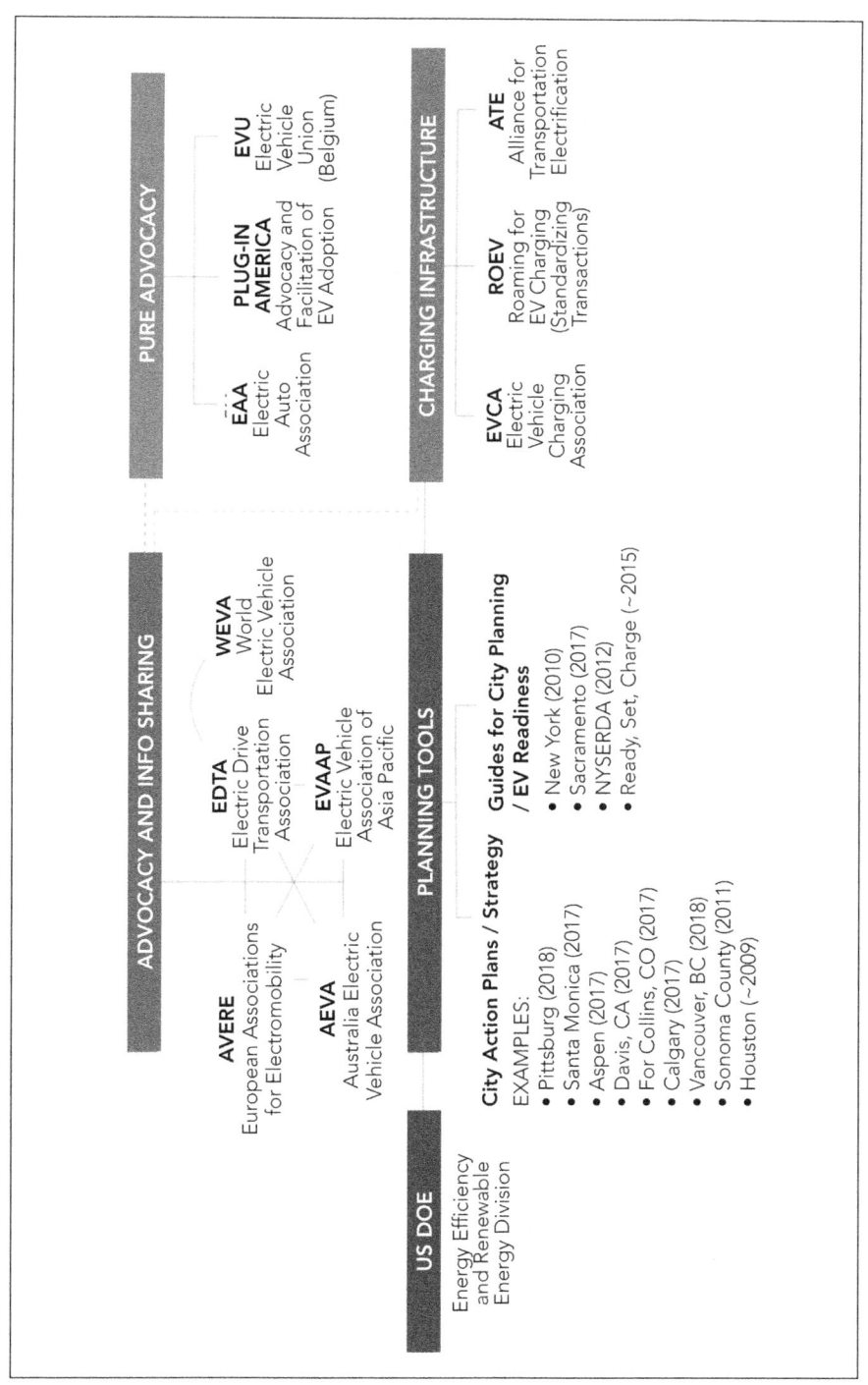

FIGURE 8.3 Main Topics for Sharing Operational Details

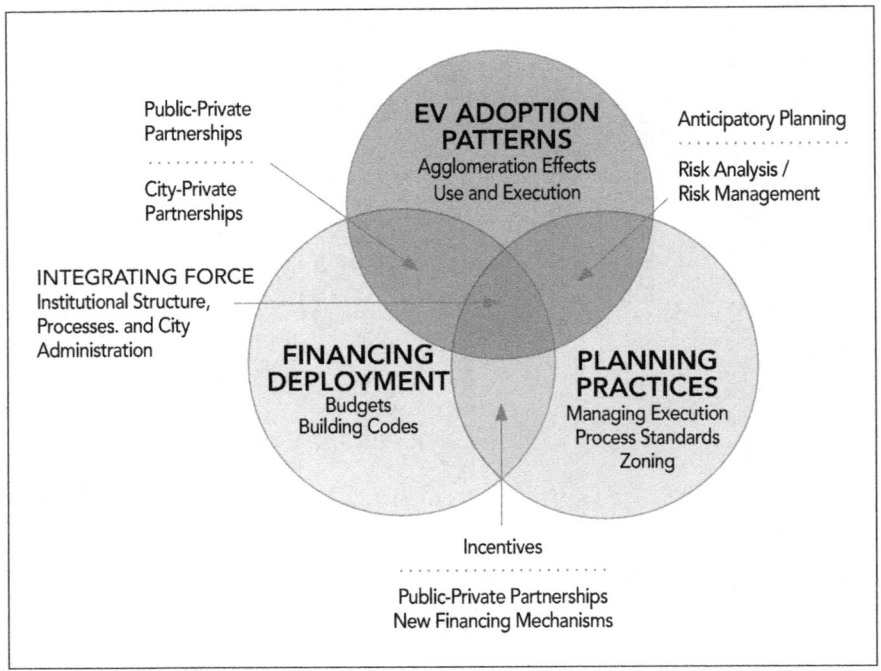

There are three main overlapping areas of information- and experience-sharing about operational activities related to EV management and deployment, which can help cities more smoothly and effectively anticipate and adapt to accelerating EV adoption.

Sharing information on EV adoption patterns. Information on how cities are experiencing EV adoption will help anticipate consumer demands as EV volumes increase. Also, such information contributes to better risk management. Managing risk when EV adoption patterns are still emerging helps to optimize limited public funding to support EV charging infrastructure. Also, it can help cities craft public-private partnerships that maximize benefits to participating parties while meeting EV owners' charging needs. There are many vehicle-related organizations (Figure 8.2 above) where information sharing occurs and several city organizations, from C40 (an international group of leading cities) to the National League of Cities in the United States, where ongoing platforms exist for ensuring relevant EV infrastructure information is shared.[278] The Institute of Transportation Engineers provides technical analysis and advice to city transportation professionals on matters related to EV infrastructure and related road management, but the linkages to assessing implications of EV adoption may merit enhanced sharing of adoption patterns and rates related to implications for EVSE infrastructure planning.[279]

Sharing planning practices. Cities always share planning practices, and through associations, conferences, and personal networks, city planners keep up with evolving knowledge and practices. The focus here is on how *operations-related* planning may warrant periodic adjustments as EV adoption increases. Operations-related planning involves city functions concerning roads and traffic management, and related infrastructure such as pedestrian sidewalks.

Cities' operational planning and execution processes vary. EV charging infrastructure poses challenges pertaining to scheduling, queuing, installation construction, ongoing operational oversight, safety, and other factors, all of which require time to execute. Refined sharing of experiences in adjusting priorities and adapting to needs for faster change will help operational planners anticipate impacts and manage related risks, ensuring that public infrastructure keeps pace with increased rates of EV adoption.

Finally, city operational planning and infrastructure execution can be constrained by other priorities, budget limitations, and stakeholder concerns; in which case outsourcing aspects of EV charging infrastructure may be the best way to keep infrastructure and EV adoption aligned. Similarly, city-level incentives for EV owners can be shaped according to their expectations as cities work to meet EV infrastructure needs. For instance, cities can create special charge points for high-frequency users; provide subsidies for installing home charging equipment; enable private-sector mobile charging units to operate with "self-registered" temporary permits; or a host of other initiatives that could temporarily satisfy EV owners' charging needs as cities contend with an expanding public charging infrastructure.

Sharing information on financial deployment. City case studies and literature impart a consistent message: City budgets tend to be structurally con-

---

278 Available at: https://www.nlc.org; C40 can be found here: https://www.c40.org/searches. A discussion of city sustainability networks can be found in Hatch, J., Cleveland, J., Silano, M. and Fox-Penner, Peter, *Cities and Climate Change: Strategic Options for Philanthropic Support*, April 2019, Boston University Institute of Sustainable Energy, Available at: https://www.bu.edu/ise/files/2019/04/CitiesStrategicOptions_Hatch_Cleveland-et-al-_Final_3.12.19b.pdf?utm_source=cities&utm_medium=site&utm_campaign=research_040319&utm_content=link.
279 Available at: https://www.ite.org/site-search/?Keywords=electric+vehicles.

strained, limiting discretionary funding during one or more budget cycles.[280] Sharing information about operating functions can inform cities on various effective uses of public-private and private enterprise models to meet EV infrastructure deployment needs. In doing so, sharing can help all cities achieve a least-cost/best-fit incremental solution as EV adoption rates, scope, locational characteristics, and traffic impacts evolve.

In cities everywhere, institutional structures, processes, and administrative practices serve to integrate urban activities, planning requirements, and financial matters.

8.3   Metrics for Managing EV Infrastructure Deployment

8.3.1 EV Charge Point Congestion and Its Mitigation

EV adoption is not the same throughout an urban area. This asymmetry means that some areas have larger concentrations, or agglomerations, of EVs than other areas.[281] Agglomerative geographic pockets can shift from location to location as EV drivers try to avoid congestion choke points on roads and high-

---

280 For an understanding of budget constraints confronting ambitions to facilitate decarbonization efforts, including consideration of EVs, see: Holscher, K., Frantzeskaki, N., McPhearson, T., and Loorbach, D., *Tales of transforming cities: Transformative climate governance capacities in New York City, U.S. and Rotterdam*, 2019, Netherlands, Journal of Environmental Management, 231, pages 843–857. For a look at how local incumbents can affect budgeting and its reprioritization, see: Susan Muhlemeier, *Dinars in transition? A conceptual exploration of local incumbents in the Swiss and German energy transition*, Environmental Innovation and Societal Transition, article in press.

281 In addition to anecdotal stories gleaned from case studies in this work, asymmetric agglomeration of EVs in specific locations within cities has been considered both directly and indirectly in research. A representative example of a modeling analysis is: Ahn, Y., and Yeo, H., *An Analytical Planning Model to Estimate the Optimal Density of Charging Stations for Electric Vehicles*, Nov. 17, 2015, Plos One, Available at: https://doi. org/10.1371/journal. pone.0141307. Another perspective helpful in understanding asymmetric agglomeration tendencies of EVs and their effect on city traffic and road management is through examining mobility demand and charge time by location: Xu, Y., Colak, S., Kara, E.C., Moura, S. J. and Gonzalez, M.C., *Planning for electric vehicle needs by coupling charging profiles with urban mobility*, April, 30, 2018, Nature Energy, vol. 3, pages 484–493.

ways. EV concentrations can arise when cities act to decongest traffic by changing road scale, altering traffic flows, adding tolls, and many other tactics.[282]

City leaders and planners should continually review the following situational factors:

- Is it time to accelerate response time as agglomerative effects change city traffic congestion patterns or create new forms of congestion around charge points?
- What decision criteria are pertinent to a particular city and best provide guidance when EV-related charging congestion must be addressed quickly, or managed with less-urgent treatment?
- How can the public be informed about possible effects of EV adoption on congestion, when the rate of adoption can eclipse public charging infrastructure needs? Are the tactics being used working? Which tactics being used by other cities merit inclusion in efforts to build public awareness?
- Can a culture of EV operations be implemented as more vehicles hit the road? This might involve encouraging behavior that rewards top-off charging modalities, thereby enabling more access—and flexibility of access—to EV users in areas where charging infrastructure still needs to expand.[283]
- How should pricing mechanisms be used to ration existing charging infrastructure while encouraging higher charge point utilization as charging systems are expanded?

Adoption metrics should focus on understanding and staying current with changing mobility patterns caused directly by increasing numbers of EVs on the road.

Tracking adoption patterns also helps cities plan for potential equity issues related to access to public charging. Doing so will minimize the unintended

---

282 There appears to be limited economic, geographic, and human ecological analysis of asymmetric agglomeration patterns in specific intra-urban locations, an area of research that may become more important as EV adoption continues to increase. One relevant article on the topic is: Oda, T., Aziz, M., Mitani, T., Watanabe, T., and Kashiwagi, T., *Mitigation of congestion related to quick charging of electric vehicles based on waiting time and cost-benefit analyses: A Japanese case study*, 2018, Sustainable Cities and Society, 36, pages 99–106. Another article with useful perspective is Zhang, A., Li, H., Zhu, L., Campana, P.E., Lu, h., Walin, F. and Sun, Q., *Factors influencing the economics of public charging for EV—A review*, 2018, Renewable and Sustainable Energy Reviews, 94, pages 500–509.

283 Short-cycle charging that tops off EV batteries is one way to reduce congestion (others argue that decongesting charge points is a simple up-pricing solution tied to time on a charger, or some other rationing practice using price). Innovations in rewards for topping off is a research area that merits further exploration.

consequence of income disparity causing uneven support of public EV adoption and infrastructure access.[284]

8.3.2 Measuring Utility Engagement in EV Infrastructure Deployment

Utilities must necessarily be involved in EV charging infrastructure design and placement because the source of electricity for such networks is predominantly the local load-serving entity (LSE).[285] While integrating EVs with rooftop solar and battery storage for home charging might in some cases reduce the role of LSEs, local distribution utilities are likely to remain important infrastructure resources enabling EV adoption for the foreseeable future. Accordingly, tracking how utilities are engaged with cities, and how they help or hinder EV infrastructure deployment pace, should be an important element on city planner and operations manager "dashboards."

Utility engagement with cities has many dimensions.[286]

- In some cases, EV infrastructure may require upgrades to distribution system equipment. For example, changing transformers, possibly undergrounding overhead wires, or repowering lighting systems if EV charging is designed to harvest power from street-lighting poles.
- Most utilities are required by regulations to pre-arrange their field operations work with customers if utility personnel must be on private property, or if power service to one or more customers is likely to be turned off as part of upgrading.
- Utilities must seek approval from public utility commissions in the case of investor-owned enterprises or from municipal utility boards if expenditures supporting EV infrastructure require new funds; and these processes can take time and require thorough justifications.

It is likely to be the case that the more closely aligned cities and utilities remain as EV adoption continues, the more likely it is that cities can keep pace with the rate of EV utilization.

---

284 284 Sovacool, B.K., Kester, J., Noel, L. and Rubens, G.Z., *Energy Injustice and Nordic Electric Mobility: Inequality, Elitism, and Externalities in the Electrification of Vehicle-to-Grid (V2G) Transport*, March 2019, Ecological Economics, vol. 157, pages 205–217.

285 LSE is a standard industry term that covers conventional wires and customer service distribution utility, retail commodity provider using local distribution utility wires, or a distribution service operator [DSO] providing wires services for a retail commodity electricity provider.

286 The three bullet points that follow this statement reflect general practices. In discussions between the authors and Southern California Edison executives managing electric vehicle operations matters in September 2018, these points were noted, as well.

Another important reason for cities and utilities to remain aligned is that utilities can finance assets or lend financial support to city investments; and the opposite applies as well—standalone municipal financing or municipal financing combined with utility financing strengthens both institutions as EVSE infrastructure is built. As EV adoption accelerates, leveraging such financing mechanisms may help prevent cities keep pace with EV owners' needs for readily accessible charging.

Utilities can and do provide other supportive activities. They support building public awareness. They must be responsive to third-party-charging vendors in a timely manner, under the terms of their regulatory compact. They help promote EV buying, without favoring any one vehicle type, brand, or dealer. They offer discounted electricity rates for home charging in many areas of the United States.

Crafting actual metrics that help cities stay aligned with utilities and EV market changes should be done on a city-by-city basis. Using various consumer preference research tools and devising measures of proactive versus reactive actions by utilities and by city administrators will be important metrics to craft and maintain. Also, such measures can help both cities and utilities coordinate their efforts to keep EV adoption moving forward.

Finally, city/utility alignments will help spotlight choke points in processes and procedures within each organization. Such alignments will also reveal problems at the interface with other entities, such as state transportation departments and other agencies, which contribute to lags in infrastructure deployment.

8.3.3 Managing Operations and Maintenance (O&M) Requirements

Public works departments are a vital aspect of all city operations. As one city staff person interviewed for the case studies in this work characterized it, "we own the roads." Owning the roads is a strength in that it means controlling one of the most critical assets on which cities function and EV charging infrastructure depends.

Owning roads is a weakness, as well, because road operations and maintenance (O&M) is complex, requires careful scheduling and budgeting, and often involves multiple city departments coordinating to make changes in a road (e.g., deploying EV chargers that may alter curbside parking and sidewalks), as the cases in Chapters 3 to 6 demonstrate. Managing and making changes to roads, and integrating new roads into a city's road network, must follow stringent laws, rules, processes, and state and federal compliance requirements.

Tracking metrics for keeping up with EV infrastructure deployment requirements should include measures that focus on the rate at which charge points are installed and the install duration of each charger deployed. Such metrics should be captured on an ongoing basis for all networks, whether public, public-private, or private. Doing so will help city operations managers identify execution inefficiencies, thereby enabling continuous improvement and enhanced execution effectiveness.

8.3.4 Tracking and Adapting to Change Through an Ecosystem Model

The EV transportation mobility ecosystem is still in its infancy; but it will become a complex system of supply chains, operational elements, and user-developed solutions that overlap and leverage existing ICE infrastructure. This will help minimize the scale, scope, and cost of new, incremental EV infrastructure needs.

For example, if existing retail gas (and possibly hydrogen fueling) stations can be modified to include charging assets, the need for on-street charging infrastructure may be reduced. The same principle applies to centrally placed charging and/or on-street wireless charging, if city or higher-level government decides to proceed with wireless charging to electrify transportation. As noted in Chapter 2, some oil companies like Shell and BP already have plans to transform their retail distribution points into multifuel sales platforms. Also, other retail brick and mortar enterprises, such as big box stores and food service chains, may move into EV charging services as an add-on to their core services.

Accordingly, an ecosystem perspective on optimal outcomes may benefit all parties involved in advancing an electrified transportation/mobility ecosystem. Tracking metrics based on an ecosystem approach should cover such factors as these:

- **Establish and maintain an EVSE system reserve capacity standard,** especially in clustered locations. Establishing a metric for sufficient reserve capacity in EV infrastructure to handle unexpected surges in demand for public charging would help planners and public works operators better prioritize work and determine best technology types to be deployed as well as best locations for infrastructure expansion. Flammini, et al., analyzed statistics of actual connected, idle, and charge times of charging stations in the Netherlands and discovered that asset performance depends on location.[287] They found that, on average, individual vehicle charging lasts for four hours, which affects local distribution grids, including voltage surges and sags. The authors note that further issues will likely appear,

---

287 Flammini, M. G., Prettico, G., Julea, A., Fulli, G., Mazza, A. and Chicco, G., *Statistical characterization of the real transaction data gathered from electric vehicle charging stations*, 2019, Electric Power Systems Research, 166, pages 136–150.

such as charging locations that are unavailable due to congestion at charging stations. Communications tools, such as smart phone apps, already are used to schedule EV charging before arrival, helping to lower the risk of congestion.[288] On the operational side, queuing will help lessen the risk of EV users not being served, which directly affects EV charging infrastructure design and scale.[289] By calculating a de facto "reserve margin" based on charge station use patterns, city planners can more precisely allocate charge stations according to capacity required at various locations (and use mobile chargers to fill in situational gaps).

- **System instability is the obverse of capacity reserves noted above.** Assessing the uncertainty in system operations and system expansion efforts can help planners (city as well as utility) protect existing assets and operations while minimizing disruptive effects of EV adoption and use patterns. Uncertainty is defined in this case as miscommunications, breakdowns in data flows, failed O&M actions that must be repeated, interruptions in charging service while charging is occurring, errors in transaction execution, and so on.[290]

Anticipating accelerated adoption should include metrics that track key technologies, which can help determine the cost and performance of EVs. Hence, as EV adoption accelerates, evolving EVSE technology, which improves EV infrastructure and related services merit tracking.

Also, city-specific measures of EV infrastructure deployment effectiveness and productivity should be tracked. Doing so will give planners and public works operators a more granular understanding of how infrastructure deployment is affecting the gap between EV sales and vehicles on the road. Also, it will help commercial enterprises with EV fleet deployment initiatives and real estate developers as they plan for and implement onsite EV charging infrastructure.

Recent research demonstrates the importance of keeping pace with evolving EV infrastructure standards. If standards lag behind infrastructure requirements dictated by evolving technologies, they could impede the pace of accelerating EV adoption. Moreover, standardizing charging infrastructure helps EV

---

288 288 For example, Gibson, R., *Top Apps and Websites to find EV Charging Stations*, April 17, 2018, Fleetcarma, Available at: https://www.fleetcarma.com/top-apps-websites-find-ev-charging-stations/.
289 Ibid., Flammini, M. G., Prettico, G., Julea, A., Fulli, G., Mazza, A., and Chicco, G.
290 Su, J., Lie, T.T., and Zamora, R., *Modelling of large-scale electric vehicles charging demand: A New Zealand case study*, 2019, Electric Power Systems Research, 167, pages 171–182. This article offers perspective on interactions between large-scale EV deployment and local grid effects.

manufacturers increase EV sales while possibly mitigating the need for more public charging infrastructure.

8.4 Conclusion

Execution is about details. A systems approach to planning for and managing details in EV infrastructure deployment will help cities stay ahead of changes driven by the increasing pace of EV adoptions. The planning index tool offered in Chapter 7 helps cities prioritize their focus and investments related to EV adoption. A systems analysis approach to EV infrastructure deployment provides several managerial benefits to city managers and executives: better risk management of EV adoption impacts on cities, and more efficient and effective deployment of EV infrastructure buildout. Further benefits include planning tools that better address challenges to resources and capital allocation requirements caused by changes in EV adoption patterns, which affect overall city operations and city roads, as well as traffic management in particular.

CHAPTER 9

Paving the Road to Accelerated Deployment

Z. Justin Ren, PhD, and David O. Jermain

9.1 Summary

In his book *Climate of Hope* (which we mention in the very opening of this book) Michael Bloomberg wrote:

> By all indications, we're just at the beginning of a revolution in city transportation that is fundamentally changing the way we get around. As cities continue growing, so will the demand for transportation. But if we keep meeting that demand with twentieth-century automotive solutions, then by 2050 the average urban resident will spend more of his or her day stuck in traffic jams, with a life expectancy shortened by air pollution, in a city whose economy is slowed by car congestion, and in a climate characterized by unpredictability and extreme weather.[291]

Indeed EVs are at the center of such a mobility revolution, and this book is a deep dive of research in this direction.

This final chapter summarizes learning and implications for planning and managing EV deployment in cities. Five distinct case studies of cities around the world (Los Angeles and Brookline, Massachusetts in the United States; Beijing and Shanghai in China; Oslo in Norway) have been coupled with the advance of an analytical approach, which can help city planners and managers better prioritize EV related efforts. These combine to form a distinctive "compass of experience."

The experience of **Los Angeles** spotlighted:

- Public awareness is important to advancing EV deployment efforts;
- Shared vision has value only if it is accompanied by shared actions;

----

291 Ibid., Bloomberg ,M. and Pope, C.

- Building codes and parking codes are essential to infrastructure deployment and enabling more EV adoption;
- Streamlined permitting is necessary, to enable quicker deployments in response to increasing (but localized) EV charging needs; and
- Leveraging existing infrastructure is critical, including roads, transit hubs, retail gasoline stations, workplaces, and in-building and surface parking facilities.

The experience of **Shanghai and Beijing** reinforced understanding of:

- The role of coordinating bodies to ensure alignment of various levels of government with local competing interests, which (if not coordinated) can disrupt smooth EV deployment efforts
- Utilization rates of charging piles in service, enabling faster and more comprehensive EV adoption
- Achieving timely and cost-effective deployment of EV infrastructure by converging local policies and state-level utility priorities
- The development of EV infrastructure serving all vehicle types, not just passenger cars, if efficiency and maximum EV adoption impacts are to be realized
- The importance of utilities to EV infrastructure deployment and national policy playing a primary role in ensuring timely and balanced engagement of utilities and local interests

Oslo's success provided insights useful to other cities as they anticipate how steady growth will affect EV adoption. A *combination* of benefits, such as low price, ease of access to charging, and others are key drivers of EV adoption, more so than *individual* benefits.

Brookline offers insights into the interfaces between policy-making and actual EV deployment:

- EVSE installation benefits when the township provides clear guidelines to private charging service vendors and building owners;
- Costs are significant for small towns and cities, so every possible funding source should be continually pursued;
- The buildings department and the planning department of a city or town can help drive adoption of EV charge points when new building plans and permits are issued, even when including EV charge points is voluntary for building owners;
- Ongoing assessment of EV charging needs is important; and
- Continual advocacy focused on barriers that slow or debilitate EV infrastructure deployment is necessary. For instance, in Massachusetts, if EV charging infrastructure is to be mandatory for buildings, it must be writ-

ten into state building codes, which are determined through legislative action.

The index tool discussed in Chapter 7 is useful for sharpening a city's focus. As noted, Beijing might benefit from focusing on home charging, Los Angeles may need more public infrastructure charging given how far vehicles typically travel in the LA basin, and Oslo may benefit from redefining what types of charging the city needs.

In the Oslo case, home charging is the preferred charging location, raising important policy questions about how much public infrastructure is needed. In most cities, "home" generally refers to single-family dwellings when in fact most "homes" are in multifamily buildings where charging is needed. However, building scale, location, and design can limit the number of charge points that can be deployed, even as the volume of EVs that need to be charged can be higher in such scenarios.[292]

The index tool offered in Chapter 7 is a first step toward a much more refined analytic framework that can help cities better prioritize their efforts related to EV adoption. In the next iteration of the index, examining the sub-categories of "home charging" will further refine the use-value of EV adoption index-based analytics for city planners and managers.

9.2 The Road Ahead

Cities are the spearpoint for EV adoption. Within their existing institutional spheres, they contain the people, processes, and technologies needed to address increasing needs for public charging. But resources do not necessarily translate into timely and effective action.

---

292 Ibid., Lorentzen, E., Haugneland, R., Bu, C., and Hauge, E., "Since the population in many cities mostly live in apartment buildings, we see a big challenge that must be addressed to move towards a zero-emission transportation system. Shared apartment buildings need to be 'Charging ready,' meaning that they provide the basic infrastructure that every owner can connect to and install and pay for a charging station at their own parking spot. The basic infrastructure should include a dynamic effect distribution system if necessary. In new buildings, it should be mandatory to install the basic infrastructure for a future 100% EV population. In existing buildings, it should be mandatory to allow EV owners to install charging stations on demand. Today we see a lot of boards of shared apartment buildings banning BEVs to park and charge because of uncertainties with new technologies, cost and fire hazard among others. It is vital that the appropriate governmental body helps spreading up-to-date, neutral, and correct information related to this. In Norway, this is handled by the Norwegian Directorate for Civil Protection, but there is still room for improvement" (page 9).

This study suggests that whether scale and scope are small or gigantic, the transition to electrified mobility at the city level hinges on how city institutions adapt to public policy, market, and sociocultural changes that emerge from widespread and accelerated EV adoption.

Every jurisdiction with transportation responsibilities faces and fosters some degree of institutional change as the pace of EV adoption accelerates. Institutional adaptation can be difficult and provoke reactive behavior. However, if decarbonization is the objective, then cities and other jurisdictional entities must be more proactive than reactive, more anticipatory than driven by surprise. Thus, policies related to appropriately synchronizing EV adoption and public infrastructure deployment are central to managing institutional adaptation to unprecedented changes stemming from the electrification of mobility.

Tomorrow's electrification successes depend on how cities modify their operations to reduce the time spent on adding to public charging infrastructure networks and systems. Incremental modifications in city organizations may be required. Institutional structures are difficult to change significantly. So, the use of *temporary organizations* with specialized transition management talent may be the best practice for ensuring that cities can work both within and around existing institutional structures to enable a more flexible means of anticipating and adapting to accelerated EV adoption.[293]

Lewin's groundbreaking research on temporary organizations can help guide city administration adaptive actions through tactics that loosen, or unfreeze, existing organizational structures. In turn, this enables task-based teams to execute effectively in a "fluidized organizational state." Once specific goals of a temporary organization are met, a reset, or refreeze, of disrupted organizational roles restores established process workflows within workable institutional structures.[294] For example, utilities use temporary organizations to address emergencies, where expertise is drawn from the entire enterprise, as

---

293 Sydow, J., and Braun, T., *Projects as temporary organizations: An agenda for further theorizing the interorganizational dimension*, Jan. 2018, International Journal of Project Management, vol. 36, Issue 1, Pages 4-11. See also, J.R. San Cristóbal and V. Fernández, E. Diaz, *An analysis of the main project organizational structures: Advantages, disadvantages, and factors affecting their selection*, 2018, Procedia Computer Science, vol. 138, Pages 791–798.
294 Lewin, K., *Frontiers in Group Dynamics*, 1947, Human Relations, vol. 1, Issue 1, pages 5-41. Lewin's work on organizational change was considered groundbreaking in the 1940s. His techniques for unfreezing and refreezing organizations to drive change remain quoted and serve as foundations for many contemporary change management practices. The literature on temporary organization design, implementation, execution, and closure is deep, stretching from the 1940s to the present day. City planners and managers may find the literature on temporary organizations helpful in creating more fluid teams to address EV related issues, as well as many other operational challenges.

needed. Emergencies often disrupt established process workflows throughout a utility. Merger and acquisition efforts across most economic sectors use temporary organizations to manage deal execution, post-merger integration, and restoring disruptions enterprise-wide as two enterprises become one.

One thing evident from the work chronicled here is the gap between best-practice analyses and knowledge sharing. As noted, there are many organizations and publications that provide rich palettes of information on most topics pertaining to EVSE technology, infrastructure design and deployment, EV charging O&M, and transaction management. The authors observe from interviews and research for this work that knowledge and practice-sharing tend to stay within professional categories (e.g., engineers, planners, and systems integration practitioners). But if EV adoption and charging infrastructure is an evolving complex ecosystem, as discussed in Chapters 2 and 8, and profiled in Figures 2.5, 2.6, and 8.1, then there may be a need for more integrated (cross-disciplinary, cross-functional) knowledge sharing. Hence, one next step for this team of researchers is to test the value of establishing an EV operations laboratory with an integrating convener service where various global operational practices can be shared, and experimental practices can be quickly tested and piloted. Another small next step into a new operations research domain that could help city planners, offered in Chapter 7, would be to create easy-to-use tools that integrate analysis, policy design, and deployment management for city planners and managers. Ideally, this work lends substance to the question of *how* EV charging infrastructure execution can accelerate and intersect with the increasing pace of ICE to EV platform shifts.

ABOUT THE AUTHORS AND EDITORS

Peter Fox-Penner, PhD

Dr. Fox-Penner is director of the Institute for Sustainable Energy (ISE) at Boston University (BU). He is also professor of the practice at BU's Questrom School of Business. His research and writing focuses on electric power strategy, regulation, and governance; energy and climate policy; and the relationships between public and private economic activity, including corporate social responsibility. He is the author of *Smart Power* (2010), a book widely credited with foreshadowing the transformation of the power industry. *Smart Power* is now used and cited all over the world, as are other books in this area written by Fox-Penner. He also teaches courses on sustainable energy and electric power at the Questrom School of Business. The work of the BU Institute for Sustainable Energy and Peter's projects through the Institute can be viewed there. In addition, since 2014 he has been a senior policy scholar at the Georgetown Center for Business and Public Policy.

Peter's career includes leadership in academia, government, and the private sector. From 1996 through 2015, Peter was a principal specializing in energy and regulated industry matters at the Brattle Group, where he remains an academic advisor. During his time there, Peter was on the firm's executive committee, directed the Washington office, and then became the firm's longest-serving chairman. In addition, he helped the Brattle Group grow from a small regional consulting boutique into a globally recognized brand with offices all over the world. He also played an integral role in designing a unique corporate governance framework that has allowed the firm to become intergenerational, self-governed, and privately held. During this period, his work was quoted as authoritative in a Supreme Court decision, and he participated extensively in litigation involving Enron and the California electricity crisis.

From 1994 to 1996, Peter was principal deputy assistant secretary at the US Department of Energy's Energy Efficiency and Renewable Energy unit (EERE) and a senior advisor in the White House Office of Science and Technology Policy (OSTP). Among other duties, he led policy and budget formulation at EERE; implemented the largest part of the first official US Climate Change Action Plan and the path-breaking Partnership for a New Generation Vehicle; represented the US government in California's power deregulation and parallel federal efforts; and defended the federal government against the unsuccessful 1994 shutdown.

Prior to 1994, Peter was a vice president at Charles River Associates, where his work centered on electric utility policy and regulation. He was also a research engineer at the Illinois Governor's Office of Consumer Services, one of the first utility consumer advocates in the United States, and he was a researcher at the University of Illinois' Energy Research Group (ERG). ERG was one of the original three interdisciplinary energy research centers in the United States and helped contribute to the first formal national energy policy adopted by the United States, President Nixon's Project Independence.

Since 1996, Peter has also been active in outside business and civic activities. He currently serves as chief strategy advisor to Energy Impact Partners, as a board member of an energy efficiency company, Lighting Retrofit, Inc., and as an advisor to EOS Energy Storage. He was previously on the board of, or an advisor to, the Solar Foundation, the Center for National Progress, the Brookings Institution Energy Program, the United Nations Foundation, the Energy Foundation, the Global Energy Group, GridPoint, and other groups. In 1977, Peter cofounded one of the original antinuclear-power groups in the United States, the Prairie Alliance, and in 2000, he cofounded Environment 2004, a political group that subsequently merged with the League of Conservation Voters. He has also been a policy advisor to numerous presidential campaigns.

Jie (Roger) Hao

Jie (Roger) Hao is an expert in China's automobile industry. His expertise is in Chinese car buyers' preferences and consumption patterns, operations management of auto dealers, and distribution channel and marketing strategy of New Energy Vehicle (NEV) in China. He is now the chief consultant of Easy-ToFortune-China. His clients include VW, Audi, Porsche, Maserati, Mazda, Volvo, Geely, and Rolls-Royce. Mr. Hao obtained his BS and MA from Remin University in China.

Jennifer Hatch

Ms. Hatch is a transportation researcher and Fellow at Boston University's Institute for Sustainable Energy (ISE), managing the sustainable transportation practice. Her research focuses on the impact of transportation on energy systems, the role of decentralized transaction systems in energy, and de-carbonization of the energy and transportation sectors. Previously, Ms. Hatch worked as an independent energy and environmental consultant, primarily in the United States and Mexico. Also, she held research positions at the World Resources Institute and the World Bank in Washington, D.C. She holds a master's degree in public policy from the Harvard Kennedy School and a BA from Wellesley College.

John P. Helveston, PhD

Dr. Helveston is assistant professor in the Engineering Management and Systems Engineering in the School of Engineering and Applied Science of George Washington University. Professor Helveston is interested in understanding the factors that shape technological change, with a focus on transitioning to more sustainable and energy-saving technologies. Within this broader category, he studies consumer preferences and market demand for new technologies as well as relationships among innovation, industry structure, and technology policy. He has explored these themes in the context of China's rapidly developing electric vehicle industry. He applies an interdisciplinary approach to research, with expertise in discrete choice modeling and conjoint analysis as well as interview-based case studies.

Dr. Helveston contributed to this work as a post-doctoral fellow at the BU Institute for Sustainable Energy (ISE) and continued his work with ISE while assuming his role as assistant professor at George Washington University.

David O. Jermain

Mr. Jermain is a senior research scientist and senior fellow at Boston University's Institute for Sustainable Energy (ISE). Also, he is an adjunct professor at Boston University's Questrom School of Business. For nearly 40 years, he has held senior energy sector executive positions and served in several consulting capacities for large and small consultancies as well as firms he has founded. He served as head of strategic planning for Pacific Power & Light where he helped drive execution of the first major utility merger in the United States in fifty years. He was vice president for corporate development of PacifiCorp's initial independent energy services company where he guided development of packaged remote power (solar, wind, battery and small backup diesel generators) for telecommunications infrastructure, and helped execute acquisitions of gas and biomass cogeneration power plants. He founded MicroGrid, Inc. with two partners, whose mission was to provide integrated energy, water, telecommunications, and waste management services to resort facilities on islands around the world as well as offering off-balance sheet financing tools for energy assets of commercial building developers.

Mr. Jermain managed international electric power restructuring projects in Russia, India, and California. He managed the project to file documents with the Federal Energy Regulatory Commission (FERC) requesting operating approval for the California Independent System Operator (ISO) and Power Exchange (PX), moving there from to assume responsibilities for market monitoring, federal regulatory affairs, and internal audit for CalPX. He managed the workout of a merchant generator in the United States. His consulting roles included a partnership he founded, work in the Arthur Andersen National Utility Practice, KPMG, Bearing Point, RCG Hagler Bailly, and Putnam, Hayes, and Bartlett.

Over the last ten years, he managed industrial and commercial demand response programs for Southern California Edison, SCE's operations-related Electric Vehicle adoption support services, and its business planning for the Customer Services division. He worked on the development of a biomass fuels start-up, as well as a retail electricity commodity services start-up. He helped write the Department of Energy's Quadrennial Energy Review 1.2, published in January 2017, thereafter joining the ISE. At the ISE, he works on US-China energy and climate change issues and researches electric vehicle adoption matters as well as energy development issues in Africa, and carbon power production decommissioning challenges.

Guillermo Ivan Pereira

Guillermo Ivan Pereira recently completed his PhD in sustainable energy systems at the University of Coimbra, Portugal and MIT Portugal Program. Previously he worked as an innovation developer for smart grid and smart home applications at Intelligent Sensing Anywhere (ISA) in Portugal. At Coimbra he collaborated with industry, universities, and governmental institutions to design and develop initiatives to advance energy efficiency across the EU. He holds a master's in energy for sustainability with specialization in energy systems and policy by the faculty of science and technology of the University of Coimbra and a bachelor's in management by the faculty of economics of the University of Coimbra. His research focuses on the electricity sector sustainability transition, smart grids, and utilities business model innovation. His research focuses on policy, technology, and business model adaptation for smart and sustainable energy systems. His contributions to the field of sustainable energy systems encompass analyses of green jobs creation in energy efficiency and renewable energy industries, assessment of energy efficiency governance, solar PV diffusion and policy adaptation, analysis of future alternatives for electricity sector transformation, and assessment of utility adaptation and business model innovation. He contributed to this volume during his appointment as a Visiting Research Fellow at the Boston University Institute for Sustainable Energy.

Z. Justin Ren, PhD

Z. Justin Ren is an associate professor of business administration at Boston University's Questrom School of Business, and a faculty researcher at the Boston University Institute of Sustainable Energy (ISE). He was also a research affiliate at Massachusetts Institute of Technology (MIT) Sloan School of Management (2009–2014).

Professor Ren's current research focuses on Electric Vehicles (EV) and infrastructure for clean energy transition. He also teaches data analytics and advises companies on tools and models that help managers gain market intelligence and make strategic decisions. His consulting clients include INTEL, Staples, BestBuy, Payless Rental Car, PWC, among others.

His research has appeared in publications such as *Management Science, Operations Research, Medical Care*, and *MIT Sloan Management Review*. He has received several recognitions, including the INFORMS George B. Dantzig Dissertation Award, INFORMS Junior Faculty Paper Competition Award, and the Production and Operations Management Society (POMS) Wickham Skinner Early-Career Research Accomplishments Award.

At Boston University, Professor Ren teaches core operations management courses, and an analytics course which focuses on tools and frameworks that help managers gain market intelligence and make strategic decisions. He also teaches in executive education in financial risk management. He is a certified teacher by the Harvard Business School Case Method Discussion Leadership Program. Professor Ren is also the founder of www.ExcelProf.com, a website dedicated to business analytics using Microsoft Excel.

Professor Ren received his MA degree from University of Wisconsin-Madison, his MS and PhD in operations and information management from The Wharton School at the University of Pennsylvania.

David B. Sandalow, BS, JD

Mr. Sandalow is the Inaugural Fellow at the Center on Global Energy Policy and codirector of the Energy and Environment Concentration at Columbia University's School of International and Public Affairs at Columbia University. He founded and directs the Center's US-China Program. During October and November 2018, he was a Distinguished Visiting Professor in the Schwarzman Scholars Program at Tsinghua University.

Mr. Sandalow has served in senior positions at the White House, State Department, and US Department of Energy (DOE). He came to Columbia from the DOE, where he served as undersecretary of energy (acting) and assistant secretary for Policy and International Affairs. Prior to serving at the DOE, Mr. Sandalow was a Senior Fellow at the Brookings Institution. He has served as assistant secretary of state for Oceans, Environment, and Science and as a senior director on the National Security Council staff.

Mr. Sandalow writes and speaks widely on energy and climate policy. Recent works include *Guide to Chinese Climate Policy* (July 2018), *A Natural Gas Giant Awakens* (June 2018, coauthor), *The Geopolitics of Renewable Energy* (2017, coauthor), *Financing Solar and Wind Power: Lessons from Oil and Gas* (2017, coauthor), *CO2 Utilization Roadmap 2.0* (2017, project chair), and *The History and Future of the Clean Energy Ministerial* (2016). Other works include *Plug-In Electric Vehicles: What Role for Washington?* (2009) (editor), *U.S.-China Cooperation on Climate Change* (2009) (coauthor), and *Freedom from Oil* (2008).

Mr. Sandalow is a member of the Zayed Future Energy Prize Selection Committee, Innovation for Cool Earth Forum (ICEF) Steering Committee, Board of Directors of Fermata Energy and Highview Power Storage, University of Michigan Energy Institute's Advisory Board, Electric Drive Transport Association's "Hall of Fame," and the Council on Foreign Relations. He chairs the ICEF Innovation Roadmap Project. Mr. Sandalow is a graduate of the University of Michigan Law School and Yale College.

Peishan Wang

Ms. Wang is a research fellow at Boston University's Institute for Sustainable Energy. She was responsible for managing the integration of work products and ensuring timely completion of the book. She holds a master's degree in systems engineering with a concentration in energy and environmental systems from Boston University. Also, she holds a bachelor of chemical engineering degree from Worcester Polytechnic Institute. Previously, she worked on developing an electrochemical wastewater sensor, taking it from a research concept to product prototype.

GLOSSARY

Battery Electric Vehicle (BEV)
A battery electric vehicle (BEV) is an electric vehicle that uses chemical energy stored in rechargeable battery packs. Battery electric vehicles use electric motors instead of internal combustion engines (ICEs).

Charging Infrastructure
Charging infrastructure tends to be defined by the voltage level of chargers. For purposes of this work, charging levels (Levels 1, 2, and 3) alone are insufficient for defining "public charging infrastructure." Public charging infrastructure includes at least the following components:
- Electricity supply—sources and delivery
- Metering and billing of power supplied and, in some cases, of parking used
- Charging assets, their placement and maintenance
- Charging service safety and security
- Equipment standards, including the vehicle-to-charger connectors to vehicles as well as actual charger dispensers
- Information related to all aspects of charging, including operational integrity of units, use patterns by charge point, chart point locations, real-time availability, and innovations in simplifying and reducing congestion caused by demand for specific charging units
- Public facilities and roadway access (e.g., curbside charging poles)
- Ownership models based on utilities, third parties, and public entities

Electric Mobility
Electric mobility comprises all street vehicles that are powered by an electric motor and primarily get their energy from a power grid—in other words: can be recharged externally. This includes battery electric vehicles (BEV) of all sizes and types, vehicles with a combination of electric motor and a small combustion engine (hybrid vehicles), plug-in hybrid electric vehicles (PHEV), and hydrogen fuel cell electric vehicles (HFCEV). Electric mobility is a system or platform that combines electricity service with EVSE and traffic-related infrastructure to yield sustainable mobility.

Electric Vehicle Supply Equipment (EVSE)

EVSEs function to supply electric energy to recharge electric vehicles. EVSEs are also known as EV charging stations, electric recharging points, or just charging points. In China, EVSEs often are referred to as "charging piles," and the connectors between charge piles and vehicles are called "guns" in common parlance.

Electrified Transportation (ET) / Electric Vehicle (EV)

Electrified transportation refers to the use of electricity from external sources of electrical power, including the electrical grid, for all or part of vehicles, vessels, trains, boats, or other equipment that are mobile sources of air pollution and greenhouse gases, and the related programs and charging and propulsion infrastructure investments.

Level 1 Charging

Level 1 equipment provides charging through a 120 volt (V), alternating-current (AC) plug and requires a dedicated circuit. Generally speaking, Level 1 charging refers to the use of a standard household outlet.

Level 1 charging equipment is standard on vehicles and therefore is portable and does not require the installation of charging equipment. On one end of the provided cord is a standard, three-prong household plug. On the other end is a connector, which plugs into the vehicle.

Depending on the battery technology used in the vehicle, Level 1 charging generally takes 8 to 12 hours to completely charge a fully depleted battery. The most common place for Level 1 charging is at the vehicle owner's home and is typically conducted overnight.

Level 2 Charging

Level 2 equipment offers charging through a 240 V, AC plug and requires installation of home or public charging equipment. These units require a dedicated 40-amp circuit.

Level 2 charging equipment is compatible with all electric vehicles and plug-in electric hybrid vehicles. Level 2 chargers have a cord that plugs directly into the vehicle in the same connector location used for Level 1 equipment.

Depending on the battery technology used in the vehicle, Level 2 charging generally takes 4 to 6 hours to completely charge a fully depleted battery. Charging time can increase in cold temperatures. Level 2 chargers are commonly found in residential settings, public parking areas, places of employment and commercial settings.

Level 3 Charging

Level 3 Charging equipment uses CHAdeMO technology, also commonly known as DC fast charging, charges through a 480 V, direct-current (DC) plug. Most Level 3 chargers provide an 80% charge in 30 minutes. Cold weather can lengthen the time required to charge.

CHAdeMO is the trade name of a quick charging method for battery electric vehicles developed by Tokyo Electric Power Company (TEPCO) that delivers up to 62.5 kW by 500 V, 125 A direct current via a special electrical connector. A revised CHAdeMO 2.0 specification allows for up to 400 kW by 1000 V, 400 A direct current. CHAdeMO is proposed as a global industry standard by an association of the same name and is included in the IEC 62196 standard as configuration AA. Competing standards include the combined charging system and the Tesla Supercharger.

CHAdeMO is an abbreviation of CHArge de MOve, equivalent to "move using charge" or "move by charge" or "charge 'n' go", a reference to the fact that it is a fast charger. The name is derived from the Japanese phrase O cha demo ikaga desuka, translating to English as "How about a cup of tea?" referring to the time it would take to charge a car. CHAdeMO can charge low-range (120 km, or 75 mi) electric cars in less than half an hour. It plans to introduce 400 kW "ultra-fast" charging in the coming years.

Plug-In Hybrid Electric Vehicle (PHEV)

A plug-in hybrid electric vehicle is a hybrid electric vehicle composed of a battery powered motor and an internal combustion engine; where the battery can be recharged by plugging it into an external source of electric power, as well by its on-board engine and generator.

Terminology in Referencing Cities

EV charging infrastructure is deployed in legally demarcated towns and cities and in metropolitan areas typically defined by the US Census as standard metropolitan areas (SMAs). General terms that reference urban areas include the use of the term "urban" for organized settlements ranging from small villages to mega-cities, like Shanghai, Beijing, Los Angeles, New York, and Tokyo. Urban planners, social and human ecologists, and economic geographers use the following terms:

- Urban—An urban area is the region surrounding a city. Most inhabitants of urban areas have nonagricultural jobs. Urban areas are very developed, meaning there is a density of human structures such as houses, commercial buildings, roads, bridges, and railways. "Urban area" can refer to towns, cities, and suburbs.

- Suburb—A suburb is a mixed-use or residential area, existing either as part of a city or urban area or as a separate residential community within commuting distance of a city.
- Rural—A rural area or countryside is a geographic area that is located outside towns and cities. Typical rural areas have a low population density and small settlements. Agricultural areas are commonly rural, as are other types of areas such as foothills and forests.

Made in the USA
Middletown, DE
26 May 2019